Michael Miller

£14.99

Alpha
Teach Yourself

Business Plans

in **24** hours

ALPHA

A Pearson Education Company

Alpha Teach Yourself Business Plans in 24 Hours

Copyright © 2002 by Michael Miller

International Standard Book Number: 0-02-864216-3

Library of Congress Catalog Card Number: 2001092335

Printed in the United States of America

First printing: 2001

03 02 01   4 3 2 1

Note: This publication contains the opinions and ideas of its author. It is intended to provide helpful and informative material on the subject matter covered. It is sold with the understanding that the author and publisher are not engaged in rendering professional services in the book. If the reader requires personal assistance or advice, a competent professional should be consulted.

The author and publisher specifically disclaim any responsibility for any liability, loss or risk, personal or otherwise, which is incurred as a consequence, directly or indirectly, of the use and application of any of the contents of this book.

Trademarks

All terms mentioned in this book that are known to be or are suspected of being trademarks or service marks have been appropriately capitalized. Alpha Books and Pearson Education, Inc. cannot attest to the accuracy of this information. Use of a term in this book should not be regarded as affecting the validity of any trademark or service mark

SENIOR ACQUISITIONS EDITOR
Renee Wilmeth

DEVELOPMENT EDITOR
Nancy D. Warner

PRODUCTION EDITOR
Katherin Bidwell

COPY EDITOR
Amy Lepore

INDEXER
Tonya Heard

PRODUCTION
Mary Hunt

COVER DESIGNER
Alan Clements

BOOK DESIGNER
Gary Adair

MANAGING EDITOR
Jennifer Chisholm

PRODUCT MANAGER
Phil Kitchel

PUBLISHER
Marie Butler-Knight

Overview

Contents

Introduction

Every business needs a plan.

You need a plan to guide your business, both now and in the future, to define the long-term strategy you'll use to help you achieve your goals and mission.

You need a plan to share with your employees, to show them where you want to go and how you want to get there, to motivate them and direct their day-to-day activities.

You need a plan to provide to potential lenders and investors, to convince them that your business is a good risk with strong potential, and to encourage them to provide the funding you need to grow and nurture your business.

The problem is—how do you create an effective business plan? You're a businessperson, not a writer; you don't even know what you need to know to pull the right information together and put your thoughts and strategies on paper. How in the world can you create a business plan that will do what it needs to do?

If you need help creating a plan for your business, you've come to the right place. *Teach Yourself Business Plans in 24 Hours* will lead you step by step through the entire business planning process, from the initial research to the final printing and presentations. You'll learn the essential elements of an effective business plan, as well as the inside tips and tricks that help you really sell your business to the people that count—the lenders and investors you depend on for funding.

And, best of all, you'll learn how to create a business plan without becoming overwhelmed with the process. That's due to the format of Alpha's *Teach Yourself* series; what you need to know is presented in 24 easy-to-follow lessons, each of which you can complete in an hour or less. It's an easy way to put together a business plan that will drive your company for years to come—and earn you the funding you deserve!

WHAT YOU'LL FIND IN THIS BOOK

Part I, "Plan for Research," presents a variety of business basics that you need to prepare for the business plan process. You'll learn how to identify the audience for your plan, define your market, define your core competencies, prepare your business strategy, and evaluate different funding options.

Part II, "Plan the Plan," launches the planning process. You'll learn the different components of a successful business plan, discover how to plan and manage the business plan project, and take a refresher course on essential financial statements.

Part III, "Plan to Write," takes you step by step through the different sections of a typical business plan. You'll learn how to create compelling text for all the sections—Executive Summary, Vision, Mission, Opportunity, Market Strategy, Business Strategy, Organization and Operations, Management, Core Competencies and Challenges, and Financials.

Part IV, "Plan the Package," helps you take your text and turn it into a highly professional business plan document. You'll learn about appendixes and attachments, tables of contents and indexes, and formatting and printing.

Part V, "Plan for Success," shows you how to put your business plan to real use. You'll learn how to turn your plan document into a compelling presentation, how to employ your plan for the day-to-day management of your business, and how to use your business plan as the basis for a full private placement memorandum.

EXTRAS

To help you prepare for the next lesson, you'll find special "Homework" sections at the end of each hour. These short sections suggest items to think about, read, or assemble before you embark on the next hour's lesson.

Following the 24 one-hour lessons are four appendixes. These supplements provide a variety of reference material that you might find useful as you prepare your first real-world business plan; included are a 20-minute recap of each hour in the book, a glossary, a sample business plan outline, and a list of key financial formulas.

Last but not least, this book has a lot of miscellaneous cross-references, tips, shortcuts, and warning sidebars. Here's how they stack up:

GO TO ▷
This sidebar gives a
cross-reference to
another chapter or
section in the book
to learn more about
a particular topic.

JUST A MINUTE

 This sidebar offers advice or teaches an easier way to do something.

STRICTLY SPEAKING

This sidebar offers definitions of words you may not know.

TIME SAVER

 This sidebar offers a *faster* way to do something.

PROCEED WITH CAUTION

 This sidebar contains a warning. It warns you about potential problems and helps you steer clear of trouble.

 This sidebar lets you know where you can find more information on a specific topic.

About the Author

MICHAEL MILLER is a successful and prolific author and consultant with a reputation for practical advice, technical accuracy, and an unerring empathy for the needs of his readers and clients.

Mr. Miller has written more than three dozen nonfiction titles since 1989. His books include *The Complete Idiot's Guide to Online Search Secrets*, *The Complete Idiot's Guide to Home Theater Systems*, and *The Complete Idiot's Guide to Playing Drums*. He is known for his casual, easy-to-read writing style and his practical, real-world advice—as well as his ability to explain a wide variety of complex topics to an everyday audience.

Mr. Miller is also president of The Molehill Group, a strategic consulting and authoring firm based in Carmel, Indiana. As a consultant, he specializes in providing strategic advice to and writing business plans for Internet- and technology-based businesses.

Dedication

To all my former colleagues in the management team of the former Macmillan Publishing, for providing numerous opportunities (not all welcomed!) to hone my business development skills.

Acknowledgments

The usual thanks go to the usual suspects at Alpha, including but not limited to Renee Wilmeth, Nancy Warner, Katherin Bidwell, Amy Lepore, and Marie Butler-Knight.

I'd also like to acknowledge Julie Shedd's contribution to the financial-oriented chapters in the book—and to my own financial savvy over the years. Thanks for the help, Julie!

PART I

Plan for Research

Hour 1

Analyze Your Objectives

CHAPTER SUMMARY

LESSON PLAN:

In this hour, you will learn about ...

- What a business plan is
- Why your business needs a plan
- What results to expect
- The plan's *real* audience
- Components of the plan

Every business needs a business plan—especially new businesses and businesses expecting significant change or growth in the near future. You obviously recognize this need, which is why you're reading this book. Good for you!

Unfortunately, most businesspeople have very little experience in creating business plans. They don't know what to include in the plan, where to obtain important information, or how to put the plan together. More important, most businesspeople don't know exactly *why* they're creating a business plan or for whom the plan is really being written. And, of course, if you don't know the why or the whom, you're going to have trouble creating a convincing plan that achieves your goals.

If the previous paragraph describes your current state, don't worry. You're starting in the exact same position as hundreds of thousands of businesses before you. The difference between you and those who came before—the thing that gives you a competitive advantage—is that you know what you don't know, and you want to overcome these shortcomings to create the most effective business plan possible.

If you want to learn how to create a successful business plan for your specific business, you've taken a good first step. *Teach Yourself Business Plans in 24 Hours* will teach you everything you need to know about how to write the perfect business plan for your business—in 24 easy-to-grasp, one-hour lessons. An effective business plan is essential to both guide and obtain financing for a growing company; read on to learn how to build the kind of plan that gets attention and achieves results.

BUSINESS PLANS: FACTS AND FICTION

First-year business school courses will tell you that a business plan provides the strategic direction for a company's ongoing activities. You write the plan to describe where you want to go and how you want to get there, and then you follow the plan you've written to achieve your goals.

Sounds easy, doesn't it?

Reality is much different from business school. If business success were as simple as following a few step-by-step instructions, we'd all be running our own billion-dollar businesses—and we're not. Building a successful business is an art, not a science, and there are no convenient substitutions for hard work, smart thinking, good instincts, and a lot of luck. No business plan in the world can deliver these resources; you have to provide them yourself.

What good is a business plan, then, if it doesn't guarantee success?

There are two main reasons to create a business plan:

- To formally articulate the strategic direction for your business
- To communicate that strategic direction to people or firms that will provide funding for your business

Let's examine each of these points separately.

ARTICULATING THE STRATEGIC DIRECTION

A business plan does not create your business's strategic direction—it records it, sets it in writing, and presents it for all to see. Looking at the proper order of things, your strategic direction comes first, and your business plan comes second. Putting things the other way around just doesn't work.

In spite of how some companies attack this issue, if you didn't have a strategic direction before, the act of writing a business plan will not create or discover one now; it's a fundamental law of physics that you can't make something from nothing. In fact, sometimes the act of writing a business plan will uncover the fact that a business has no overall guiding strategy. If that happens, it's probably a good thing; it's better to know now rather than later that your company is drifting aimlessly.

Assuming that your company actually does have a strategy, creating a business plan helps to make that strategy official and communicate that strategy to others, both inside and outside your organization. A strategy that exists only in the mind of the chief executive is not an official strategy—it's just a thought, often uncommunicated. The act of putting that thought on paper makes it official, gives it authority, gives it a *weight* that it didn't have previously. And, of course, putting it on paper makes it easier to share that strategy with others; pieces of paper can be distributed more easily than can your private thoughts.

COMMUNICATING WITH POTENTIAL INVESTORS

One group of people with whom you most definitely need to share your strategy is the people with the money—your current and potential future investors. The reason you need to share your strategic direction with these folks is simple: You want them to give you more money, and the more they know about your business strategy (and the more they're sold on that strategy), the more likely they are to invest.

This holds true no matter where you get your money. Your funds may come from your local banker, from friends and family, from venture capital firms, or even from private or public stockholders. Any type of potential investor will want to know a few facts about your business before he or she writes a check. In essence, you need to convince your investors that they're making a good investment. They want to know that they'll get a good return on their investment and that the chance of losing their investment is small. A good business plan serves this purpose of informing, selling, and reassuring potential investors that your company is a worthy recipient of their funds.

WHO THE TARGET AUDIENCE *REALLY* IS FOR YOUR BUSINESS PLAN

There are three potential constituencies for your business plan:

- Customers
- Employees
- Investors

Let's look at each of these and assess how important a business plan is for each.

BUSINESS PLANS AND CUSTOMERS

In theory, a business plan can be used to communicate your company's mission and message to your customer base. This may be more important for some types of businesses than it is for others.

For example, if you're a retailer, it's unlikely that you're going to hand out copies of your business plan to every customer who walks in the door or picks up the phone to place an order. On the other hand, if your business caters to corporations and government entities, it may be necessary to provide some degree of background information before you can sign a large sale—or even just to get in the door. In these instances, some subset of your full-scale business plan (minus the detailed financials, at least) might serve as a marketing piece you can use to establish your credibility.

JUST A MINUTE

Many large corporations view their annual reports—which contain many of the same elements as a good business plan—as a marketing tool for both their investors and their customers. This is why most annual reports are glossy, highly professional, four-color pieces with lots of attractive pictures and graphics.

On the whole, however, you probably wouldn't create a full-blown business plan just for your customers. If you can reuse portions of an existing plan, that's great, but this constituency alone will not likely drive your company to create a business plan.

BUSINESS PLANS AND EMPLOYEES

In some first-year business school courses, you might be told how important a business plan is to drive the strategic direction of a business. Every employee should receive a copy of the business plan, the courses say, so that everyone knows where the company is going and how you're going to get there.

This is all very nice in theory, but in reality, it is practiced more in the breach than the observance.

Hundreds of thousands of companies have written very elaborate business plans. Hundreds of thousands of companies have distributed these business plans to key employees, presented them at company meetings, and read them from front to back. Hundreds of thousands of companies have then taken these business plans and sat them on their shelves, never to be opened again.

Despite good intentions, most internal business plans are written, read once, and ignored. Day-to-day operations and ever-present crises get in the way of strategic management, and improvisation takes precedence over long-range planning. It probably shouldn't be that way, but it is, and there's no use pretending otherwise.

Knowing this, it's unlikely that you'd create a business plan purely for internal consumption—although it wouldn't be such a bad idea, if you could really follow through on it.

GO TO ▶
See Hour 23, "Use the Plan," for some thoughts on how to use your business plan in the course of running your day-to-day business.

BUSINESS PLANS AND INVESTORS

Of the three potential constituencies for your business plan, we're now left with number three: potential investors. This constituency, as you will soon see, is *the* target audience for the vast majority of business plans written today.

Most potential investors—and lenders—require that you present a detailed business plan before they will even consider making an investment or a loan. Since your business plan contains information about your market, your business, your strategy, and your company's performance—both historical and projected—any investor or lender can read the plan to get a quick snapshot of you and your business.

A strong business plan can help convince an investor or lender to give you the capital you seek; a poorly written business plan will reflect negatively on you and your business and could sink any pending deals. The stronger your business plan—the more professional and persuasive it is—the more likely it is that you'll be successful in your quest for capital. Where business plans are concerned, both substance and appearances count.

GO TO ▶
See Hour 2, "Analyze Your Audience," to learn what lenders and investors expect to see in a typical business plan.

So, when you create a business plan, make sure you know for whom you're creating it (investors and lenders) and why (to generate capital). That knowledge should drive every step you take as you start to create your plan.

WHY *YOUR* BUSINESS NEEDS A BUSINESS PLAN

Okay, you may be thinking, you can see why a business plan might be important for a company just getting started, one that needs a massive cash bankroll, or one that plans to go public at some time in the future. But your business is *different*—why does *your* company need a business plan?

If your company is entirely self-funded, if you never have occasion to take a short-term or long-term loan, if you would never use a revolving line of credit, if you never need to finance inventory, and if you never plan to grow any bigger than you currently are, then you're right—you *don't* need a business plan. (Not for investors, anyway—you still might need an internal business plan for your management and employees.)

However, if your business has need for a large cash infusion—to make it through the startup phase, for example, or to fund a planned expansion—then you most definitely *do* need a business plan. You'll be spending a lot of time and effort before potential lenders or investors, and these folks will want to see a detailed business plan before they'll fork over any cash.

Why do lenders and investors want to see your business plan? Here are four very good reasons:

1. Your business plan contains all your financial information—historical, current, and projected—and numbers guys always want to see your numbers.

2. Your business plan explains your business and your market. A potential lender or investor might not know enough about your business to make an intelligent decision without the help of this information.

3. Your business plan contains your plan, your strategy for success—and both lenders and investors need to assess your chances for success.

4. Your business plan tells your potential financial partners a little bit about *you*—who you are, why you're doing what you're doing, whether you have good ideas or bad ones.

In short, a business plan should contain everything a potential lender or investor needs to make an informed decision about whether or not to lend or invest. Without a business plan, you won't even get in the door.

But wait, some of you are saying, why do I need to go to all the time and trouble of writing a fancy plan? I have my financials (in this stack of papers somewhere), I know my business (and I'll be glad to tell you about it), and I have a plan for success (in my head). Why can't I just walk into the lender/investor's office, hand over my financial papers, and tell them why they should give me their money?

Making an investment or a loan based on a personal meeting and gut reaction is a nice concept, but it's one that went out of favor back when George Bailey quit running his family's savings and loan back in Bedford Falls. If you need any substantial funding, you'll be dealing with professionals—professionals with rules and regulations and procedures and processes that must, *must* be followed. More than likely, you'll be dealing with more than one individual, and you'll need to pass some rigid qualification procedures *just to get in the door*. The more professional your presentation—both personally and in terms of the information you provide—the better you'll be received, and the better your chances for success. Enter the world of high finance on a wing and a prayer, and that's all you'll leave with, too.

THE COMPONENTS OF A SUCCESSFUL BUSINESS PLAN

Now that you know *why* your business needs a business plan, let's take a quick look at what information goes into a successful plan.

Although different types of businesses might need to fine-tune this list a bit for their unique circumstances, most business plans will include some variation of the following sections:

- **Executive Summary.** This is the first part of the plan, the very first section the reader sees. It should encapsulate the main points of the entire document in a short (ideally one page), bulleted, easy-to-grasp style.

- **Vision.** This part of the plan, typically just a sentence (or at most a paragraph) long, tells the reader your dream for your business—why you're doing what you're doing.

- **Mission.** If the Vision is the why, the Mission is the what. Sometimes called a Mission Statement, this is a short (also typically a sentence or a paragraph) section that describes, as clearly as possible, just what your business is trying to accomplish.

JUST A MINUTE

A mission is different from a goal in that a mission defines a general direction, while a goal defines a specific target. A business will have but a single mission but can have many individual goals.

- **Opportunity.** This section, sometimes called the Market or Market Dynamics section, describes the compelling reason for your business to exist. Typically, this section includes a wealth of market data that presents a picture of immense market opportunity.

- **Market Strategy.** This section describes how you'll exploit that immense market opportunity described in the previous section, and puts forward your current and potential market activities—your product development, your marketing, your sales. This section also details your competitors and how you'll respond to them.

- **Business Strategy.** This section describes your business—what business you're in, what you make or sell or offer, and how you'll make money (otherwise known as your revenue model).

- **Organization and Operations.** This section—sometimes broken into separate Organization and Operations sections—describes your company structure as well as the backend operations you use to bring your products and services to market. (This is where you'll find all sorts of details about warehouses and computer systems and the other "behind the scenes" parts of your company.)

- **Management.** This section of the plan tells the reader all about your management team members—their backgrounds, their strengths, the reasons why this is the right team to lead the company to marketplace success.

- **Core Competencies and Challenges.** This section lays bare your business's strengths and weaknesses—and uses both to define the specific competitive advantages you have in the marketplace.

- **Financials.** These are the numbers—at minimum, a profit and loss statement and a balance sheet, both historical and projecting forward three to five years.

Your particular business plan can contain more or fewer or different sections than presented here, but it should contain the same information because that's what investors and lenders are looking for.

WHO WRITES YOUR BUSINESS PLAN?

How you attack the process of creating your business plan depends on the unique structure of your organization.

If your organization is just you, then you get to write the plan. (Although you may want to bring in a consultant to help you with some of the work.)

If your company is small and your management layer thin, you probably still have to shoulder the majority of the burden of creating your business plan. However, you can probably offload some of the details to other members of the management team—and it's sometimes a good idea to get the ideas and buy in of other managers during the process. (You still might want to bring in a consultant—someone who specializes in creating business plans—to help you over some of the rough spots.)

If your company is large and your resources many, you probably have a dedicated staff member or department for strategic planning or business development. Use this resource but keep your fingers in the pie. This is *your* plan, after all—just because you have someone else who can do a lot of the grunt work doesn't mean you should extricate yourself from the process completely.

HOW TO MOVE FROM IDEA TO REALITY

However you decide to proceed, the following are some definite steps you need to take to bring your business plan from idea to reality:

- **Develop your strategy.** You can't write a strategic plan if you don't have a business strategy. Use this opportunity to develop, fine-tune, or articulate your company's long-term strategy.
- **Gather your facts.** A business plan has to be built on a bedrock of solid information. Before you write a word of your plan, you need to assemble all manner of market facts and figures—including, when available, information about your competitors.

GO TO ▶
See Hour 7, "Create Your Outline," to learn about the recommended sections for your business plan. In addition, Hours 10 through 18 discuss each section in detail and show you what you need to include in each section.

GO TO ▶
See Hour 8, "Marshal Your Resources," to learn the best ways to plan and execute your business plan.

GO TO ▶
See Hour 5, "Analyze Your Strategy," to learn how to determine your company's vision, mission, goals, strategies, and tactics.

GO TO ▶
See Hour 3, "Analyze Your Market," to learn how and where to find all types of market and competitive information.

GO TO ▶
See Hour 9, "Build Your Numbers," to learn how to gather all the financial information you need and how to build a five-year plan from the ground up.

GO TO ▶
See Hour 21, "Format and Print," to learn how to use Microsoft Word or specific desktop publishing software to turn your words into a truly professional-looking business plan document.

GO TO ▶
See Hour 22, "Present the Plan," to learn the best ways to present your business plan to various audiences.

- **Build your numbers.** This is where your financial people come in. Not only do you have to assemble past and present financials, you need to plan the growth of your business over the next three to five years. These numbers don't come out of thin air, of course; there must be a reasonable basis for your projections, as well as a "sales" aspect to appeal to your potential investors.

- **Write the plan.** Once all your homework is done, someone has to do the actual writing. You can do this yourself (especially if you're a good writer), but you might be better off hiring a professional, *marketing-oriented* writer to do the job.

- **Publish the plan.** You want your business plan to look as professional as possible. To that end, you may want to contract with an individual or a firm to "publish" your plan. Page layout, paper choice, number of colors, and use of graphics are all important decisions at this stage.

- **Print the plan.** Find a printer; print the plan. Enough said.

- **Present the plan.** You might find that creating the business plan was the easy part. Now you get to present the plan to potential lenders and investors—which can involve anything from a simple one-on-one discussion to a full-blown dog-and-pony show complete with multimedia Microsoft PowerPoint presentation.

And that is how business plans are created. Keep reading for more details.

How to Define Success

What makes for a successful business plan? Is it one that's sleek and attractive and extremely professional looking? Is it one that's big and thick and extremely comprehensive? Or is it one that's short and sweet and easy for everyone to comprehend?

Actually, it's none of these. A successful business plan is one that accomplishes your main goal of attracting new funding for your business. It doesn't matter if the plan is thick or thin, pretty or plain, easy to read or densely written. If the plan convinces investors or lenders to provide the capital you asked for, it is successful.

Remember, the business plan is just a tool, a means to an end—not an end itself. And a tool is a good tool only if the job is successfully completed.

So don't go patting yourself on the back just because you created a stunning business plan document. Wait until the tool does its job and the money is in the bank—and *then* give yourself a hearty congratulations for a job well done!

HOMEWORK

In this hour, you learned why your business needs a business plan. In Hour 2 you'll learn more about who will be reading your plan—and what they expect to read.

To prepare for the next hour, you may want to think about the following:

- Who will be receiving copies of your business plan?
- What are their backgrounds?
- What other types of businesses do these investors fund?
- What expectations are these investors likely to have?
- Can you obtain copies of business plans for companies similar to yours?

HOUR 2

Analyze Your Audience

CHAPTER SUMMARY

LESSON PLAN:

In this hour, you will learn about ...

- Writing for a specific audience
- Researching competitor's plans
- Different types of investors and lenders
- What your audience expects to see

The biggest mistake most companies make when creating a business plan is to write the plan without a target audience in mind. These businesses can follow all the rules and go through all the steps, but what they end up creating is something generic, without a purpose or a defined goal.

It is much better to know who will be reading your plan (and why) so you can craft your plan to that particular audience. When you know who your target audience is, you know what you can leave out (because they either know it already or don't care about it) and what you should beef up (because they either expect to see it or are particularly interested in it). When you know your audience, you know whether your plan should be short or long, plain or fancy, and simple or complex. In short, if you know who your audience is and what your audience wants, you can build a plan that fits like a custom-made glove.

It's just like the way the best businesspeople run their businesses—know the customer and deliver a product that exactly meets that customer's wants and needs. In this case, your customers are the readers, and your product is the business plan. Just as you wouldn't want to deliver a product that didn't match your customer base, you don't want to create a business plan that is less than ideal for its target audience.

Looking at it another way, if you don't know who your audience is, you really don't know why you're creating a plan—and a plan with no purpose is a plan for failure.

DETERMINING THE AUDIENCE FOR YOUR BUSINESS PLAN

All this talk about creating the type of business plan that best suits your audience begs one question: Who is your audience?

As you learned in Hour 1, "Analyze Your Objectives," in general terms, there are three potential audiences for your business plan:

- Your customers
- Your employees
- Potential lenders and investors

Common sense leads to the conclusion that, although some of your customers might be interested in your company's business plan, most customers are more interested in the products and services you're selling and the prices you're charging. In short, you're not creating a business plan for your customers' benefit.

Creating a business plan that provides honest-to-goodness strategic guidance for your employees—particularly your key managers—is a noble idea, spoiled only by the fact that the vast majority of internal business plans end up sitting on a shelf collecting dust. While your business definitely needs a strategic direction (which a good business plan can provide), you're probably not going to go to all the time and trouble to create a business plan purely for internal use.

That leaves, for your target audience, the people that you'd like to lend you money. This audience of lenders and investors can consist of several different types of entities, depending on your particular business and its financing needs:

- **Bankers and loan officers.** You'd typically go to a bank or a lending firm for a loan if you're a local business, if your capital needs are small, or if you want to maintain complete control over your business.
- **Small investors.** Small investors, typically called (and culled from) "friends and family," are individuals who put up relatively small sums

of money (certainly under $1 million and often under $100,000) in exchange for an appropriate ownership stake in your company.

JUST A MINUTE

When you accept money from investors, you cede some degree of control over your business. In essence, an investor becomes a co-owner of your business, with specific rights and responsibilities. When you accept a loan from a lender, you cede no control over your business; you simply assume a legal obligation to repay the loan, and the lender has no involvement with the management of your business.

- **Strategic investors.** Strategic investors typically are large companies that invest larger sums (typically in excess of $1 million) in return for a larger equity stake in your company—and with some sort of synergy in mind for your two firms.
- **Venture capitalists.** Venture capital (VC) firms are companies that specialize in investing both money and their own expertise in startup businesses, in return for a significant equity position in the company. VCs most often expect relatively large rates of return on their investments.

WRITING FOR YOUR AUDIENCE

GO TO ▶
See Hour 6, "Analyze Your Options," to learn more about the different options you have for injecting money into your business.

Although each of these different audiences has its unique wants and needs, they all have one thing in common: They're in the business of handing out money—and you want some of it!

To that end, each of these target audiences expects that a business plan will contain the information and strategy that will convince them that your business is either a good loan risk or a good investment. They expect your plan to be in a specific format, to contain specific data, and to resemble similar plans from other businesses in your market niche. To some degree, they expect you to follow an outline, a boilerplate of sorts, in which everything is in the right place and format so that they (the investors) can quickly and easily find the information that is important to them.

This may sound a little restrictive, but in fact it makes your job easier. It's just like it is in the day-to-day running of your business—when you know what your customer wants, you know what kind of product you have to deliver.

What happens, you may ask, if you *don't* write your business plan for a specific audience? In the worst of all possible scenarios, if you don't give the audience what it expects (in terms of content and format), it may simply toss your plan aside without even a cursory read. That outcome is not only possible, it is likely, especially if a lender or investor has dozens of other similar proposals on his or her desk at the same time. These people are looking for a reason—*any* reason—to whittle down the stack of proposals by rejecting unworthy candidates. Making the first cut is important, and any deviation from standard operating procedure marks your business plan for the outbox.

YOU ARE NOT THE AUDIENCE

The first thing to keep in mind when writing for your audience is that you're *not* writing for yourself—or for your staff or advisors or friends or family. It doesn't matter what you'd like to see included in the business plan; if your audience doesn't want to see it, you shouldn't include it.

The opposite is also true, of course. There may be information that you feel is irrelevant, common knowledge, or (more likely) boring. Your feelings, in this case, don't matter. If the audience expects to or needs to see this information, it should go in the plan—no questions asked.

Remember, you're writing for your audience (your banker, the VC firm, and so on) and not for anyone else. Your audience might be a single person (in the case of your banker), or it might be many different people or groups of people. It doesn't matter. What they want to see is what goes into the plan. Nothing more, nothing less.

It's important to note that your audience probably doesn't know as much about your business as you do. (That's one of the reasons they need to read your plan.) You may need to include some very basic information about your market, the type of business you're in, and the like, just to bring your audience up to speed. Don't assume that your audience knows as much as you do—unless, based on past experience or similar investments, you're *sure* they do.

Along the same lines, you need to avoid using buzzwords and acronyms that are foreign to the uninitiated. If you're in the cellular phone industry, you're familiar with terms like CDMA and TDMA and GSM; your potential investors probably aren't. (Unless, that is, they're VCs who have invested in other cellular firms.) If you must use the buzzwords—and some of them can't be avoided—you should take the time to define and explain them on first use.

JUST A MINUTE

If your business uses a lot of industry- or technology-specific buzzwords and acronyms, consider including a glossary in the back of your business plan so that uninformed readers can look up words they're unfamiliar with.

Your Employees Aren't the Audience

It's often hard, when writing your business plan, to keep your focus on the target audience. At any point in the process, you may feel the need to make the plan palatable to others in your organization, all of whom have their own interests and agendas and few of whom are capable of focusing solely on what lenders and investors want and expect to see.

You will invariably run into a situation in which someone (probably a respected high-level manager) will read a draft of your business plan and question why certain information wasn't included (probably information about his or her particular department). In some such situations, the other person will *insist* that this information be added to the plan. Even worse, this person might insist on writing that section him- or herself!

The temptation will be to respond to this individual's concerns by adding the information in question, either to keep the individual quiet or to build "buy-in" for your plan. In most cases, this would be the incorrect response.

First, you don't need buy-in from your employees. It's your plan, written for your audience of lenders and/or investors. The plan is not being written for your employees—even your most trusted senior staff. If they don't agree with something in the plan, you have to explain to them that you understand their viewpoint but that the company's potential investors expect to see what you've included. If you were writing the "real" plan for internal consumption, the argument goes, you'd do it another way. But since this is for the investors, you have to play it along those lines. ("I appreciate your input, but ....")

Second, although acceding to your employee's demands will get that employee off your back (or make for a happier employee, if you want to think in those terms), adding irrelevant or improper information can and will detract from the effectiveness of the business plan. Adding a section on the HR department's new employee review process might seem like an acceptable bone to throw to your HR manager, but in a document in which every word counts, that extra paragraph or page or section can be just enough to throw off the delicate mix and convince potential investors that management is focused on the wrong issues. There should be nothing—*nothing*—in your business plan that doesn't advance your goal for achieving funding.

JUST A MINUTE

 This doesn't mean that your staff shouldn't help you prepare the plan or that their opinions aren't wanted. Your staff can often make suggestions (that you didn't think of yourself) that will improve the effectiveness of your business plan. It's only when those suggestions are self-serving and ignorant of the plan's true audience that they (the suggestions, not the staff) should be dismissed.

If the business plan you create ends up producing too much cognitive dissonance among your management or staff, it's possible you're selling something to investors that really doesn't exist—which is not a good thing. Your business plan should be a highly sanitized, extremely positive version of what your business really does on a day-to-day basis; it should *not* reflect some sort of altered reality that is unrecognizable to the rank and file. In other words, it's okay to put a positive spin on things—it's not okay to outright lie.

If you want to distribute the completed business plan to your employees but are concerned about their response, consider creating a second, *edited* business plan for internal consumption. You may want to delete some sections of the plan that are of interest only to investors, or to add sections that would be of more interest to your employees. Since an internal business plan would have a different audience than your investor-driven plan, it makes sense to create a plan that is personalized for that different audience.

YOUR CUSTOMERS AREN'T THE AUDIENCE

In the course of running your business, you're accustomed to putting a customer-focused spin on everything you do. If you have to drop a product line or raise prices, you're capable of spinning those actions in a way that sounds like you did them for the customers' benefit.

That's just good business.

The reality, of course, is that you make many business decisions because they'll have a positive impact on your business—not necessarily because they'll directly benefit the customer. Some of these decisions may be irrelevant to your customers (the grade of toilet paper you use in the employee restrooms, for example); some are relevant to your customers but directly benefit the business (changing suppliers or raising prices).

For the purposes of the business plan, you don't have to worry about putting a customer focus on all your information and strategies. In fact, some of your strategies might sound offensive if read by some of your customers. (Let's face it—part of what you do in business is exploit the customer to generate higher revenues and profits.)

Having a strategy of "improving customer satisfaction," for example, sounds very noble and market focused—but probably won't buy you much from a jaded investor. Investors want to know, in explicit detail, what you do that sets you apart from your competitors, how you're going to increase your market share, and how you're going to generate (and increase) profits. "Improving customer satisfaction" is a strategy that can be found (or at least implied) in virtually every business plan ever written. It is not a unique strategy, nor is it truly a strategy that will take business away from competitors (who are all trying to do the same thing) and increase your profits.

This does not mean you should not be customer focused, nor that you shouldn't strive to improve customer satisfaction. It merely means that you need to be business-like in your approach and be ruthlessly focused on achieving marketplace success in your plan. Even though you'd never tell your customers this, it's okay (and desirable) to include in your plan that you intend to increase selling prices 10 percent a year over the next five years. That's an accepted and acceptable business strategy, even if it wouldn't make a good headline for your next customer advertisement.

YOUR AUDIENCE IS THE AUDIENCE

The only audience you should be writing for—the only opinions that really count—are the people and firms that you want to put money into your business. Your goal in producing this plan is to entice these entities to make a loan or an investment. Everything in your business plan—every section, every graphic, every *word*—should be targeted at this audience and should work toward accomplishing your goal.

The better you know your audience, the better you can target your business plan. If your audience is a single individual (the loan officer at your bank, for example, or a particular partner at a VC firm), write your plan *for that individual*. Don't even pretend to create a plan with global application; make sure every page of your plan is meaningful to your target individual.

If your audience is multiple individuals or multiple *types* of individuals, your job is slightly more complex. It's possible that you're presenting your plan to two different banks or two different VC firms, each of which have slightly different hot buttons. That's a tougher task but not an impossible one. Remember, they're both investors (or lenders), and both are driven by similar factors.

Your task only becomes untenable when you try to target your business plan to two totally different constituencies. For example, if you expect your plan to do double duty with both investors and employees, you're setting yourself up for failure. You will end up compromising your success with at least one of the two constituencies—if not both of them! In this example, you're likely to not get the investment you want *and* alienate your employees, all in one fell swoop.

If you *must* distribute your business plan to two totally different audiences, consider creating two different business plans. This isn't an accounting-type situation, in which creating two sets of books will get you in hot water with the Feds. It's perfectly acceptable—and particularly recommended—to create two different audience-specific business plans, one to spur investment and the other to guide your employees.

To this end, it's a shame that the business plan you share with potential investors is actually called a "business plan." If this document were subject to truth-in-labeling laws, it would be called an "investor enticement plan" or a "stock sale infomercial." The fact that it's called a business plan—which is commonly perceived to be a type of internal strategic plan—is misleading, especially to those charged with creating the document.

JUST A MINUTE

Not all business plans are labeled as such. It's not uncommon for a business plan to have an alternate title, such as strategic plan, business overview, strategic overview, or even a "goals and opportunities" document.

UNDERSTANDING SPECIFIC AUDIENCES

As you write your plan, you need to know what your specific audience expects to see. What drives your audience—what information does it need before it can say "yes" to writing a check?

Let's take a look at the four different types of potential lenders and/or investors and how you can fine-tune your plan for greatest appeal.

JUST A MINUTE

There is actually a fifth type of investor—the public stockholder. However, once you're a publicly traded company, the information you provide to investors becomes tightly regulated by the Securities and Exchange Commission (SEC). It is highly unlikely that you will be providing simple business plans to public stockholders.

BANKERS AND LOAN OFFICERS

When you need a loan, you go to your bank or another lending institution. You're not asking your banker or loan officer to invest in your business; you're asking him or her to give you a loan and to assume some degree of risk regarding the repayment of that loan. (The smaller the better!)

The driving force behind a yes or no decision by a banker or loan officer is how he or she assess the risk—that is, how likely is it that you won't be able to repay the loan? Again, lenders are not interested in getting a return on their investment, they only care that their loan gets repaid (plus interest, of course). To that end, how fast and how far you can grow your business is not as relevant to a lender as it is to an investor; of more interest is the stability of your business and your ability to generate sufficient cash flow over the loan period.

Here, then, is a mini-checklist of the types of things you want to include in any business plan targeted at bankers, loan officers, and other lenders.

Important Business Plan Elements for Bankers and Loan Officers

- ☐ Historical cash flow statement
- ☐ Historical balance sheet
- ☐ Historical profit and loss statement
- ☐ Projected cash flow statement
- ☐ Projected balance sheet

continues

Important Business Plan Elements for Bankers and Loan Officers   (continued)

- ☐ Projected profit and loss statement
- ☐ Successful prior experience in management bios
- ☐ Evidence of stability (market stability, business stability, management stability)
- ☐ Detailed plan of how the loan will be used

PROCEED WITH CAUTION

In most instances, lenders will not look favorably on loans that are used to pay for existing and recurring business expenses. (For example, they won't loan you money just to make payroll.) Most lenders make loans to finance expansion products, or (in the case of lines of credit) to even out seasonal fluctuations or other natural ebbs and flows of the business.

SMALL INVESTORS

A small investor is typically a friend, family member, or business associate who is putting his or her personal funds into your business. People may do this out of a sense of obligation, because they trust your abilities, or because they sense an opportunity to make a substantial return. Remember, though, that they're often investing their *personal* funds—so the return of principle is probably equally as important as return on investment.

It's likely that you have an existing personal relationship with any individuals who are thinking of investing in your business. They're interested in investing because they know you and because they know your track record. In some instances, they may not know you personally but may be a "friend of a friend" who knows you. In any case, there often exists the feeling of a personal obligation to small investors, especially those "friend and family" investors, to ensure that they don't lose their money if things go bad and that they get a good return if your business really takes off.

What drives the small investor? One driver is the safety of their money; many small investors would like as much of a guarantee as possible that they won't lose their funds. On the opposite end of the scale are those who are really looking for a killing by getting in on the ground floor of a new business and being able to cash out at huge multiples when the company goes public or gets acquired. You need to balance both of these drivers when you construct a business plan for small investors.

Here, then, is a mini-checklist of the types of things you want to include in any business plan targeted at small investors.

Important Business Plan Elements for Small Investors

- ☐ Historical profit and loss statement
- ☐ Projected profit and loss statement
- ☐ Detailed information about market potential
- ☐ Examples of similar companies that have thrived in this or similar markets (especially any that have subsequently gone public)—with the goal of convincing the reader that your company represents a similar investment opportunity
- ☐ Detailed information about your company's products and services
- ☐ A detailed three- or five-year growth plan, focusing on strategies to grow revenues over that period
- ☐ A detailed examination of the business's revenue and profit models, focusing on achieving and surpassing the breakeven point
- ☐ Management bios, with a focus on prior entrepreneurial experience
- ☐ Information about other major shareholders, including (if advisable) a table of share holdings

STRATEGIC INVESTORS

Strategic investors are driven by many of the same factors as drive small investors—with a little more emphasis on return on investment and a little more tolerance for risk. The investors themselves are typically companies, not individuals, and thus can afford to pony up bigger bucks without putting their own net worth at risk.

An additional factor driving strategic investors is the strategic importance of the investment. Does your firm have some sort of market or operational synergy with the other firm? Is getting into this market segment particularly important to the investor? It may be that just being in this segment is more important than which firm they're aligned with—or there may be some strategic significance behind partnering with your particular firm.

Here, then, is a mini-checklist of the types of things you want to include in any business plan targeted at strategic investors.

Important Business Plan Elements for Strategic Investors

☐ Historical profit and loss statement

☐ Projected profit and loss statement

☐ Detailed information about market potential

☐ Detailed information about your company's products and services, with a focus on any alliances you have with other companies

☐ Information about the strategic importance of your products/services/business to the potential investor

☐ A detailed three- or five-year growth plan, focusing on strategies to grow revenues over that period

☐ Management bios, with a focus on prior industry experience

☐ Information about other major shareholders, especially if you have other institutional or strategic investors

---

VENTURE CAPITALISTS

Venture capitalists, or VCs, are a unique breed of investor. These businesses raise money from other investors (either individuals or institutions) to create an investment fund; that fund is then used to place investment in a number of worthwhile startup companies.

VCs invest large amounts of capital and expect a lot in return. They typically want a significant equity position, a seat on your board of directors, a say in the day-to-day management of your company (including, in some instances, their own guy on the management team), and a substantial return on their investment. What's a substantial return to a VC? Five times their initial investment is good, 10 times is better. Fortunately, most VCs are relatively patient when it comes to expecting their payout; some will wait up to 10 years before they cash out and return their gains to the investors in their funds.

What inspires a VC firm to invest in a specific business? In a phrase, *growth potential*. They want to own 20 percent of a firm that will increase its market share and sales by a factor of 10 or more over a given period. They're not interested in slow-growth businesses, and they recognize the risks involved in riding the rockets. They like to see driven individuals with a vision—and a unique business proposition that can own (or make!) a market.

Here, then, is a mini-checklist of the types of things you want to include in any business plan targeted at VC firms.

Important Business Plan Elements for Venture Capitalists

- ☐ Projected profit and loss statement
- ☐ Detailed information about market potential (unless they're already familiar with the market; in that case, this section can be abridged)
- ☐ Your unique vision for this market, and for your company
- ☐ Detailed information about your company's products and services, with a focus on what makes them unique in the marketplace
- ☐ A detailed three- or five-year growth plan, focusing on strategies to grow revenues (significantly) over that period
- ☐ Management bios, with a focus on prior entrepreneurial experience
- ☐ Information about other major shareholders, especially if you have other big-name or strategic investors

---

RESEARCHING WHAT OTHERS HAVE DONE

There is one last, but vitally important, step you need to take as you determine how best to target your business plan for a particular audience. Since there is no benefit to be gained by reinventing the wheel—and no penalty to be paid for learning from the work of others—you should seize the opportunity to examine a number of business plans from other companies.

PICKING A PLAN

What types of business plans should you seek to examine? Here's a short list:

- **Competitors in your industry.** If you can obtain them, the business plans of your direct competitors can be extremely informative. Not only will you learn about your competitors' strategy and positioning, you can also "borrow" some of their market data and general industry information and analyses. You'll also benefit from the views and opinions of people who know your industry inside and out—and, if you ask the right people the right questions, you can find out how the competitors' plans were received by their lenders or investors.

- **Companies in related industries.** While it may prove difficult, if not impossible, to obtain business plans for other companies in your specific industry, you can probably find business plans for companies in industries that are noncompetitive, but similar, to yours. Although you won't be able to use the market data in these plans, you can learn from how the companies developed their strategies and positioned themselves to potential lenders and investors.

- **Similar companies in other industries.** Sometimes the company is more important than the industry. Find a company of similar size, in the same stage of development, with similar strengths and weaknesses, and with similar investment needs—in other words, a mirror image of your company but in a different industry. You may be able to position your company in a similar fashion, especially if the other company was successful in attaining the type of funding you also desire.

FINDING A PLAN

Where can you obtain business plans to examine? The first place to go is to the company itself. While you probably can't obtain a business plan from a direct competitor (unless you're in an unusually cooperative industry), you'll find that many entrepreneurs are eager to help other entrepreneurs get up and running. The other advantage to asking directly is that you now have the opportunity to strike up a relationship with another business leader who can provide valuable advice and guidance, both professionally and personally.

Friends and family are also good sources of business plans, especially if they're active investors. Ask them about any private investments they've recently made or considered; chances are, they have a business plan or two filed away that you can borrow.

Another good source of business plans are the very people you're asking for money. Most potential lenders and investors are eager to give advice and provide guidance; all you have to do is ask for it.

Finally, take the opportunity to evaluate the *S-1* filings of public companies that fit your profile. These initial public offering (IPO) filings are similar in many ways to private business plans and contain much of the same market data and financial information. Plus, S-1s are publicly available, so no subterfuge is required.

STRICTLY SPEAKING

An **S-1**, sometimes called a public filing, is a document required by the SEC of any company filing for an initial public offering. It contains a variety of information specified by the SEC, in a set format.

FYI Since S-1s and other SEC-required documents are publicly available, you can use a number of sources to obtain copies of these documents. Two of the best Web sites for S-1s and other documents are the EDGAR database at the SEC's site (www.sec.gov/edgar.shtml) and FreeEDGAR (www.freeedgar.com).

STUDYING A PLAN

Once you obtain a copy of a business plan, you should study the plan intently. Sure, you may be able to "borrow" some of the market information and specific wording to insert into your plan, but—more importantly—you can learn from the style and approach adapted by the plan's creators.

What, in your opinion, works for that plan? What stands out as being unique or particularly effective? What doesn't work or stands out as irrelevant or inappropriate? What is directly applicable to your business?

A good approach, after an initial read-through of a plan, is to go through and mentally insert your business in place of the original business. Is this a good way to present your business? Are there factors that need to be added—or things that aren't relevant? Most importantly, would this plan *work* in presenting your business to potential investors?

Of course, examining a single plan can only tell you so much. A better approach is to obtain several plans from several different businesses in several different industries to get a better feel for different approaches and styles. When you have multiple plans to compare, you'll quickly learn what works and what doesn't—and you'll get a wealth of ideas on how to approach *your* business plan.

Learning by example is a good thing.

HOMEWORK

In this hour, you learned why and how you should target your business plan to a specific audience. In Hour 3, "Analyze Your Market," you'll learn more about how to define your market and how to perform effective market research and analysis.

To prepare for the next hour, you may want to think about the following:

- How would you define your company's industry?
- Who are your key competitors—and how much do you know about them?
- What sources of information exist for your industry? (Think about trade publications, research reports, information databases, and the like.)
- Are there any market research firms that focus on your industry?
- In terms of dollars, how big is your industry—and what is your company's market share?

HOUR 3
Analyze Your Market

LESSON PLAN:

In this hour, you will learn about ...

- Market research and analysis
- Defining your market
- Quantifying market size and share
- Estimating market growth

As you will learn later in this book, a good business plan tells a story—and the first part of the story defines *why* you want to pursue this particular business opportunity. The reason why has to do with the revenue and profit potential represented by a particular market. There's an attractive market opportunity, your story goes, and this business plan describes how we're going to get our share of that opportunity.

To make your case about market potential, you have to tell your investors about the market—what it's all about, how big it is, who the major players are, and how it's going to grow. However, to impart this information with any degree of authority, you have to become extremely familiar with the dynamics of your particular market.

Knowing your market is a business requirement that, unfortunately, many businesspeople take too lightly. It's very easy to get caught up in the day-to-day operations of your business, get sucked into the high-profile world of conferences and high finance, or get lured into the "inside" thinking of your product development team and thus lose track of the customers and the market that really drive your business. Keeping in touch with your customers is hard work, but it's not work you can neglect or delegate.

Why Market Analysis Is Important

You have a full-time job just running your business—why do you have to spend time digging up information about what other companies are doing? How could what your competitors are doing possibly affect what your company does?

The reality is that market research and analysis is vital to the success of any business; its importance to the construction of a successful business plan only highlights that overall significance.

The Market Drives Everything

Why should you have a constant focus on market research and analysis? There are several important reasons.

First, let's not overlook the obvious. As discussed in Hour 2, "Analyze Your Audience," there are certain types of information that potential lenders and investors expect to see in your business plan. One of these items is a section on your market—how big it is, who plays in it, how it's going to grow, and so on. So, at the very least, you need to engage in some rudimentary market research and analysis to create this section of your business plan.

Second, and more important, the more you know about your market, the better you can focus your business, your products, and your services. "Market," after all, is just another word for the total universe of potential customers for your goods and services. Knowing your market means knowing your customers—and every businessperson worth his or her salt knows that knowing your customers is the single most important factor in business success.

Some would go so far as to say that knowing the market is—or, at least, should be—second nature to every successful businessperson. Truly market-focused businesspeople live and breathe the market; they know their customers' needs and whims, they know the fads and trends, they know what's happening in each and every distribution channel, they even know what their competitors are doing—before it happens. To a successful businessperson, the market is his or her life.

That's because the market drives your business. Everything you do is to serve the market. If *you* lose touch with the market, then your business is also out-of-touch—and an out-of-touch business quickly becomes a failing business.

That is why knowing your market is vital to the success of your business. It's not just for the business plan; knowing your market helps you to create the long-term strategy that drives your company's current and future actions.

HOW TO KEEP IN TOUCH

Aside from sporadically gathering information when you absolutely have to—like the creation of this business plan—how do you keep in touch with your markets on a day-to-day basis? There are several things you can do to make sure you're as market-savvy as you need to be, including the following:

- **Read.** Most industries have at least one trade publication that provides periodic information about the companies and customers of that specific industry. Find your trade publications and read them—religiously.

- **Surf.** More and more information is shifting from print to online. Make sure you browse the Web several times a week, stopping at all the industry-related sites you can find. Some of the major portals, such as Yahoo!, let you define company- or industry-specific searches that can be placed on their customizable home pages; use these features to alert you to important industry news as it happens. It also doesn't hurt to use Yahoo! or the other search engines to do periodic searches on industry-specific terms (including the names of your competitors), just to see if anything new has popped up since your last search session.

- **Participate.** If your industry has a trade association, join it. If your industry has trade shows or conferences, go to them. In other words, participate in everything your industry has to offer—and make sure you mingle with your peers while you're there!

- **Visit.** Force yourself to get out of your office and visit your major customers or the stores where they shop. Make an effort to walk in your customers' shoes; do what they do—and how they do it—to get a better feel as to their current wants and needs. Don't let yourself get trapped into observing the market from an ivory tower—get out into the marketplace and be as one with your customer base.

- **Listen.** Salespeople, customer support reps, even the guys on the loading dock all have contact with parts of your market and your business that you might not touch on a daily basis. Listen to these people. Make yourself available for all types of feedback, from employees and customers and even competitors, if the opportunity arises. Let the world be your eyes and ears to keep you more connected with the marketplace.

Keeping abreast of marketplace trends is a full-time job—and it's too important to completely delegate to someone else on your staff. Think of it this way—if a potential investor asks you a market-related question, you want to be able to answer it off the cuff without referring to your printed materials. Your investors want to be assured that you know your market—and to be successful, you really do need to be in touch.

Your market is your business. Know it!

DEFINING YOUR MARKET

A market is typically defined by the goods and services it offers and by the types of customers that exist for those goods and services.

For example, if you offer four-color printing services to small and medium-size businesses in the greater Chicagoland area, you would define your market as "the market for four-color printing services for small and medium-size businesses in the greater Chicagoland area." If you're creating a Web site to offer investing advice and information to females aged 25 to 45, you would define your market as "the market for Web-based investing information for female investors, aged 25 to 45."

Of course, there may be better ways to describe your market. If there's an accepted market shorthand, use it. For example, instead of describing your market as "the market for washers, dryers, refrigerators, ranges, and dishwashers that are packaged by new home builders to new home buyers," you could use acceptable industry shorthand and describe your market as the "builder appliance market."

If you're unsure of what to call your market, look to your industry's trade publications and research reports. Chances are, the press and the analysts have a phrase for the place where you play; if so, use it.

YOUR COMPETITORS' MARKET IS YOUR MARKET

If you're unsure exactly what market it is that you play in, take a look at your direct competitors. If your competitors are focused, that focus will likely describe the same market you're targeting. You can describe your market, then, by the customers your competitors target and by the types of products and services that they offer.

Know, however, that defining a market based on what your competitors do is not the same as defining a market by your competitors. A market is defined by its customers and products, not by the companies that play in the market. (It's not the IBM and Toshiba market—it's the portable computer market.) So take care to avoid a competitor-focused description of your market.

BROAD OR NARROW?

A market can be defined as broadly or as narrowly as you wish. In fact, you may want to set distinct market parameters that best match the specific products and services offered by your company.

For example, defining a market as the "communications market" is fairly broad and includes all sorts of communications products and services— everything from cellular telephone networks and landline phone services to cordless telephone handsets and walkie-talkies. A more narrow definition would be the market for "mobile communications devices," which would cut out all the networks and services (along with all desktop phone products) to focus specifically on mobile phones and walkie-talkies.

Obviously, the broadest market definitions would describe the largest revenue opportunities, along with the largest number of competitors. It's easy to get lost in this type of market definition; you become a very small fish in a very big pond, and it will look like you're competing with a number of established industry behemoths.

The narrowest market definitions, on the other hand, run the risk of describing very small (and potentially uninteresting—to investors, at least) revenue opportunities. If you define your market too narrowly, you may paint yourself into a corner; future growth may be dependent on expansion in a fashion that appears to exceed the restrictive bounds you've described for your market.

YOUR MARKET—AS OTHERS SEE IT

When you define your market, take care not to slice the pie in a way that differs too much from common perception. While a new and unique definition of a particular market (or, more likely, a subset of a market) might appear to benefit your business (by defining market parameters to favor the precise product mix of your company), most neutral observers will see the ploy for what it is—and proceed to define the market in the same fashion they've always used.

For example, no matter how strenuously you insist that the market for left-handed fishing poles is a distinct and separate market, most industry observers will contend that the real market (or is that the *reel* market?) is the broader one for fishing poles of all types and sizes. All the fancy prose and multicolored charts in the world won't be able to convince investors that you're right about the left-handed market if it's just a convenient way to spin your company's prospects. Creating an artificial market division won't get you too far with investors—and could possibly damage your chances for funding.

The bottom line is that if all the analysts and investors think one way, it's not a good idea for you to think another. This isn't some sort of contest in which you win by thinking smarter or more uniquely than everyone else; this is a game with a preexisting set of rules, and you have to play by those rules. Any attempt to rewrite the rules will be viewed with suspicion at best—and will be outright rejected, in all likelihood.

QUANTIFYING YOUR MARKET

Once you've defined your market, you need to size it. You need to quantify how big your market is in terms of either gross or net revenues—typically measured in terms of the total industry-related revenues generated by all companies competing in the market.

While you're gathering information, it helps to have industry revenue data for at least the past three years, if not longer. (This way, you can do some historical trends analysis.) Any granulation of the data (by customer, customer type, distribution channel, product type, and so on) might also prove useful.

FINDING THE DATA

GO TO ▶
e Hour 12,
portunity," to
list of poten-
rces for mar-
ed data and

In many instances, however, sizing a market is easier said than done. Just where do you obtain these revenue numbers?

If you're lucky, all the companies in your industry belong to some type of trade association that closely monitors sales from all companies. This data can be self-reported, tracked by a third-party firm (such as the music industry's SoundScan service), or estimated by the trade group. If this is the case in your market, you can go to the industry trade group to obtain all the market data you need.

Even if your industry doesn't have an industry trade group or accurately reported trade data, it may still be an industry that is covered by one or more market research firms or analysts or even by an especially diligent and aggressive trade press. Research firms, analysts, and the press typically won't have access to actual revenue data, but they might undertake their own estimates and analysis. In this type of industry, you're relying on third-party "guesstimates"—which may be flawed but at least represent an intelligent attempt to provide accurate numbers.

TIME SAVER

 You may be asked to purchase a high-priced market research report (or join an industry trade group) to obtain the market data you seek. If you'd prefer not to incur this expense, try searching through the organization's database of press releases; chances are, the data you seek has been publicly announced at some point in the past.

Creating Your Own Data

What do you do if there isn't *any* public data about your particular market? This is often the case, and it requires a bit of work on your part to pull the numbers together.

If no good data about your market exists, you have to make your own intelligent estimate based on information that does exist. The way to approach this is to identify the largest companies in your industry, make a guess as to what percentage of total industry revenues are generated by these big players, and then determine these companies' revenues.

Let's go through this step by step.

First, you have to identify the industry's largest players. This shouldn't be a long list—typically, the top three or four players contribute at least half of the total revenues for any given industry. If you're unsure who the big players are, ask some of your customers—they'll know.

Once you've identified the big boys, now you have to guess how much of the market they control in total. As stated previously, the top three or four players *typically* generate about 50 percent of the industry's total revenues. The precise number in your industry may vary, and you probably won't be able to find out the real number anyway, so you'll just have to go ahead and guess.

Now comes what appears to be the really tough part—estimating your competitors' revenues. This may be easier than you might think, however.

First, if a company is publicly traded, its revenues are part of the public record. Just look up the company's most recent 10-K filing with the SEC or search its Web site for a copy of its annual report. The company's annual revenues (and profits!) will be right there for all to see. Easy.

PROCEED WITH CAUTION

In many cases, a single company might compete in several different markets; the total revenues of that company would include revenues for your specific market—*and* revenues for other, unrelated industries. Since it would be inaccurate to count all of the company's revenues when calculating the size of your market, you'll need to get a breakout of revenues for that large company or at least estimate the specific revenues generated in your market.

Even if the company isn't publicly traded, it still might have released its revenue numbers publicly. Naturally, a private company doesn't have to release this data, but some companies can't resist a little bragging at the end of a good year. Search the Internet for press releases from the company, and scan the releases for any annual revenue information. For that matter, searching the company's Web site (use the About the Company links) can sometimes reveal this sort of information.

Your industry's trade press or research reports might also contain a clue as to the revenue data you want. It's not uncommon for company executives to make comments to journalists and analysts that provide clues to the company's revenue or profit numbers—at least in round terms.

It also wouldn't hurt to talk to some other companies in your industry or some major customers. They might have an idea as to the size of a specific company—even if it's third-hand information or data derived from other sources. For example, a customer might recall hearing the company's salesperson say something about the customer representing five percent of the company's total business. If this is true, and if you know how much business the customer did with the company, the information you seek can be generated with a little simple math.

As a last resort, you may just have to guess. If you do this, be sure to label any guesstimate-type market data as coming from "company analysis" or "internal research."

DETAILING THE MARKET

Sizing your market is part of the equation. The other part is describing your market—how it's built and how it works.

There are several components of a comprehensive market description:

- **Products and services.** For your business plan, you'll need to describe the types of products and services offered within your industry.

- **Customers.** You'll probably need to describe the types of customers your industry targets (consumers, corporations, and so on), the demographics of these customers (men between 25 and 45 with incomes above $100,000, for example), and—if a few major customers represent a large percent of sales—the names of the industry's key customers. (This last point would come into play if you're a manufacturer selling to wholesalers or retailers—your largest customers would be the major distributors or retailers who stock and sell your product.)

- **Competitors.** What are the biggest companies in your industry? What are their estimated revenues? (You might have to guess at this.) What are their individual *market shares*? What are their individual strengths and weaknesses? Are they gaining or losing ground in the marketplace? To compete effectively, you need to know as much about your competitors as you can.

STRICTLY SPEAKING

Market share is the percentage share of industry revenues generated by a specific company. You compute market share as follows: Total industry revenues divided by individual company revenues.

- **Distribution channels.** Do you sell directly to consumers, do you sell to retailers (two-step distribution), or do you sell through wholesalers that then sell to retailers (three-step distribution)? Or do you sell via mail order, direct mail, telemarketing, a Web site, or through a dedicated sales force or third-party sales reps? However things get sold in your industry, it needs to be described.

- **Promotional activities.** How do companies in your industry promote their products and services to prospective customers? Do the companies advertise—and, if so, where and how much? However your industry supports its sales needs to be described.

- **Average margins.** How much profit does the typical company in your industry generate, as a percent of sales? Knowing an average industry profit margin will help you better build your own financials and will lend an air of credibility to the financial projections you make to potential investors.

- **Other analytics.** If you have the numbers, there are several other interesting data points you can calculate. These analytics can be useful for making comparisons between your company's performance and industry averages: sales per employee, profit per employee, advertising as a percent of revenues, development cost as a percent of revenues, and so on.

The important thing is that you need to know how your market ticks, even if you don't have precise numbers—not just to create your business plan but, more importantly, to help you develop your overall business strategy. You can't figure out how to get from point A to point B unless you know the landscape!

PROJECTING THE FUTURE

Let's assume you can gather enough data and information to paint the picture of your market as it exists today. That's all well and good, but where things are today doesn't help you figure out what you're going to do tomorrow. To fully develop your long-term business strategy, you need to have a good idea of how your market is going to develop over the next several years.

Gazing into the future might seem like the province of crystal-ball gazers and Tarot card readers, but it's also a skill that's essential to building a successful business. Unless you have a good sense about how the market is going to look next year, or five years out, you won't know in which direction to steer your business to take advantage of (or avoid the repercussions of) any coming changes.

How, then, does one go about predicting the future?

CONSIDERING THE PUNDITS

A good place to start is with people who get paid to predict the future—market analysts. If your industry is fortunate enough to be covered by one or more market research and analysis firms, you'll find that their industry reports always contain a section that predicts future trends and projects future industry revenues. It's their job to tell other people what's likely to happen in the future, so their reports are driven by their predictions and projections.

JUST A MINUTE

Other sources for similar market information are the industry and individual company reports issued by various financial analysts. You can find these reports at the best financial Web sites, such as Motley Fool (www.fool.com), or you can obtain them from your personal stockbroker.

The only thing is, when you go back and look at how accurate they've been in past predictions, you'll find that the market analysts are often way off base; what they say will happen and what actually does happen are often two wildly different things. Most typically, the analysts end up being too optimistic about the future. When the future comes, it seldom lives up to the analyst's expectations.

Why is this? Why do analysts always guess high?

It's because market analysis firms make their money by selling their research reports—often at very high prices to a select few high-paying clients. These clients (either large investors or large industry players) buy a research report because they're interested in the opportunities presented by a particular market. If they didn't think there was money to be made, they wouldn't be interested—and thus wouldn't buy the high-priced research report. (This is the variation on the theme that people only pay for good news—or, in the case of big business, good news that will make them money.)

So, in order to sell their high-priced reports, the research firms have to sell their clients on the high potential of the industries covered in the reports. If a firm reported that an industry was going down the toilet, that firm wouldn't sell too many of their high-priced reports about that industry. The result is that just about every report you read paints an extremely rosy picture of the industry at hand, with lots of fancy charts showing revenues growing—significantly—year after year after year. That's what their clients want to hear, so that's what they tell them.

Now, this sounds like a cynical take on what is a very large and important industry service. If you think this really isn't the case, take a look at some past industry reports and see for yourself how predictions compare to reality. You'll be surprised at how optimistic most of these reports really are.

That's not to say that research reports don't have value. Most of the time, the underlying trends and information presented in the reports are true. It's just that, when preparing the numbers, the analysts tend to emphasize the positive points and gloss over the negative ones.

So when you're making your own predictions for the future of your market, use any existing market research reports as a base for your own analysis. Interpret the facts and trends in your own manner and draw your own conclusions. Just beware of the tendency of the professional analysts to overestimate future potential.

EXTRAPOLATING CURRENT TRENDS

A quick and easy way to predict future industry revenues is to look at what's happened in the past. Use Microsoft Excel or your favorite financial analysis software to plot a trend line based on the past five years (or more) of total industry revenues. Extend the line forward, and you have your future industry projections.

The problem with this method is that it assumes that things continue in the future the same way they have in the past. For many industries, this is a valid assumption; for other, more dynamic industries, this has the potential of painting a false picture of the future.

If your industry is too nonlinear to rely on long-term trend analysis, try performing the same analysis but based on a shorter historical period. Maybe you only take the last two years of data instead of five. Or maybe you perform your analysis on *quarterly* data and then create a series of quarterly industry projections. When things are volatile, use more granular data—and make shorter-term projections.

ANTICIPATING FUTURE DEVELOPMENTS

More important is the ability to anticipate new developments that significantly impact the dynamics of your industry. Is there a new technology coming your way that will impact what you sell or how you make your products? Is there a new player entering the market—or an old one exiting? Are conditions ripe for a series of mergers and acquisitions? Is your customer base changing in some way—growing older, perhaps, or earning higher incomes? All these factors—and many others—can significantly alter an industry's shape and performance and should be taken into account when putting together your long-term projections.

How do you know what is going to happen in the future? It's simple—keep your ear to the ground *today*. Observe your customers—*individual* customers, if necessary—and see what's changing in their lives. Read the trade journals, as well as publications dedicated to new technology, with an eye for developing trends. Talk to the insiders in your industry, including your own product development and market research people, to find out what new things they have their eyes on. Read, listen, and absorb—so you'll know what trends are coming *before* they hit.

PUTTING IT ALL TOGETHER

With all this information under your belt, you can now make an educated guess about how your industry will perform over the next three to five years. If your industry always grows at 5 percent year after year after year and there are no big developments on the horizon, then put together a projection that shows a 5 percent compounded annual growth. If your industry is about ready to be hit with a brand new technology that will cut your costs in half—and thus enable you to sell your products for half their current price—then factor in a substantial increase in consumer demand along with that lower average selling price. If your industry caters to an older audience with shrinking incomes, then plan for revenue shrinkage over time.

Use what you know, and what you feel, to make the best predictions you can. Don't sweat the details too much; focus on big picture changes and come up with some good, round number projections.

KEY MARKET INFORMATION

Summing things up, the following checklist details the market information that is key to the development of your company's long-term strategy, and to the preparation of your business plan.

Important Market Information

- [ ] A precise definition of the industry, in terms of markets, customers, products, and services
- [ ] Current market size, in revenue dollars
- [ ] Historical industry revenue and growth numbers
- [ ] Estimated market growth for the next three to five years
- [ ] A list of leading companies within the industry
- [ ] Market share estimates for the largest industry players
- [ ] Estimate of average industry margins
- [ ] Customer and distribution channel profiles
- [ ] A list of the largest industry customers (if appropriate), with estimates of annual purchases
- [ ] Current and projected industry trends

HOMEWORK

In this hour, you learned how to define your audience and gather market research and information. In Hour 4, "Analyze Your Strengths," you'll learn how to assess your company's competitive advantages—and unique business challenges.

To prepare for the next hour, you may want to think about the following:

- What does your company do well?
- What does your company do poorly?
- What do your competitors do well—and poorly?
- What things (products, services, processes, and so on) are unique to your company?
- What unique benefits do you, personally, bring to the company?
- What one thing could happen that would bring your company to its knees?

HOUR 4

Analyze Your Strengths

CHAPTER SUMMARY

LESSON PLAN:

In this hour, you will learn about …

- Unique competitive advantages
- Potential business challenges
- Exploiting your strengths
- Minimizing your weaknesses

As you develop your company's long-term business strategy—and prepare to mold that strategy into a business plan—not only do you need to know your customers and your competitors (as discussed in Hour 3, "Analyze Your Market"), you need to know your company. You need to know what your company does, of course (what products and services you sell and to whom), but you also need to know all about your strong points and your weak points.

You can be sure that your competitors know your strengths and (especially) your weaknesses and are right now plotting how to defend against your strengths and target your weaknesses for offensive action. If you're up on your market, you're doing the same for *your* competitors.

If your competitors can (and do) identify your strengths and weaknesses, so can (and should) you. Once you have this information in hand, you can develop a strategy to build on your strengths and strengthen your weaknesses —both of which are essential for long-term success.

There's another reason for identifying your strengths and weaknesses—you'll need this information for your business plan. Most business plans include a section called Competitive Advantages (or Core Competencies or something similar) that details your company's strengths; most plans also include a section called Competitive Challenges (or Potential Liabilities or the like) that details your weaknesses. So you'll need to have a handle on your strengths and weaknesses before you start writing your business plan.

IDENTIFYING WHAT YOU DO WELL

The things you do well are your strengths, or your core competencies. The things you do uniquely well, or demonstrably better than your competitors, become unique competitive advantages.

It's important to differentiate between *simple* strengths and *unique* strengths. A simple strength is something you're inherently good at; a unique strength is something you're better at than your competitors.

In the course of defining your company's strengths and weaknesses, you should count your simple strengths and your unique strengths as two separate items. This is because one of your simple strengths may also be a strength for one or more competitors, whereas a unique strength is something your company alone possesses. A unique strength can be turned into a competitive advantage; if you can do something your competitors can't, that gives you some degree of advantage in the marketplace. And, as you know, you'll take every marketplace advantage you can get.

DIFFERENT KINDS OF STRENGTHS

What types of activities represent strengths? Although there are literally hundreds of different areas in which your company can excel, you can group those activities into five main types:

- Product strengths
- Brand strengths
- Marketing and advertising strengths
- Sales and distribution strengths
- Operational strengths

PRODUCT STRENGTHS

A product strength is one of the most important strengths to attain because it's directly seen by your customers—and should directly impact your sales. There are many ways to establish a product strength: Your product can be of higher quality than the competition; it can be available in a wider variety of outlets and channels; it can be available in a wider selection of colors or sizes or options; it can be lower priced than the competition; it can have a better reputation than the competition. The key is that the strength is directly attributable to the product.

For example, the drumset part of the musical instrument market in the 1980s was plagued by cheap, poorly constructed products. In the 1990s, a company named Drum Workshop came along and raised the bar, producing better-made and better-sounding products than the competitors of the time. Today, Drum Workshop is known for its high-quality (albeit expensive) drumsets, and has rocketed to a top-three position in the market. Other companies that didn't innovate and improve their products suffered by comparison; the once-venerable Slingerland company, as an example, had all but disappeared from the scene by the turn of the millennium. Drum Workshop developed the product strength, and benefited from it; other companies didn't, and suffered.

JUST A MINUTE

Strengths are fleeting and often easily duplicable; few advantages last forever. After all, if you can build a better mousetrap, so can your competitors. When you identify a unique advantage, don't rest on your laurels—start working on developing the *next* great product or competitive advantage.

BRAND STRENGTHS

A brand strength is similar to a product strength, but the quality is held by the overall brand rather than the individual product. Individual products sold under that brand often (but not always) share the brand strengths by association. A brand might be known for quality, price, innovation, fun, status, or lots of things.

For example, the Rolls Royce brand is known for high quality; that's a brand strength. Within the Rolls Royce line, specific models are also perceived as being of high quality, because the Rolls Royce brand is high quality—they share the strength of the brand, by association.

Brand strength is especially valuable in those industries in which individual products have become commodities. Thus, any perceived benefit associated with the brand serves to distinguish that brand's products from other similar products on the market. For example, almost all low-end audio/video receivers have practically identical performance and features. Sony's receivers, however, stand out from the others because of the strength of the Sony brand, which stands for quality and innovation. It doesn't matter that the Sony receiver is virtually indistinguishable from the JVC or the Kenwood; in the eyes of the customer, it's a higher quality product because it's a Sony.

JUST A MINUTE

Sometimes the brand and the product are so closely associated with each other as to be virtually indistinguishable. For example, Kleenex the brand is, in most consumers' minds, indistinguishable from Kleenex the facial tissue.

Marketing and Advertising Strengths

Some companies know how to market their products and services; others don't. A great marketing or advertising campaign will increase awareness of your product and (in some cases) your company; greater awareness should, at least in theory, lead to greater sales.

A good example of marketing strength can be found in the automobile market. Over the years, Honda has demonstrated marketing and advertising strengths that set it apart from competitors like Nissan and Mazda. Are Honda's cars any better than similar models from Nissan and Mazda? It doesn't matter, because their marketing makes you *think* that they are. That's a marketing strength—and it's accomplished partly by brute force (Honda outspends these competitors by a considerable margin) and partly by what can only be described as institutional marketing and advertising savvy. It's likely that you're aware of the Honda Civic; you know it's a good, inexpensive little car. It's also probable that you're less aware of the Mazda Protegé or the Nissan Sentra. The difference is Honda's marketing strength.

Sales and Distribution Strengths

If your sales force can get more items stocked than your competitors' sales forces can, then you've just identified a sales/distribution strength. If your sales force can push your product into more channels than your competitors can, that's another sales/distribution strength. The ability to get your product stocked—or, in the case of direct-sales models, to make a sale directly to the end customers—is a necessity; if you can do it better than your competitors, it's a strength.

In the consumer electronics industry, Thomson Electronics (the parent company of RCA and GE) exhibits significant sales and distribution strengths. Not only can you find RCA televisions in traditional consumer electronics stores, such as Best Buy and Circuit City, you can also find their products in mass merchants (Wal-Mart and Target), warehouse clubs, and in Radio Shack. What other television manufacturer has the strength to sign an exclusive distribution deal with Radio Shack? It's a real strength for Thomson.

JUST A MINUTE

If you're in a business that deals directly with your customers, your sales and distribution strengths will be related to the number of customer contacts you can initiate—and how effectively you can turn those customer contacts into revenues.

OPERATIONAL STRENGTHS

Operational strengths relate to processes that occur behind the scenes. You may be able to ship your products faster than your competitors; that's an operational strength. You may be able to produce your product at a lower cost; that's an operational strength (that can also translate into a product strength—lower prices). If you have a more efficient warehouse operation, that's an operational strength.

In mass-market retailing, Wal-Mart claims numerous operational strengths. By requiring all manufacturers to comply with Wal-Mart's proprietary inventory systems, Wal-Mart can run a much more efficient warehouse and distribution operation than its competitors—who must contend with a hodge-podge of labeling and packaging standards from their various suppliers. If you sell products to Wal-Mart, you use their labeling and bar-coding systems, and you pack your boxes according to the quantities that Wal-Mart dictates. The result is a distinct operational strength for the Wal-Mart operation, which translates into lower stocking and handling costs, and shorter restocking times from warehouse to store shelves.

OTHER STRENGTHS

There are many other types of strengths that your company could possess. Your firm could have a strategic vision that always gets you to new opportunities sooner than your competitors; in this instance, your strategy is your strength. Your firm could be so well known in your industry that you're always getting interviewed by the trade and consumer press; in this case, your public awareness is a strength.

Your employees can also be a considerable strength. Do you have more seasoned employees than your competitors? That could be a strength. Do you compensate your employees in ways that improve their output or efficiency? That could also be a strength. Maybe your company culture is a strength or the perks and plans that enable you to have a high employee-retention rate. Maybe it's just the fact that you're a good guy (or gal), and everybody knows it. Sometimes your personal strengths translate into business strengths; this is especially true in smaller businesses in which, to the eyes of the community, you *are* your business.

Look around; anything you do better than competing companies—and that directly impacts your top-line sales or bottom-line profits—could be a strength.

DETERMINING YOUR STRENGTHS

How do you know when your company has a bona fide strength—and not just something you *think* you do well?

The first thing to do is look at everything your company does, all its processes and activities, from top to bottom. Note which activities appear to be running smoothly and which appear to have some rough edges. Focus on the smooth-running operations, and you've made your first cut.

Next look at each of those smooth-running operations and ask yourself what impact each one has on your revenues and profits. (Remember that an activity that reduces costs increases profits.) Rank these operations by their monetary impact and get ready for the next step.

Now, in order of importance, start comparing your best operations to those of your competitors. If you think you have a particularly impactive sales force, compare your sales force's results to those of your chief competitors. If you think you get products to market extremely fast, compare your time-to-market with that of your competitors. If you think your product is of higher quality, *test it*. Do whatever you need to do to prove (to yourself, if to no one else) that you really are doing this one thing better than anyone else in your industry.

JUST A MINUTE

If you're starting up a new business, it will be more difficult to identify your strengths and weaknesses. You may need to think in terms of *potential* strengths and weaknesses as well as strengths and weaknesses that relate to the people you've hired for your management team.

LEARNING FROM YOUR STRENGTHS

Once you've found a bona fide competitive advantage, tear it apart. Look at that advantage from every angle. Figure out why it exists and what your company has done to create that advantage. Answer the question, "Why is this thing so good?"

If you *don't* examine your strengths, you'll never be able to replicate them. The goal is to determine what you've done right so you can do something similar elsewhere in your organization.

A related goal is to preserve your strengths. Again, if you don't know how the strength came about, if you don't know what you're doing right, then you probably won't know how to keep doing it right. Analyze your strengths just as a competitor would; when you understand what you're good at, you'll get even better.

Finally, you need to *exploit* your strengths. If you can ship products to customers one day faster than any of your competitors, then make that one day a big issue. Play up not only how fast you ship but also how your customers benefit by getting your product one day sooner. Turn your company's strength into a consumer benefit, and you'll get the full benefit of your competitive advantage.

JUST A MINUTE

If you don't draw attention to your strengths, they lose their value. A strength is only a strength—and a consumer benefit is only a consumer benefit—when others know about it and when you make it matter to them.

BROADCASTING YOUR STRENGTHS

When you start to put together your business plan, you'll need to feed some information about your strengths into the Competitive Advantages section of the plan. Just what advantages do you include—and which do you leave out?

First, include only those strengths that are real strengths. If you say you have the fastest time-to-market, you'd better be able to back it up. A single "mistruth" can damage the credibility of your entire plan.

Second, include only those strengths that have significant impact on your sales and profits. Yes, you may buy the softest toilet paper for your employee restrooms, but that probably doesn't impact your market share or operating margin. Stick to the big things whenever possible.

It also helps if you include the competitive advantages that are easily understood by potential investors—or at least describe them in a way that is easily understood. If you tell investors that you utilize the new X-23 antistatic conveyor belts in your warehouse because they provide more friction at curves and intersecting corners, you'll probably get a few yawns and quizzical looks. If, on the other hand, you tell them that you use state-of-the-art conveyor technology to reduce product damage during packing, you'll make a bigger positive impact.

JUST A MINUTE

As will be discussed quite often later in this book, it's important to convey information in terms of benefits rather than features. It's just like good advertising copy; stress the impact that your competitive advantage gives you instead of talking about the advantage itself.

It may be important to limit the amount of detail you convey about specific strengths. If you have a top-secret formula that you use in your best-selling product, you probably want to tell investors that you have such a formula—but you don't want to divulge the formula itself. (We all know that Coca-Cola has a secret formula, and we know it's a product advantage, but no one outside of Coke's Atlanta labs knows the formula's exact composition.) After all, it's quite likely that one or more competitors will get their hands on a copy of your business plan; you don't want to reveal all your business secrets if you don't have to!

FIGURING OUT WHERE YOU'RE WEAK

Just as your company has its strengths, it also has its weaknesses. For every thing you do well, you probably do an equal number of things not so well. It's a fact of life; no one's perfect!

Determining your company's soft underbelly is of equal importance to determining your strengths—and may, in fact, be more important over the long run. When you discover a weakness, you now have a project—to either mitigate or improve the thing that is weak. The more weaknesses you can eliminate, the stronger your company will be.

UNDERSTANDING DIFFERENT KINDS OF WEAKNESSES

Any area that can be a strength can also be a weakness. Obviously, some areas are more critical than others; a rotten product will ultimately derail even the best sales force or advertising campaign. Here, then, are the key areas in which to look for inherent weaknesses:

- **Product weaknesses.** Product quality is probably the biggest killer. If your product or service doesn't deliver as promised, everything else you do will also suffer. You have to ensure that your product is *at least* as good as your competitors' products, just to stay in the game.

  Product quality isn't the only possible product weakness, however. Your product can be too pricey or not expensive enough. (Too low a price can sometimes convey poor quality.) Your product might not be available in the right colors or sizes or other variations, it might not be available in as many different outlets, or it may be outdated. (Last year's product available this year is of little use.) Worst of all, your product might simply not be available at all; if your competitors beat you to market with the latest thing, that is a huge product weakness.

- **Brand weaknesses.** Just as you can have strong brand names, you can also have weak brand names. When it comes to quality and reliability, do you want to be known as the Volvo of your industry or the Pinto? Pinto is an equally recognizable brand, but it's a brand with a *bad* reputation. Given the choice of having a bad brand image or no brand image at all, you might want to choose the no-image option.

  This leads into the other, more common type of brand weakness—the lack of brand recognition. If your primary competitor has a recognized brand and you don't, you have a brand weakness problem. It doesn't matter how good your product is; if customers flock to a competitor's product because of its brand image, you're out in the cold.

- **Marketing and advertising weaknesses.** There are two major types of marketing/advertising weaknesses: bad marketing and no marketing. With the first type, it doesn't matter how big your budget is if your ads are ineffective. With the second type, it doesn't matter how effective your ads are if no one (or not enough people) sees them. You have to know what you're doing, and you have to actually spend the money to do it. Anything less—especially if your competitors are constantly out there in front of customers—is a competitive weakness.

- **Sales and distribution weaknesses.** If your competitors consistently achieve better stocking than you do, you have a sales weakness. If your competitors are in more and different outlets and channels than you are, you have a distribution weakness. It doesn't matter how good your product is or how effective your advertising is; if your product isn't on the shelves, nobody can buy it.

  You face similar issues whether you're a retailer or you sell directly to your customers. If your customers can find the products they want—or if they're thwarted in their attempts to purchase those products—you'll lose those sales. Anything that stands in the way of your customer and the sale is a sales weakness that must be overcome.

- **Operational weaknesses.** The best business ideas are too often sabotaged by operational weaknesses. Maybe you have a great idea for a new product; if you can't get it built on time or at the right cost, you have a big problem. If orders or restocks sit in your warehouse for days and weeks without being fulfilled, you have a problem. If your systems are so poor that you end up with twice as much inventory as your competitors, you have a problem.

  Your company's operations support everything else you do. At the very least, you need to be on an operational par with your major competitors. The best businesses recognize the importance of smooth-running operations and strive for operational advantages in the marketplace. These successful businesspeople realize that getting a product to market faster, and at a lower cost, provides a tremendous competitive advantage. Not doing so can have a tremendous impact on a business's bottom line.

- **Other weaknesses.** Many other types of weaknesses could plague your company. If you have poor relationships with your employees—or if you don't pay them enough—you could have trouble holding on to experienced staff, with its resultant ill effects. If nobody in the industry (including your key suppliers) returns your phone calls, that's a weakness. If you're constantly playing catch-up because you're not savvy to market trends and developments, that's a weakness. If your company has a bad reputation in the industry (whether it's earned or not), that's a weakness that you have to work hard to overcome every day.

Cast a critical eye at everything your company does on a day-to-day basis. Anything you do poorly, or anything you don't do as well as your competitors, is a potentially devastating weakness.

Determining Your Weaknesses

You determine your weaknesses in the same way that you determine your strengths. Start by examining all of your company's processes and activities, as well as its image in the community, the workplace, and the marketplace. Note the negatives you find and isolate them for further examination.

Now look at the activities that *appear* to be positives. These activities might be running smoothly in your eyes but might not be as efficient or as effective as similar activities from your competitors. If you find that your competitors are doing something better than you are—no matter how well you *think* you're doing it—that activity becomes a competitive weakness.

Once you've assembled this list of weaknesses—you can call them "things to improve" if you want—you need to rank the list by importance. Put the items that most put your business at risk at the top of the list and toss the minor annoyances to the bottom. Now you know what you need to attack.

JUST A MINUTE

You should also rank your weaknesses in order of how easy they are to fix. There may be benefit in doing some easy fixes—even if they're fixing relatively unimportant items—just to get them off your plate, and to get the ball rolling with an aura of accomplishment.

Fixing What's Wrong—Or Minimizing Its Impact

Some things that are broken can be fixed. Some things that are weak can be strengthened. Some things that you're number two in can be improved so that you become number one. However …

Some things that are broken *can't* be fixed. Some things that are weak *can't* be strengthened. And some things can't be improved, no matter how hard you try. This means you might never be number one in that area.

One of the key skills of successful businesspeople is knowing which issues are worth spending their time on and which to just let go of. Maybe you're stuck with an old, inefficient warehouse that would cost too much money to bring up to snuff. Maybe you have a brand that was tarnished by some unspeakable event in the past. Maybe your management team is so young it lacks vital experience in your particular market.

If you can't fix something, learn to live with it. Maybe you can compensate for the weakness by exploiting your strengths in other areas. Maybe the area you're weak in isn't vital to your ultimate success. Maybe you just have to drop back 10 and punt. (Remember that a strategic retreat is still a viable strategy.)

If you have an inefficient warehouse, maybe you can speed up other parts of your operation—such as your product development or your shipping—to compensate. If you have a bad brand, maybe you should just kill it or let it die a natural death. If you have an inexperienced management team, maybe that means they can think outside the box and come up with new ways of doing old things.

Whatever your particular case, you need to recognize your weaknesses—and then incorporate those weaknesses into your overall strategy. Your strategy might be to fix the weaknesses, live with them, or cut your losses—but whatever you come up with, your response has to be strategic.

You can bet that your competitors are strategizing about how to exploit your weaknesses. It behooves you to strategize from the other direction and cut them off at the pass.

ACKNOWLEDGING YOUR WEAKNESSES

Just as your business plan should have a section for your strengths, it should also have a section for your weaknesses. This section is sometimes called Risks, Competitive Challenges, or something along those lines. (*Never* call this section Weaknesses—unless you add the word "Potential.")

In an S-1 document, tradition (and the SEC) dictates the sort of information that goes into this section. It's typically a laundry list of "what ifs"—

what if your product doesn't perform as planned, what if projected sales don't materialize, what if you get sued, what if your key managers quit or die, and so on. You probably don't need to put these rather obvious risks in your business plan; they're pretty much assumed to be the standard business risks facing any company.

FYI The reason an S-1 (the required filing document when a company is planning an IPO) has to include so many more—and more obvious—risks and weaknesses relates to the concept of "full disclosure" from public companies to their potential investors. Private companies have less of a requirement in this area.

Instead, you should focus on those obvious weaknesses that could have significant impact on your ability to achieve your financial goals. You shouldn't list too many of these weaknesses—a half dozen would be a lot—but you also shouldn't pull your punches. If you know you have a big weakness, your potential investors will recognize the problem as well—whether you tell them yourself or not. So you might was well tell them; being forthright counts for something.

When you present a weakness (or a "competitive disadvantage") in your business plan, don't just let it sit there—tell the reader what you're going to do about it. This is your opportunity to turn a potential concern into a benefit; if you tell investors how you plan to deal with a major issue, they'll feel more secure about your overall business savvy and abilities and will be more inclined to give you the financial support you're looking for.

So spend a paragraph talking about a weakness and then a second paragraph describing your strategy for working through or around the problem. You'll come off as both totally honest (by disclosing the issue) and foresighted (by having a plan to attack it). Thus your weaknesses become strengths—at least in the eyes of your potential investors.

COMPLETING THE STRENGTHS AND WEAKNESSES CHECKLIST

To help you identify both your strengths and your weaknesses, use the following Strengths and Weaknesses Checklist. Put a checkmark in the Strength column if you think an item is one of your company's particular strong points; put a checkmark in the Weakness column if you think this is an area that your company needs to work on. Leave the line blank if you feel your company is no better or worse than your competitors in this area; put an "NA" next to any activity that doesn't apply to your business.

STRENGTHS AND WEAKNESSES CHECKLIST

Activity	Strength	Weakness
Community visibility and support	_____	_____
Corporate (employee) communications	_____	_____
Customer communications	_____	_____
Customer focus	_____	_____
Customer service and support	_____	_____
Distribution/warehousing/shipping	_____	_____
Employee compensation	_____	_____
Employee quality	_____	_____
Employee recruitment and retention	_____	_____
Employee relations	_____	_____
Financial analysis	_____	_____
Funding	_____	_____
Industry visibility	_____	_____
Internal operations (including HR)	_____	_____
Internal systems and processes	_____	_____
Management	_____	_____
Market awareness	_____	_____
Market research	_____	_____
Marketing/advertising	_____	_____
Product development	_____	_____
Product mix	_____	_____
Product pricing	_____	_____
Product quality	_____	_____
Public relations	_____	_____
Sales	_____	_____
Speed to market	_____	_____
Other:		
_____	_____	_____
_____	_____	_____
_____	_____	_____

Be completely honest when completing this checklist. If you put checkmarks in the Strength column beside every activity, you're either blissfully ignorant of reality, or your company is the best damned company in the history of Western-style capitalism. Don't overestimate your strengths; one of the most common management failures is believing your own BS. Be realistic and check only those activities in which you do a significantly better job than the other companies in your industry.

If you're totally honest with yourself, you'll end up checking only a handful of Strengths—and about the same number of weaknesses. You should discover that your company performs the majority of activities at about the same levels as your competitors. That's nothing to be ashamed of; it's just the way it is. Most companies do most things equally well (or equally poorly, if you're a perfectionist). To make your mark, however, your company must do at least one thing better than the competition. Pick the activity that matters the most to success and focus on making it one of your unique strengths. *That's* the path to success.

HOMEWORK

In this hour, you learned how to identify your business's major strengths and weaknesses. In Hour 5, "Analyze Your Strategy," you'll learn how to develop a long-term strategic direction for your business.

To prepare for the next hour, you may want to think about the following:

- Where do you want your business to be in one year? Two years? Three years? Five years?
- Why are you in business—and in this particular business?
- Why does your business exist?
- How do you want your business to get from point A to point B?

HOUR 5

Analyze Your Strategy

CHAPTER SUMMARY

LESSON PLAN:

In this hour, you will learn about ...

- Vision, mission, goals, strategy, and tactics
- Setting goals for your business
- Developing a clear path to the future

A well-written business plans sets down, in ink and paper, your business's long-term strategy. That alone is reason enough to develop a strategy before you start writing your business plan.

More important, however, is the fact that a business without a strategy is a business without direction or purpose. If all you do is come into the office at nine in the morning, make widgets all day long, and then leave at five, you're not really going anywhere—you're just making widgets.

If, on the other hand, you know you want to reach a certain revenue number in three years, and to do that you have to make a certain quantity of widgets each day, and they have to be of a certain quality and at a certain cost, then you have a purpose for everything you do. Yes, you'll still come in at nine and leave at five and make a bunch of widgets in between, but now you'll know why and how, and you'll ultimately be able to inject new methods and processes to help you better get to where you need to get.

Strategy, then, is important—so take this hour and learn how to develop a long-term strategy for your business.

WHAT YOU ARE—AND WHAT YOU WANT TO BE

There is a hierarchy of direction that drives every business. This direction starts with an overriding vision and filters down to specific tactics in the following manner:

- **Vision.** The dictionary definition of this word is "a mental image or imaginative contemplation." Applied to the business world, the vision is the reason you're in business; it's what drives your company and everything your company does. Even though visions are meant to be unquantifiable and ultimately unachievable, organizations without a driving vision quickly become rudderless and unfocused. It's the vision that guides the way; without a vision, your business isn't going anywhere.

- **Mission.** The mission is the overall purpose of your business, more specific than your vision but not necessarily quantifiable. Missions are often presented in the form of a mission statement, which is a short, succinct, often single-sentence statement of what your business is trying to achieve.

- **Goal.** A goal is an end or objective, specific to your mission, that your business strives to attain. Unlike your vision and mission, your goals are quantifiable.

- **Strategy.** Your strategy is your plan of action, designed to achieve your business goals. Put another way, strategies describe how to meet your goals and objectives.

- **Tactics.** A tactic is a method used to implement your strategy. Tactics, in a sense, are the details of your larger strategy.

Everything starts with the overriding **vision** you have for your business. This vision is then translated into a specific **mission,** which is quantified by one or more specific **goals** or objectives. These goals are reached by implementing an overall **strategy,** which is executed via individual **tactics.**

Here's an example of how these five drivers interact.

You might start out by saying that the **vision** for your company is to be a global innovator in information technology. That's sufficiently vague to provide a general business direction, without being so specific as to be limiting.

You might then say that the **mission** of your business is to solve the networking problems of large- and medium-sized businesses. Again, this is unquantifiable, but it's also narrower in scope than the vision, and thus provides more specific direction.

Now you need to set a specific, measurable objective. You do this by stating that the **goal** of your business is to double its market share within five years. This goal is quantifiable, and is a way of measuring how successful you are in pursuing your mission.

How do you achieve your goal? By stating that your **strategy** is to increase the value of your products while holding the line on pricing. Notice that no specifics are mentioned, even though you have set a general course of action.

Now it's down to the details. Your final statement is that your primary **tactic** within your strategy is to reduce manufacturing costs by sourcing key components from overseas suppliers. When you put it correctly, the tactic is a marching order for the troops, a specific step-by-step instruction for how to implement the strategy that achieves the goal that follows your vision and mission.

VISION

The vision you have for your business defines what you do and how you do it. It sets the culture for your company and, when translated into a written statement, sets the entire tone for your business plan. In short, your vision describes your company—and why it exists.

Do you tell people that your company makes widgets (even though that might be a factual statement), or do you say that your company helps manufacturers produce lower cost, higher quality finished goods? Put another way, you don't make widgets just to be making widgets; you make widgets because you have a vision of helping manufacturers (your customers) make better products. The widgets you supply are part and parcel of your vision.

Your vision is the dream you have, the reason you went into this business, the thing that drives you and all your employees. Everything you do in business should be in the service of that dream, that vision.

JUST A MINUTE

If you're having trouble seeing the vision or mission of your business, you're probably too involved in the day-to-day running of things to see the big picture. Take a few days off—and a few giant steps backward—to gain a clearer perspective of what you're *really* doing, all the normal buzz of activity aside.

MISSION

Your mission is narrower than a vision but broader than a goal. Your mission is what you want your company to do, what you want it to become. Not in terms of achieving a specific revenue or profit number, but rather in terms of achieving something more general and less quantifiable.

A well-written mission statement, placed near the front of your business plan, defines the focus of your business. If you have a vision of a world of peace and harmony, your mission might be to eliminate all wars. (Your individual goals, then, might include reducing tensions in the Middle East and ending the civil war in Kosovo.)

It isn't so much that your mission restates your vision; it's that it *focuses* your vision. If your vision is, by nature, ultimately unattainable, your mission provides a focus that *is* attainable, even if you can't exactly quantify it in terms of numbers of this or that. Like your vision, however, your mission should be short and sweet, devoid of flowery prose, and as to-the-point as you can make it.

GOALS

Your goals are the first quantifiable drivers you have for your business. If your vision and mission tell you in which direction to head, your goals define precisely how far you want to go and by when.

Relating to your company and your business plan, you should set specific, measurable goals for each important area of your business. Your goals will probably be at least partially financial; you want to achieve $1.5 million in revenues during year two, for example. In fact, every revenue and profit number you plug into your financial projections is a specific goal.

Goals can also measure how you're performing in the overall marketplace; they don't have to be entirely internal. Setting out to be number two in the marketplace by year three is an example of an external goal, as is the goal of attaining a 20 percent market share within 12 months.

For a goal to be viable, it must be measurable. Saying you want to be "number one," without defining what "number one" is, creates a nonviable goal. If you define "number one" as having the leading market share, or the highest revenues, or the least number of defects, then you've set a more viable goal—assuming, that is, that the metrics necessary to measure your goal are readily available. Don't, for example, set a goal of attaining the number-one position in market share if revenue numbers aren't available from your leading competitors. Unless you can measure it, you shouldn't make it a goal.

JUST A MINUTE

Interestingly, your goals—at least those that are defined in financial terms—don't appear until the very last section of your business plan.

STRATEGY

If your goals tell you how far you want to go, your strategy tells you how you want to get there. Thinking in terms of a roadmap, your goal is to travel from point A to point B; your strategy is to drive the western route, via Interstate 70, via car.

Strategies don't worry themselves with a lot of detail, however; that's why you need tactics. If your strategy is to drive via car on I-70, your tactics define what kind of car, how fast you're going to drive, when you're going to stop for lunch, and how many rest stops you're going to allow.

If you're the grand strategist, you don't care about whether you stop at a Stucky's or a Nickerson Farms, you only care that you follow the assigned route to get from here to there. You fail in your strategy if you take a different route; going north on I-65 is not the same as going west on I-70, and it is likely to generate different results. You pick a specific because you know that, when executed properly, that strategy is the best way to get from here to there. If circumstances change, you'll consider a different strategy.

In business terms, your strategy defines how you're going to achieve your financial and other goals. If your goal is to achieve 20 percent market share, your strategy might be to produce a higher quality, lower cost product than your competitors. (Your tactics would then describe specifically how you're going to lower costs and increase quality.) There are many ways you could achieve your market-share goal; your strategy describes the one way you've picked to do it.

JUST A MINUTE

Another difference between strategies and tactics is that strategies are typically longer-term, whereas tactics are of a specific shorter-term duration.

TACTICS

Tactics are the day-to-day details of what your business is doing. They're low-level enough that they might not find their way into the business plan you present to potential investors; they're important enough, however, that they need to be clearly communicated to those employees who are charged with the execution of the plan.

In our driving from point A to point B example, you already know that the strategy is to hop in a car and take I-70 west. Your tactics might be to leave at 8:00 on Monday morning, average 65 m.p.h., stop once every two hours for gas and refreshments, and end up the first evening at the Holiday Inn in Salina, Kansas. If you're describing your trip to a friend, you'd leave out those details; you'd just convey the strategy of taking I-70 west. But once you're behind the wheel, the details are vitally important.

And that's how tactics help to drive your business.

FIGURING OUT WHERE YOU WANT TO BE IN THE FUTURE

Now that you understand the differences between vision, mission, goals, strategies, and tactics, let's focus on the long-term goals for your business. (Strategy will follow in the next section; you have to have a goal, however, before you can devise a strategy.)

You can set many different goals for your business, many of them very specific and short term in nature. (Saying that you want to decrease travel expenses by 10 percent in the next quarter is a very specific short-term goal, for example.) When it comes to building your business plan, however, you want to concentrate on the broader, longer-term goals you have for your business.

One of the best ways to determine your true long-range goals for your business is to ask one simple question: "What will my business look like in five years?" When you answer this question, you define your five-year business goals.

JUST A MINUTE

Picking a five-year timeframe is somewhat arbitrary. Depending on the type of business you're in—and the demands of your potential investors—you may want to plan out two, three, or four years instead. (Anything more than five is probably just guessing.)

When you think about what your business will look like five years out, consider the following:

- **What business will you be in?** This might sound like an obvious question ("I make widgets, so I must be in the widget-making business"), but how you define your business in the long term could prove either liberating or unnecessarily confining. For example, if you ran a railroad at the end of the 1800s, you could have defined yourself as a railroad company or as a transportation company. The first definition would have been sufficiently narrow as to ensure your probable demise with the coming of the automobile; the second definition would have empowered you to investigate other forms of transportation as they developed. So make sure you see the big picture when you describe what it is that you do—and try, as much as possible, to anticipate any major changes in your industry that could also impact your core business model.

- **Who will your competitors be?** This question anticipates changes in the general make-up of your industry—and helps you focus on who to worry about as the years go by.

- **Where will your business be?** Here you can think both about physical expansion and about how much of your business will be nonphysical—that is, conducted over the Internet and other yet-to-be-invented virtual channels.

- **How big will your business be?** Answer this question in terms of revenues, profits, number of employees, number of locations, or any other quantifiable metric that makes sense for your industry.

- **What kinds of products and services will your company be offering?** This question is related to question number one but with more specifics attached. If you produce skateboards today, will you also be producing roller blades and anti-grav hoverboards five years from now? Also think about the pricing of your future products as well as their quality level, variety, and so on.

- **Who will your customers be?** Many companies find that their customer base changes over time; consider factors such as aging, changing demographics, regional migration, and so on, as you draw a picture of your future customer.

- **How will you reach your customers?** When you answer this question, consider marketing and advertising, sales forces (do you sell direct or through distribution?), sales channels (what's retailing going to look like five years from now?), and distribution (how will you get your product to the consumer?). Remember to consider the impact of the Internet and any other developing channels and technologies.

- **What will *you* be doing?** This is a personal question, and it has to be answered. Just how involved with this business will you be five years from now? Do you want to stick around that long, or will you have moved on to the next big thing? If you do stay involved, in what capacity will that be? If you're not involved—or if you see your role dramatically changing—who will fill your place? If you do see yourself leaving, what's your specific exit strategy?

- **What about your investors?** Five years from now, your current investors might be long gone—or they might still be hanging in there, still waiting for you to do something that will generate a big return for them. In any case, what will be your capital needs in the future—and how do you anticipate meeting those needs? Will your company be private or public—or will you be an acquired part of a larger firm?

This process can be a lot of fun, but it requires a clear mind and a bit of concentration. You may need to go away for a weekend or a week to develop your view of the future—and then spend a few days writing it up in the appropriate detail.

JUST A MINUTE

A good way to approach this imagining exercise is to write about your future business as if you were actually in the future, providing a description for a future business plan. Write it as if it's already happened, and it will really come to life.

FORGING A PATH TO YOUR FUTURE BUSINESS

Once you've described your future business, you have to figure out how to get from here to there. That path is your company's long-term strategy, and it's one of the most important elements of an ongoing successful business.

Remember that your strategies will tell you—and your staff—what you're going to do to build your future business. They don't have to (and shouldn't) go into a lot of detail because details are notoriously difficult to predict and are changeable. (Besides, details are tactics—and your tactics will get decided on the way.)

An example of a well-defined long-term strategy would be to say that you're going to increase your product mix for the 10- to 14-year-old market. This is clear enough that anyone reading the plan will know what to do, without providing a bunch of details that might not be relevant two or three years from now. You don't define the specific products to produce (that's a tactic), you merely say you need to produce more products in order to achieve your goals. Clear, concise, and compelling.

As you define the paths you want to follow, you'll need to consider separate strategies for different operational parts of your business. The following sections go into more detail about these individual strategies.

GROWTH STRATEGY

Assuming that your company will be larger five years from now than it is today, you need to strategize how to accomplish that growth. Will the growth come from stronger sales of current products, or from higher prices, or from new product lines, or from new channels of distribution? What about international growth? Will all your growth be internal, or will you grow, to some degree, by acquisition?

Once you delineate your overall growth strategy, you'll see that you now have to develop several related strategies to ensure this growth. If you're growing via an expansion of your product mix, that dictates the development of a new product strategy. If you're growing via new distribution channels, you'd better work on your distribution strategy. If your growth will double the size of your business, you'd better strategize for stepped-up employee recruitment—and a larger management team.

In short, your strategy for how you grow feeds all the other strategies you need to develop. Let your future vision drive where you want to go, and then develop the individual strategies to make sure you get there.

PRODUCT STRATEGY

When you define a long-term product strategy, you're really interested in defining the type of *product mix* you'll have over the specified time period. Will your mix shift to higher-quality products, or to lower-priced products, or to a greater variety of products, or to products that all incorporate a green stripe down the middle?

When you consider your product mix, also consider how you're going to build or buy all those products. (This will feed a separate manufacturing strategy, if you're a manufacturer.) What investment will be required to affect a new product mix? Do you need to figure out a way to make these products for a lower cost—or to a higher quality standard? Will you need to keep more SKUs on hand, or can you increase your days-on-hand to build or buy higher quantities at a lower cost?

As you can see, your product strategy, without going into specific tactics, needs to be relatively far-reaching in its scope. It's called a product strategy, but it applies to whatever it is that generates revenues for your company—products, services, or whatever.

Pricing Strategy

For planning purposes, we've separated pricing from product, although they're definitely related in the real world. Look at your future plan, and see where you think average selling prices will be five years from now. Obviously, if prices are wildly different (higher or lower), you'll need a strategy for how to get to there from today's current levels.

Equally important is where you want to play in the pricing range. If your goal is to be a leading mass-market supplier, you'll want to develop a strategy that incorporates pricing in the lower and middle parts of the future pricing range. If you want to be the quality provider, consider developing a higher-price strategy. Naturally, you'll need to synergize your pricing strategy with your product/manufacturing strategies, even though the pricing you adapt will do most of the driving.

Marketing Strategy

How will you reach your future customers? You don't have to devise specific ad campaigns (that's a short-term tactic), but you should strategize about how much you want to advertise (in general terms) and in what media.

When developing your marketing strategy, you should also think about product packaging and in-store displays (if you sell at retail). If you sell a service, consider how you reach potential customers to tell them about what you offer. Do you need to develop a direct direct-marketing operation? That's a strategy. Do you want to increase your Internet-based promotion, to drive more sales over the Web? That's another strategy.

Think through all your product and sales needs, and make sure to develop a marketing strategy for each.

SALES STRATEGY

How will you get your customers to buy your products? Do you need a direct sales force, or a catalog, or hired reps, or telemarketers, or an e-commerce Web site, or something different? If you use sales reps, will you need more or fewer of them, going forward? Just how do you intend to sell what you sell?

Related to your sales strategy is your discount strategy, if you sell in that manner. Will your big accounts demand a higher discount? If so, you'd better develop a strategy to handle it. Will you be moving into a different distribution channel that operates on a different discount schedule? Will you have different sales needs? Strategize for it.

Whatever you do, don't get caught by surprise. Be prepared for any changes in the way you sell, and develop a strategy to handle the changes.

DISTRIBUTION STRATEGY

We'll define distribution as the channels where you sell your products and services. You know where you sell your products today; how is that going to change over the next five years? Do you want to add new channels of distribution? Do you want to cut out some of today's less-profitable channels? Or will there be new channels for your product five years from now?

Think back to the advent of the Internet in the mid-1990s. Some companies saw the Internet coming and developed strategies to exploit it as a sales/distribution channel. Other companies were caught flat-footed, and weren't able to benefit from the creation of a new e-tail marketplace. Make sure your strategies recognize developing channels—or are flexible enough to adapt to any future channels, when they develop.

PROCEED WITH CAUTION

Just because a new channel develops doesn't mean that your industry or your company is capable of exploiting it. The Internet, as an example, proved a good way to sell small, low-cost products—the types of products that have always sold well through catalogs and direct mail. It proved less suited for selling big, bulky products—such as furniture, housing, and automobiles. Make sure that any new channels you identify are truly suited for the business you're in, and for the capabilities of your particular company.

INTERNAL OPERATIONS STRATEGY

It's important to have a strategy for what you do in the marketplace; you should also have a set of strategies for what you do within your own four walls. To properly prepare for five years' worth of changes, you'll need to develop strategies for all sorts of internal operations—attracting new employees, retaining old employees, managing your existing facilities, building new facilities, creating an IT infrastructure, communicating between locations, you name it.

Whatever changes you see for your internal operation over the next five years, you'll need to develop strategies to match.

MANAGEMENT STRATEGY

When you're talking about internal strategies, you also need to consider strategies related to the management of the business. If you plan for your business to grow (and you probably do), you also need to plan on attracting additional management. Where will you find new managers—will you promote from within or will you seek experienced management from the outside? Just where will you need new management in your organization? How will you compensate—and retain—these folks?

Management goes beyond people—you also need to consider the structure of your organization. If your company doubles in size, will your current structure still work? Do you have to reorganize your operations or business units? How will you handle management communications in a larger, more complex operation? Do you need to beef up your infrastructure to handle the increased load? And who's going to take your place as your role changes?

Many companies get blindsided by the increased management needs of a larger organization. Don't expect your current management team and structure to suffice if your company grows significantly; you'll need more (and, perhaps, better) management to run a larger and more complex business.

You need to develop a farsighted strategy for how you manage the larger and different company of five years from now. This may be a strategy, however, that you don't share with your current management team—especially if the strategy effects affects them personally. Develop your management strategy and then keep it locked in your upper upper-left-hand desk drawer, until it's time to implement it.

Funding Strategy

Your final strategy needs to guide how you'll finance your business of the future. You'll have to spend money to grow your business—so where will that money come from?

Your funding strategy needs to address some fundamental issues. Do you want to keep your company private, or do you want to go public at some point? Do you need additional capital to fund physical expansion or acquisitions? Will your competitors be going public—and if so, do you need to follow, in order to have competitive capital at your disposal? How supportive will venture capitalists or the public equity markets be for your particular market segment, five years from now? If you already have equity funding, will your current investors stick around for the full five-year period, or do they have a different exit strategy? Is it feasible to execute a strategy that ends with the sale of your business to a strategic partner?

The more ambitious your plans for your future business, the more ambitious your funding strategies need to be. Don't neglect this part of your strategy— you may have to start planning now to attract adequate planning several years in the future.

Elements of a Sound Business Strategy

As you develop your business strategy—and prepare to create your business plan—work through the strategic elements in the following checklist.

Business Strategy Checklist

- ☐ Growth strategy
- ☐ Product strategy
- ☐ Pricing strategy
- ☐ Marketing strategy
- ☐ Sales strategy
- ☐ Distribution strategy
- ☐ Internal operations strategy
- ☐ Management strategy
- ☐ Funding strategy

GO TO ▶

The strategies you develop here will feed into different parts of your business plan document. Turn to Hour 7, "Create Your Outline," to learn which strategies go where.

If you can write at least a paragraph on each of these points, you're well on your way to developing the right strategy to drive your business forward over the next few years.

HOMEWORK

In this hour, you learned how to develop a long-term strategy for your business. In Hour 6, "Analyze Your Options," you'll learn how to evaluate the various sources of funding available for your business.

To prepare for the next hour, you may want to think about the following:

- If you're running an existing business, where have you obtained funds in the past?
- To achieve the financial goals you've set for the next two to three years, how much additional money (above and beyond normal operating profits) will your business need?
- How much of your own money can you—or do you want to—put into the business?
- What sources of financing are typical for the type of business you're in?
- Whom do you personally know that has a lot of money?
- How much control of your business are you comfortable ceding to outside investors?

HOUR 6

Analyze Your Options

CHAPTER SUMMARY

LESSON PLAN:

In this hour, you will learn about ...

- Calculating your financing needs
- Equity and nonequity financing
- Choosing the right financing
- What different investors want

As you learned back in Hour 1, "Analyze Your Objectives," the primary reason you're creating a business plan is to raise money. You share your business plan with potential lenders or investors and hope it does a good enough job of selling your business that they give you the funds you're asking for.

All businesses need money, even if it's just to pay the rent, keep the lights lit, and make sure your employees' paychecks don't bounce. Sometimes, though, a company needs extra money—to get a new business off the ground, to fund an expansion of an existing business, or merely to cover operating costs during a slow streak. When your business needs an infusion of cash, where do you go?

There are several funding options that any business can pursue. Which particular option (or options—they're not mutually exclusive) you pursue depends on the needs of your individual business, the amount of money you need, what you want to do with that money, and what you're willing to pay to get it. Read on to learn about your various funding options and how to choose the funding that's right for your business.

DETERMINING HOW MUCH MONEY YOU NEED— AND WHY

Before you go seeking new funding, you first have to determine how much money you need. This isn't as easy as it may sound.

WHY DO YOU NEED THIS MONEY?

First you need to establish *why* you need this funding—because the why will sometimes determine the who (to ask for money). Here are some questions to ask that will help you determine why you need the funds and how you'll use them if you get them:

- **Is your business a pure startup?** If so, you'll need enough cash in the bank to pay for all your *operating expenses* until the time when you start generating real profits—which could be a period of months or even years.

STRICTLY SPEAKING

Operating expenses can be defined in several different ways, depending on how the phrase is used. For our current purposes, operating expenses are defined as the ongoing, day-to-day expenses of the business—rent, payroll, utilities, advertising, and the like. Operating expenses do *not* include costs related to the manufacturing of a product.

- **Are you buying an existing business or a franchise?** If you're acquiring a business that's already up and running, you'll still need a large amount of upfront cash to pay for the business itself—or, in the case of a franchise, the upfront franchise fees.
- **Is your business entering an expansion mode?** If you're planning any type of expansion, you'll need extra cash to pay for it. This may include funding to build new physical facilities, to hire a new sales force, or to blanket a new territory with advertising.

PROCEED WITH CAUTION

It's easy to underestimate the costs of starting up or expanding a business. Make sure you count *everything* associated with the new initiative, from payroll to rent to advertising to legal expenses.

- **Is your business entering a period of heightened competition?** If so, you may need a one-time cash infusion to step up your promotional activities.
- **Is your business getting ready to introduce an important new product?** It takes money to launch a new product. Not only do you have heightened product development costs, you may also need to add new manufacturing capabilities or capacity, your warehouse might need to

be upgraded, your sales force will definitely need to be trained, you'll need to fund an introductory advertising budget, and (if you're distributing through retail channels) you'll probably have to buy some shelf and display space. All the expenses, of course, will take place before the new product starts generating new revenues—which is why you need the cash infusion *now*, not later.

- **Is your business getting ready to enter a cyclical downturn?** Some businesses go through natural cycles. Retail businesses, for example, make a lot of money in the three months before Christmas, but have trouble keeping their doors open during the summer doldrums. If you're anticipating any of these cyclical downturns, you may need to stockpile some extra cash just to meet your basic operating expenses.

- **Is your business having trouble meeting its basic operating expenses?** This is probably the worst reason to seek funding; unless you have a plan for recovery, you'll find it difficult to get anyone to lend you the money you should be generating normally.

HOW MUCH MONEY DO YOU NEED?

Once you've determined why you need the money—and how you'll use it—it's time to figure out how much you need, and for how long. This process is one you're probably familiar with; it's called *budgeting*.

STRICTLY SPEAKING

Budgeting is the process of creating a month-by-month (or, in some cases, week-by-week) expense budget. This is a plan for how much money your business will spend during a specific time frame, and may include several variations, based on alternate scenarios.

The key to funding a new initiative is to create an expense budget strictly for the initiative, without factoring in any costs for your existing business. (Existing costs should already be paid for out of current operating profits.) Factor in any new facilities, employees, and activities related to the new entity. Make sure you include advertising, promotion, sales costs, and anything else that is directly related to the new initiative. Don't leave anything out. How long your budget period should be dependents on how long it will take your new initiative to start generating adequate profits to start funding itself. If the initiative's breakeven point is two years away, create a two-year budget. If the initiative will be self-funding within six months, create a six-month budget.

PROCEED WITH CAUTION

Don't load up a new initiative with an allocation of existing costs; you're already paying those expenses. Make sure you look only at new costs—and new revenues—directly associated with the new business initiative.

Next you should work up a revenue plan for the same time frame. On a month-by-month basis, estimate how much revenue your new initiative will generate. Do *not* count any existing revenues in this plan; treat the new initiative almost as a separate business entity.(Be *very* conservative when creating a revenue plan; one of the most common business mistakes is to overestimate the amount of time it takes for a new initiative to start generating revenues.) Once you've developed your revenue plan, add the associated product costs to the revenues to create a *gross profit* plan. Hopefully, you're selling your product for more than it costs you to build or obtain; that difference is your gross profit, which can then be used to pay your operating expenses.

STRICTLY SPEAKING

Gross profit is the difference between a product's revenues and its cost of manufacturing. For example, if a product costs you $5 to make (not counting all your fixed operating expenses) and you sell it for $7, you make a $2 gross profit.

Now put together a profit and loss statement for the new initiative for the budgeted time period. The first month your gross profits cover your operating expenses, you've reached the *breakeven point*.

STRICTLY SPEAKING

The **breakeven point** is that point in time when expenses and gross profits become equal. Any business conducted before that point was done at a loss; any business after the breakeven point is generating an operating profit.

You may decide that this is the date when you can cut off the external funding of your new initiative's operating expenses. If your funding was in the form of investment, that may be true; you don't have to pay back an investment. However, if your funding was in the form of a loan, you have to pay back the money you received—plus expenses. So make sure you've included loan payments as part of your operating expenses; when you reach breakeven with loan payments included, then you're in the clear!

To determine how much total funding you need, add up all the losses prior to the breakeven point. This number represents the funding requirements for your new initiative. You may want to pad this number a bit, for safety's sake—and you can certainly see why you want to make sure you include *every* possible new expense, and why you want to be conservative in your plans for revenue generation.

While you're working up these numbers, you probably want to create budgets based on several different scenarios. Create a best-case scenario, in which everything goes better than planned; a worst-case scenario, in which things don't take off as fast as you'd hoped; and a most-likely scenario, which is what you think will actually happen. When it comes time to obtain financing, consider asking for the worst-case amount; that way, you'll be protected if things don't go completely according to plan.

In essence, you want to obtain enough funding to pay for all your expenses until the new generation becomes self-funding through operating profits. Anything above that figure is a safety net; anything less is a disaster waiting to happen—or a plan-in-the-making for a second round of financing.

GO TO ▶
See Hour 9, "Build Your Numbers," to learn more about building budgets, revenue plans, and profit and loss statements.

Now What?

Now that you know how much money you need, how do you go about obtaining those funds?

The first thing you need to do is develop a funding plan, which should include how many rounds of financing you want to engage in and how much money you want to raise in each round. The thinking here is that you don't always need to generate all of your funding in one go; in some instances—especially when you have a startup that requires massive amounts of funding—it may be easier to generate smaller amounts at several different points in time.

One advantage of a multiple-round funding plan is that you can use different types of investors for different rounds. You may want to get the business off the ground with a small first round from friends and family. Then, once you can demonstrate some operating results, you open up a second round of financing from venture capital firms and larger investors. You may even plan for a third round, once your company achieves a higher valuation, before you file for an initial public offering (IPO).

Of course, a single round of funding is much simpler to deal with. If you have any experience in this at all, you know how time-consuming it can be to go stumping for funding. If you can get it all over with in one round, that's more time you have to actually run your business. A one-round funding plan should be a definite option for companies requiring smaller amounts of financing, and it is the norm for companies seeking loans rather than investments. The larger your funding needs, the more likely it is that you'll have to take a multiple-round approach.

Once you have your funding plan in place, the only thing left is to determine what kind of funding you want. Read on to learn more about the funding options available to different types of businesses.

NONEQUITY FUNDING

There are two basic types of financing—equity and nonequity. Equity financing (discussed in its own section later in this hour) requires you to sell partial ownership of your business in return for the capital investment. Nonequity financing enables you to retain full ownership of your business; you receive your funding in the form of a repayable loan rather than an investment.

For many small businesses, nonequity funding is the way to go. It's a lot easier to ask your banker for a loan than to put together all the paperwork and do all the legwork necessary to sell stock to investors. In addition, when you run your business, *you* run your business; you don't have a lot of investors with their own expectations, looking over your shoulder every time you announce your quarterly results. (This points out another advantage of using all nonequity funding—you're not obligated to announce your operating results to anybody except the government!)

There are two main sources of nonequity funding—you and your banker. Both are discussed next.

BANKS AND LENDERS: BORROWING THE MONEY YOU NEED

The most popular source of funds for small businesses is your friendly neighborhood bank or lending company. When all you need is money (without the contacts and advice you sometimes get from venture capitalists or strategic investors)—and you don't want to share a stake in your company to get it—your best option is to take a small-business loan.

PROS AND CONS OF BORROWING MONEY

When you borrow money, there is no pressure to grow your business quickly (or at all), nor do you have to manage the expectations of a group of stockholders. All you have to do is promise to repay the loan (plus interest) within a predetermined period of time. Looking at it this way, a lender's expected return on investment is considerably less than that of an investor.

JUST A MINUTE

If you have trouble getting a bank to loan you money, you can enlist the services of the Small Business Administration (SBA). The SBA offers a number of different types of loans as well as loan assistance. Learn more at the SBA's Web site at www.sba.gov.

The main disadvantage of borrowing money, of course, is that you have to pay it back. When an investor puts money into your business, there is no obligation at all for the money to be returned; investors make their money by selling their equity stake to someone else, hopefully at a higher price than they paid for it. You don't have to give the investor anything.

Lenders, however, require you to give them back the money you borrowed—which means you have to include the loan payback in your financial plans. You also have to factor in interest payments, which can be significant. This means, of course, that when you're putting together your financial plans, you have to make sure you generate enough profits to cover the loan and interest payments.

Let's look at this comparison. Let's say you raise a million dollars from friends and family investors. You now have a million dollars, and it's all yours—you don't have to give any of it back, ever. If you borrow the same million dollars, you have to pay it back—*all of it*—plus a specified rate of interest on the money borrowed. If you took out a five-year loan, that's a million dollars that your company has to generate in profits over that time period just to pay back the loan principle; with interest added in, your payments will run in the neighborhood of $25,000 a month.

On the other hand, if the million dollars was an investment, you wouldn't have that million-dollar profit pressure. Or, looking at it another way, the difference between a million-dollar loan and a million-dollar investment would be about $25,000 per month—which would certainly go a long way toward easing your day-to-day stress.

Still, if you're a small business or a business with modest funding needs, taking out a loan may be your only option. If this is the case, make sure you borrow no more (or no less) than you really need and that you can realistically pay back on a regular basis.

JUST A MINUTE

If you decide to look for a loan, make sure you shop around for the best rate possible. When you're talking about the large amounts typical of business loans, a difference of a quarter or an eighth of a point can significantly impact your total payback and your monthly payments.

What Lenders Look For

When you're preparing to approach a banker or a loan official to ask for a loan, remember that lenders aren't expecting some huge payback on their investment; they merely want their principle back along with the designated amount of interest. What they're interested in, then, is your ability to repay the loan. They don't care about lofty plans for market domination and triple-digit revenue growth. Stability is more valued because a stable business is a lower risk.

Here are the key points, then, to keep in mind when presenting to a lender:

- **Show stability.** Show your personal stability. Show the stability of your business model. Show the stability of your company (or past companies you've run). Show anything you can that says "stable" and "low risk."

- **Concentrate on cash flow.** Lenders are less interested in your profitability (although they *are* interested in that, too) than in your ability to make loan payments. This means you want to stress your cash flow, which hopefully is positive and hopefully is large enough to cover your loan payments.

- **Minimize the flash.** Venture capital firms like their presentations with a lot of flash and "gee whiz" appeal. Bankers don't. You still want to look professional, but tone down the fancy printing effects and state-of-the-art presentation tricks. You might not need a PowerPoint presentation; a one-on-one meeting, accompanied by your business plan document as a leave-behind, will probably be sufficient. When you're dealing with bankers and loan officers, think staid, think low-key, think *conservative*.

- **Show a real use for the money.** Bankers won't want to lend you money without a good justification for it. (On the other hand, they also won't want to lend you money if you're so down on your luck that you really need it to survive; you'll have to strike a balance.) Show exactly how the money will be used: to build this new thing, or to enter this new market, or to fund this new initiative. And be precise; bankers are nothing if not detail oriented.

SELF-FINANCING: GOING IT ALONE

One option that entrepreneurs sometimes forget to think about is the option of paying for your new initiative yourself. If your funding needs are modest and your bank accounts (and stock funds and college savings funds and piggy banks) are large, there's nothing stopping you from financing everything with your own funds.

The advantages of a self-financed initiative are obvious. You don't have to spend time wooing a multitude of lenders and investors, you don't have any obligations (legal or financial) to anyone else, and you don't have to cede any management control to any other entity. The disadvantage, of course, is that it's all your money—and you could lose it all if the new initiative fails.

It's also possible that you don't have enough money to completely fund your initiative; that's a probability if you're building a fast-track startup. So self-funding isn't always a viable option; if you have the money, however, it's the fastest and least-complex option available.

EQUITY FUNDING

When you need more funds than you can get with a simple loan—when you want to raise larger amounts of funds to grow your business—you need to consider equity funding. It's called equity funding because you sell equity in your company in return for the funding dollars. The people or companies that buy shares of equity are called investors; they're investing their money with the hope that their equity position will be worth more at a later date than it was when they purchased it.

When you take on investors—of any type—you're gaining partners. An investor buys a share of your business and thus has a lasting equity stake. Even though that equity stake can be small (in the case of "friends and family" investors), it's still there—which means for every investor you add, the business adds a new co-owner.

The stake of the business that an investor purchases is called a share. Each share of your company's stock that you sell is assigned a specific price; this price can vary for different types of investors and will vary over time. As long as your company is private, you set the value of your shares. Once your company goes public (and it doesn't ever have to, of course), the value of the shares is set on the open market of a stock exchange.

Let's look at how someone makes an investment, and the different ways they can make money on their investment. The scenario starts out when you value each share of stock at a specific price; let's use $5 per share for this example. Our investor decides to invest $50,000, and thus receives 10,000 shares of your company's stock. The investor holds on to this stock until one of the following happens:

- You sell the company to another company, which offers your existing investors a set price for each share of stock that they own. If the acquiring company offers $6 per share, as an example, your investor makes $1 per share for 10,000 shares, or a $10,000 profit.

- Your company enters the public equity markets, and begins trading on one of the major stock exchanges. At that point, your investor can sell his or her shares anytime and, for whatever the going price is at that time. Since the price of publicly traded stocks can vary wildly, it's now up to the investor to sell at the right time to maximize the initial investment. (The investor doesn't have to sell, of course; he or she can hold on to the stock for as long as he or she likes.) If the investor sells on a day when your stock is trading for $12 per share, the profit will be $7 per share over the 10,000 shares, for a total profit value of $70,000.

- You neither sell your company nor take it public. In this instance, your investor doesn't make anything—unless the company issues stock *dividends* in the course of its normal operations. If you offer a 5-cent-per-share dividend in a specific quarter, the investor would make $500 in profit that quarter. (Dividends are issued only when the company makes a profit, and they don't have to be issued at all.)

STRICTLY SPEAKING

A **dividend** is a payment made by the company to each of its stockholders, typically based on some percentage of the profits generated during a specific time period. Dividends are typically offered in terms of cents per share.

- You do a lousy job of running the company, and it goes out of business. In this worst-case scenario, the investor loses all of his or her investment—the entire $50,000—unless there are sufficient assets left when the business closes to sell or distribute to shareholders. For all practical purposes, though, when a business folds, the shareholders lose—*everything*.

There are many types of investors you can pursue for equity funding, the most important of which are discussed next.

JUST A MINUTE

Although your business plan is a good document to use when looking for a loan, it is just one of the documents you need to prepare when pursuing equity funding. Any time you sell stock in your company, the SEC requires that you prepare and distribute a private placement memorandum (PPM), which must contain some very specific information in a very specific format. Your business plan can accompany your PPM, or you can use your business plan as the cornerstone of your PPM. To learn more about PPMs, turn to Hour 24, "Create a Private Placement Memorandum (PPM)."

SMALL INVESTORS: FRIENDS AND FAMILY FUNDING

Small investors, typically made up of people you know (hence the "friends and family" designation), are good sources of capital for small companies. Assuming you have friends and family (and assuming they have money), it's often easy to entice them to participate in your business success.

JUST A MINUTE

Small investors don't have to be friends and family. Many startups canvas their local business community for prominent private investors who can serve as a cornerstone for first-round equity funding.

Depending on your future plans for the business, you can pitch one of two different plans for these small investors.

If your plans are to eventually sell the business or take it public, then pitch a strict investment scenario. The small investors pony up a specific amount of money for a specified number of shares, with no guarantee of return. The investors make money when their shares can be monetized—when the business is sold, or is taken public. Until then, the investors own a piece of paper, and not much more.

If your plans are to keep the business pretty much as-is and *not* sell it or take it public, you'll have to pitch a different deal for your friends and family investors. In this scenario, you pitch something that resembles, to some degree, a type of profit-sharing plan, through the promise of continued stock dividends to accompany future profits.

Pros and Cons of Dealing with Small Investors

The upside of dealing with friends and family is that you're dealing with friends and family. The downside is also that you're dealing with friends and family. Although each investor is typically too small to warrant a voice in the company's management, because you know the investors personally, they'll probably share their opinions with you anyway. It won't be a formal management dilution, but it still could turn into a dilution in practicality.

In addition, dealing with multiple small investors can be extremely time consuming. Not only do you have a lot of investors to communicate with, you probably have to deal with each one of them personally. (Friends and family *hate* getting form letters!) If you fully exploit the friends and family network, expect to spend a lot of time on the phone and in business lunches—especially during any periods in which your performance lags expectations.

What Small Investors Look For

You'll probably run into two types of small investors—those who have lots of spare cash to invest and those that have to work hard to scrape up the funds. While both groups are investing because they smell a killing (in the form of a big payback in the future), the later group will also be concerned about the possibility of losing what might have been their life savings.

Keeping all that in mind, here are the key points to remember when court-ing small investors:

- **Keep it personal.** One of the key reasons these investors want to give you money is because of *you*. They know you (or they've heard of you from a friend of a friend), they trust you, they believe in you—and your ability to create a successful business. Don't bother with a lot of formal meetings and presentations; do your presenting one-on-one, casually if need be, and make each person feel like he or she's the most important investor in your entire company.

- **Be reassuring.** Especially when you're dealing with the smallest of your small investors, you need to reassure them that they're making a good decision—without actually promising, in legal terms, that they'll definitely get all their money back. Let your personality do the reassur-ing for you and have some follow-up conversations; don't let them get buyer's remorse.

- **Tell a good story—and paint a big picture.** Your business plan should serve the purpose of telling the story of your business, but with these investors, your plan document is just a presentation aid and a leave-behind. The real star of the show is you, and you have to be a good storyteller. You have to sell these investors on the huge potential here, on the high return on investment that is possible. Be compelling, be exciting, and (without actually lying, of course) paint the most favor-able picture that you can.

- **Show a little flash.** Since you're meeting these investors one-on-one, you're probably not using a formal PowerPoint presentation. (Although you can if you want to—as long as it doesn't take away from the personal nature of your pitch.) Where you *can* get flashy is in the business plan document itself—use lots of graphs, charts, and pic-tures and definitely consider springing for a professional four-color print job. Leave a great-looking document in their hands, and you'll help to close the sale.

STRATEGIC INVESTORS: BIG MONEY FROM BIG BUSINESS

It's possible that your business might be of interest to a strategic investor. This would likely be a larger company that sees some synergies between what it does and what you do. These companies typically look at strategic investments primarily from their strategic value rather than their investment value—and then invest a large sum of money for a significant equity position in your firm.

Where do you find strategic investors? If there are any to be had, they're probably people you're already dealing with—as suppliers, as customers, as partners in various projects. They may also be big industry players that you contact via trade organizations or through other business associates. They may contact you (if you've received a lot of positive press), or you may need to contact them and sell them on the benefits of a strategic relationship involving an equity position. In either case, be prepared for long, drawn-out negotiations; you'll end up dealing with the merger and acquisition, finance, legal, and other operational departments of the company, as well as with most of its senior management team.

PROS AND CONS OF STRATEGIC INVESTORS

Strategic investors can often be less demanding, in terms of expecting high returns on their investments, than either small investors or venture capital companies. That's because part of their return is measured by the strategic part of their strategic investment.

Know, however, that this strategic part of the investment is likely to come with strings. Not only will you be giving up a good chunk of equity in your business, you'll probably have to sign some sort of agreement guaranteeing the other firm *something*—exclusivity, or favored-nation pricing, or a specified dedication of resources for a joint project, or something else of the like. If you already have a good working relationship with the strategic investor, this might be an acceptable compromise; if your two firms are relatively new to each other, beware of creating obligations that may be difficult to keep.

In addition, that long, drawn-out process you went through to make the investment (which alone can be a good reason not to proceed) will probably be repeated on a regular basis for as long as the relationship between your two firms exists. Big companies bring with them big bureaucracy, and you will likely get caught up in it. Although a good personal relationship with a key player in the other business can go a long way toward alleviating these headaches, if that key player ever leaves—and he or she will eventually— expect a new set of operational and organizational headaches.

If possible, you may want to negotiate some sort of hands-off agreement between your two firms so that you won't get pulled into their bureaucratic processes. Try to negotiate a set number of meetings per year or a specific individual (or position) for you to deal with. Your ability to do this will depend on just how badly they want to do business with you—versus how badly you need their money.

Look at it this way—if you started up your new company to get away from corporate hassles, you don't want to get involved with a strategic investor. If, on the other hand, you thrive in a corporate environment, you'll probably be able to handle the relationship and bureaucracy issues inherent with this type of partnership arrangement.

What Strategic Investors Look For

First and foremost, strategic investors look for some sort of strategic benefit that your business can bring to their business. Implicit in that is some degree of control; if you're really good at what you do, they want a big—and possibly exclusive—piece of that. Any monetary return is secondary to this.

Here are the key points to keep in mind, then, when courting strategic investors:

- **Push the strategic benefit.** This advice is obvious. Identify why it is they want to partner with you—what you can do for them, in other words. Then push it, hard.

- **Push your similar cultures.** Since your two firms will spend a lot of time working together, stress how similar the company cultures are in your two firms—even if they aren't. If they're a suit-and-tie company, make sure you wear your suit and tie whenever you meet. If they're frugal, take a cab instead of a limo. Do whatever it takes to make them think that you're one of them.

- **Prepare to present … and present … and present.** You're deep in corporate-land now, which means you have to tell lots and lots of different people your story. And, in corporate-land, you do that via formal presentations. So brush up on your PowerPoint and get ready to give the same presentation over and over and over.

- **Flash counts.** You can impress corporate guys with fancy documents and flashy presentations. Pull out your entire bag of tricks; style might be as important as substance in this environment.

- **Numbers count.** The one exception to the style-over-substance argument is the company's financial team. (And it's never one person; it's always a team.) Make your financials as detailed and as buttoned-up as possible and then be prepared to go back and cut the numbers a dozen new ways, at their request. And they will request, so make sure you have the financial backup to give them what they want, however they want it—and as quickly as they want it.

VENTURE CAPITAL: BETTING ON GROWTH

If you're starting up a high-growth company, a company that plans to be a major player in a big industry, you're going to need a lot of funding. And when you need a lot of funding, there's one place to look—the world of venture capital.

Venture capital (VC) firms exist solely to make investments. They create venture funds (which have their own investors) and then use the money in those funds to fund high-potential startups and other interesting opportunities.

VCs aren't your normal hands-off investors, however. When a VC makes an investment, it becomes your silent (and not-so-silent) partner. A VC will give you a lot of money, but it'll want a lot in return—a large equity position, a seat on your board of directors, a large say so in the makeup of your management team, and even a strong voice in the day-to-day management of your company. Once you get in bed with a VC, you're *really* in bed; you may not be able to make any major decisions without first getting the VC's approval.

 FYI To learn what goes on behind the scenes of a successful venture capital firm, read *eBoys: The First Inside Account of Venture Capitalists at Work* by Randall E. Stross. This book details a year or so in the life of Benchmark Capital, one of Silicon Valley's hottest VCs—and the company that funded eBay, Webvan, and other notable Internet startups.

PROS AND CONS OF VENTURE CAPITAL

The biggest benefit of attracting venture capital, of course, is the large amount of funding you can inject in one fell swoop. Attracting $10 million from a single VC is a lot less work (at least initially) than attracting the same amount of funding from hundreds of smaller investors.

Not only does a VC represent big money, it also represents *smart money*. A dollar you get from a VC is worth more than the same dollar from a smaller investor because the VC firm brings tons of valuable contacts and advice to the table. Do you need to find a partner to help you enter a specific channel? The VC will know somebody. Need to generate some positive P.R.? The VC knows whom to call. Want to offer some joint services with a firm in a related industry? The VC just happens to have an investment in a company that fits the bill. Need to hire a new CFO? The VC already has somebody in mind. That's what smart money brings to the table.

STRICTLY SPEAKING

Smart money is money that comes from a source that can provide other benefits to your business. VC investments are often referred to as smart money because the VC firm can provide contacts and services above and beyond the monetary investment.

In addition, a VC can help you attract more money when you need it. Bring in a name VC in your first or second round of financing, and it'll pull some of its VC pals along for the ride in your next round.

Unfortunately, VC funding comes with a price, and that price is control. When a VC makes an investment, it becomes your silent (and not-so-silent) partner. More so than any other type of investor, a VC investor demands a huge stake in your company, a seat (or two) on your board of directors, and a huge say in your company's management. Once you get in bed with a VC, you're *really* in bed; you may not be able to make any major decisions without first getting the VC's approval.

The VC presence can be so strong that you, the founder, can be forced out if the VC doesn't like the job you're doing. It's quite common for a VC to force out the founder and put its own CEO in place, especially when the company is nearing the IPO stage. You may find yourself on the outside looking in just when things are getting good, all because you signed your soul away for a few million VC bucks.

Some VCs won't even make an investment without some sort of guarantee. (Others are more comfortable with the risk; there are definitely different styles of investing found at different VC firms.) It's not unusual to be asked to sign a "living dead" clause that requires you to return the VC's money if, after a certain length of time, your company has little chance of going public or getting acquired—the two ways that VCs recoup their investment. Another kicker to look out for is a "liquidation preference" clause, which specifies that, if and when you sell the business, the VC will not only recover its entire investment, it'll also receive some multiple of its investment as profit—and it'll get its money before any other investors get paid out.

As you can see, bringing in a venture capital investor will bring about dramatic changes to your business. Make sure they're changes you can live with.

What VCs Look For

When you're dealing with a VC, you're dealing with some of the best and brightest people in the business. Chances are, they know more about your part of the market than you do—which is why they're interested. You don't have to sell them on the market's potential; you *do* have to sell them on *your* potential. Why is your company—why are *you*—the horse they should bet on? What do you bring to the table that will help them get the five-to-ten-times returns that a VC typically looks for?

Here are the key points to keep in mind, then, when courting a VC firm:

- **Think big.** VCs expect a return on investment much higher than any other type of investor. If they put in $1 million, they want $2 million or $4 million or $10 million back; if they put in $10 million, they want $20 million or $40 million or $100 million back. That means you have to think big, talk big, and act big. They're comfortable with high risk—that goes with the high rewards. It's important, then, that you focus on growth—industry growth, customer growth, and revenue growth. (Profit growth is also important but less so—at least in the early stages of your company's development.)

- **You gotta have a vision.** To grow big and to grow fast, you have to have a grand plan. You have to see things as they will be, not as they are. In short, you have to have a vision—and the VC has to buy into it.

- **Flash counts.** Spend the time to develop a flashy presentation and great-looking documents, but then ...

- **Be prepared to go off-topic.** Don't be surprised if you get about five minutes into your canned presentation and then get interrupted by a barrage of questions from all sides of the table. These guys know how to cut to the quick, and they'll dive right into what interests them. If you're an overly linear type of person, you'll have trouble handling this.

- **Be one of the boys.** When you invite a VC into your company, you're going to be living with it for a long time and on a very intimate basis. Make sure you and the lead person at the VC are compatible and then play up that compatibility. If the VC is a denim and khakis group, wear denim and khakis. If they're into suits and ties, it's time to play dress up. If they shoot from the hip, learn how to shoot faster. If they're slow and deliberate, learn how to ponder before pontificating. In other words, tailor your presentation—both professionally and personally—to best fit in with your audience.

 To obtain a list of available venture capital firms, use the Venture Capital Resource Library located at www.vfinance.com.

WHICH IS THE RIGHT OPTION FOR YOUR BUSINESS?

Among these various funding options, which are the best for you and your company? Now is the time to get down to work and do some comparisons.

COMPARING THE OPTIONS

You can use the following table to compare various aspects of the different types of funding available to your business.

Funding Comparison

	Bank/ Loan	Small Investor	Strategic Investor	Venture Capitalist
Equity or nonequity?	Nonequity	Equity	Equity	Equity
Guaranteed return for investor?	Yes	No	No	No
Fixed period for return?	Yes	No	No	No
Exit strategies	Repayment of loan	IPO or sale	Acquisition of company	IPO or of sale
Values growth or stability?	Stability	Growth	Growth	Growth
Requires dilution of management control?	No	No	Yes	Yes
Requires possible seat on board of directors?	No	No	Probably	Yes
Offers strategic benefits to you?	No	No	Yes	Yes
Amount of time/ effort required to obtain investment…	Low	Low (for each; high in total)	High	High
Probability of successfully obtaining funding…	High	Medium	Low	Low

One of the line items in the preceding table is labeled *exit strategy*. An exit strategy defines how you ultimately end your involvement with your business—or, if you're an investor, how you end your investment and collect your profits. It's important to know the exit strategy of a potential investor; if the investor expects to exit after a sale of the business and you don't intend to sell the business, you have a conflict that needs to be addressed.

THE BEST OPTIONS FOR SMALL BUSINESSES

If you're a relatively small business, a strictly local business, or a business with modest funding needs, you're probably not large enough to show up on the radar of the big venture capital firms. This is probably for the best, as it's unlikely you want to cede the control (and the equity position) that a VC firm would demand.

Taking a strategic partner could be an option, especially if you manufacture components or provide services that are used by the larger firm. The strategic investor might take an equity position in your company to ensure a future (or an exclusive) supply of whatever it is you provide. If a strategic investor is interested and you can live with whatever nonfinancial obligations the partner company might impose, this could be a good way to finance your operations.

Friends, family, and other local investors are also popular sources of funding for small businesses. However, you'll probably have to structure some sort of dividend-based or profit-sharing payout for these small investors because it's unlikely that selling your business or taking it public is in your plans. You'll also have to plan for the time dilution inherent in managing many small investors—especially folks you know who'll insist on talking to you *personally* about every little issue that crops up. Still, when you need to raise a lot of cash and you know folks that have greenbacks to spare, using small investors to finance your business isn't a bad idea.

The most popular source of funding for small businesses, however, is the bank. It's often easier to get a loan than to solicit investments; taking a loan is also preferable for those entrepreneurs who don't want to cede any control of or equity in their companies. Borrow enough money to get up and running, make sure you pay it back in time, and then you're free of all obligations.

THE BEST OPTIONS FOR FAST-TRACK STARTUPS

If you have high growth expectations for your business, however, you probably won't be able to borrow enough money to get you where you want to go. Lenders aren't that interested in high-growth businesses because those types of businesses also come with high risk. (If there's anything bankers and lenders really like, it's low risk.) So if you're thinking big, you need to think about some sort of large investment.

A large investment can come from multiple small investors, of course—especially if each one ponies up at a significant level. If your business plan is sound and the promise of future rewards is great, everyone you know will want to get on board. The problem with small investor money, of course, is that it isn't smart money; still, you can probably raise enough from friends and family for your first-round needs and then hit the VCs for later rounds.

Strategic investors are another potential source of seed capital for a fast-track startup. The advantage here is that you only need one or two large investors for your first-round needs, as opposed to dozens (if not hundreds!) of smaller investors. The disadvantage comes if the strategic agreements you'll no doubt sign in any way hinder your growth; you'll have to determine how hands-on you'd like your strategic partners to be.

The holy grail for fast-track startups, of course, is venture capital funding. These big guys invest big bucks and provide the kind of jumpstart that most entrepreneurs would kill for. VCs not only provide money, they also provide advice and contacts—but they require a big say in both the strategic direction and the day-to-day management of your business. You'll probably have to give up a seat on your board to each VC investor, and the VC firms will inevitably have an opinion about how well you're running things. It's not uncommon for the founders to be forced out of their own companies by VC investors, who often prefer to put their own management in place in preparation for taking a company public. If you can live with this potential outcome, bringing a VC onboard can be a substantial boost for your business—and can help you grow a lot faster than you would otherwise.

THE BEST OPTIONS FOR GROWING EXISTING BUSINESSES

The previous scenarios have detailed relatively new businesses; what if you run a more established company that needs additional capital to fund some type of growth initiative?

If your funding needs are modest and of relatively short duration—and if you can't fund the expansion out of operating profits—then it's time to hit up your local banker or lending officer. Assuming your business has a good track record and decent cash flow, this shouldn't be a difficult process.

If your funding needs are larger—if you're trying to double the number of locations, for example, or start up an entirely new product line—then seeking a group of small investors might be a better course of action. The only issue here is that you're selling shares in your existing business to finance a new business initiative; if that doesn't bother you, then investigate this route.

If your expansion is directly related to a particular supplier, customer, or part of the market, you may be able to partner with a strategic investor for funding. For example, if you need to build a new factory to supply General Motors with windshield wiper blades for one of its new vehicles, it's possible that GM (or the equivalent in your industry) might be willing to partner with you to fund the expansion. You won't always be able to find a strategic investor, but when you do, they're worth considering.

Venture capital businesses typically aren't too interested in existing businesses unless you're really still in the startup stage. That is, a VC might be interested in coming in as part of second- or third-round funding, but it won't be interested once your company's valuation starts to rise. In most instances, then, existing businesses can rule out venture funding.

THE BEST OPTIONS FOR CASH-STRAPPED BUSINESSES

What do you do if you *really* need the money—just to keep your doors open? The problem here is that when you really need it, nobody wants to give it to you. VCs won't fund existing operations; they're only interested in growth. Strategic investors might, in some instances, step in to bail you out, but you'll pay a big price (in terms of both equity and control) for the rescue. And small investors want to get in on a good thing, not a questionable one, although some local investors might lend a hand in the name of community interest.

That leaves your friendly neighborhood banker, and he or she could go either way. If your books don't look good, the banker probably won't want to throw good money after bad. On the other hand, if you can guarantee the loan in some way—put up your home or property as equity—then you might stand a chance. You also might want to investigate SBA options, if your local banker begins to balk.

Know, however, that if things get really bad, you're probably on your own. That's just the way it is.

HOMEWORK

In this hour, you learned how to evaluate different financing options for your business. In Hour 7, "Create Your Outline," you'll start the initial planning for your business plan by learning about the pieces and parts of a typical plan document.

To prepare for the next hour, you may want to think about the following:

- Have you obtained and read sample business plans from other businesses?
- How do you think you should present your business to potential investors?
- What do you think outsiders need to know about your business in order to lend money or invest?
- How do you typically tell the story of your business?

PART II
Plan the Plan

HOUR 7
Create Your Outline

CHAPTER SUMMARY

LESSON PLAN:

In this hour, you will learn about …

- Telling your story
- Organizing your information
- Determining the elements to include in your plan

You may think that a business plan has to be a complicated document, full of complex sentences, overly technical terms, convoluted legalese, and detailed financial data. Nothing could be further from the truth. If you can talk about your business—and you no doubt can, at length—then you can create an effective business plan.

The best business plans are conversational in tone, are easy to read and understand, avoid as much legalese as possible, and only include financial data that is necessary to paint an accurate picture of the business's potential. In fact, you could probably dictate the bulk of your business plan in a single setting, based on your inherent knowledge of what it is you're trying to accomplish and why.

TELLING THE STORY

Imagine you're sitting in a restaurant or a coffeehouse, and someone you know comes up and asks you what you're up to these days. You answer that you're in the process of starting up a new business, and then you start to tell a little story. You tell this person what your business is all about, why you've decided to get into this particular type of business, what kind of opportunity you see, and how you intend to exploit that opportunity. If you're on good terms with the person you're talking to, you might even share the revenues and profits you hope to generate.

Here's the type of story you tell:

Let me tell you about my business. We supply widgets to colleges and universities across the United States, which is a pretty big market, and we hope to generate $12 million in revenues within the next three years.

I've always had this vision of every college in America using widgets to improve the learning experience of its students, and I've made it my mission to supply the college market with the widest variety of high-quality widgets available in the U.S. You see, every college should be supplying widgets to its students, one per student per semester. This creates a market for more than 10 million widgets per year. At an average selling price of $15 per widget, that's a $150 million market, at retail.

My plan is to create a line of widgets that are customized for the college market. Each widget will be available in the school's colors, as well as a variety of other fashionable colors and designs. I plan to hire a sales force to sell the widgets to college bookstores and then use on-campus marketing to get the word out to the students.

I intend for my company to produce its own widgets, from a new factory we're building in Iowa. By utilizing this new, state-of-the-art facility, as well as labor from farmers working off-season, we can produce our widgets for an average cost of about $3 per widget—which is about 10 percent less than our competitors. We sell the widgets to the bookstores at a 50 percent discount, for an average net price of $7.50. That gives us a gross profit of $4.50 per widget.

Our organization will be lean and mean and be focused entirely on making and selling widgets. All of our computer systems will have the latest widget-tracking software installed, and our new facility will have a special packing and shipping system designed especially for shipping widgets. My senior management team is a mix of experienced widget makers and managers with experience in marketing products directly to college students.

Our real strength is our ability to produce widgets in custom colors and designs and with a higher gross margin than our competitors. Now, I know we're new in the business, so we'll have to overcome that with some splashy marketing and promotions. Still, I think we're bringing a lot of new ideas and ways of doing things to the industry, and we'll be successful because of that.

My projections are that we can attain a 16 percent market share by year three. In that year, we'll sell 1.6 million widgets at an average net price of

$7.50, which will generate $12 million in revenues. With our low-cost structure, I estimate that we'll operate on a 15 percent net margin and generate $1.8 million of profits in our third year.

As you can see, this short story (fewer than 500 words) tells your audience members everything they need to know about your business. They know why you're starting the business, they see the opportunity presented, they understand how your company expects to profit from that opportunity, they sense the unique things that your company intends to do, and they learn how much money you expect to make if you follow your plan. It's all there, presented in a logical order; everything important is included, with nothing extraneous added.

THE ELEMENTS OF A TYPICAL BUSINESS PLAN

The simple story you tell about your business represents the basic framework of what will become your business plan. Every major point in your story corresponds to a section in the plan; all you have to do is elaborate a bit on the important parts, and you'll have a comprehensive, well-organized business plan document.

THE BASIC OUTLINE

Although there are many different ways to organize the information in a business plan, they pretty much all boil down to the following general outline:

- **Executive Summary.** This is a one-page overview of the major points in your plan—from your Vision and Mission all the way through your key financial goals. If your audience members read nothing but this one page (which is all some will read), they'll absorb the salient points of what your business is all about.

- **Vision and Mission.** As discussed in Hour 5, "Analyze Your Strategy," your Vision (sometimes called a Vision Statement) is a one-sentence statement of the dream you have for your business. Your Mission (sometimes called a Mission Statement) is a one-sentence statement of your business's chief purpose. Some business plans combine the Vision and Mission onto a single section and a single page; others separate them into separate sections/pages for clarity.

PROCEED WITH CAUTION

The most common mistakes made by overenthusiastic entrepreneurs is to make the Executive Summary, Vision, and Mission statements longer than they need to be. If the Executive Summary goes longer than a page, it isn't effectively summarizing; if the Vision and Mission statements go longer than a sentence each, the company's vision and mission are not clearly focused.

- **Opportunity.** This section presents the market opportunity you've identified. Typically, this section starts out by identifying the target market, sizing it, presenting growth opportunities, and discussing how other companies are pursuing this opportunity. This is where you use the market data and analysis you gathered back in Hour 3, "Analyze Your Market."

- **Market Strategy.** This section refers to the preceding section, and describes how your company will pursue the identified opportunity. This section typically includes information about the products or services you'll be offering, as well as your sales, distribution, and marketing strategies for those products.

- **Business Strategy.** In this section, you finally get to talk in more depth about the business itself. You should present your business model and your revenue model—in other words, you tell the reader how your business plans to make money.

- **Organization and Operations.** This is a detail-oriented section in which you describe (and show via an org chart) your company's structure, as well as the workings of key departments (manufacturing, warehousing, systems, and so on).

- **Management.** This section enables you to elaborate on (and brag a little about) your senior management team. You may also use this section to present members of your board of directors, as well as key strategic and institutional investors, if appropriate.

- **Core Competencies and Challenges.** This section more or less sums up what's come before by listing your unique strengths and presenting potential challenges or weaknesses.

- **Financials.** This final section of your plan is where you put all relevant financial information including profit/loss statements, balance sheets, multiyear revenue projections, and the like.

MAPPING THE STORY TO THE PLAN

Let's go back to the story we told at the beginning of this hour and pair the different parts of the story with the different elements of a typical business plan. The following table shows how this maps out:

Mapping the Elements of a Business Plan

Business Plan Section	Story Element
Executive Summary	Let me tell you about my business. We supply widgets to colleges ...
Vision	I've always had this vision of every college in America using widgets to improve the learning experience of its students ...
Mission	... and I've made it my mission to supply the college market with the widest variety of high-quality widgets available in the U.S.
Opportunity	You see, every college should be supplying widgets to its students, one per student per semester ...
Market Strategy	My plan is to create a line of widgets that are customized for the college market ...
Business Strategy	I intend for my company to produce its own widgets, from a new factory we're building in Iowa ...
Organization and Operations	Our organization will be lean and mean ...
Management	My senior management team is a mix of experienced widget makers ...
Core Competencies and Challenges	Our real strength is our ability to produce widgets in custom colors ...
Financials	My projections are that we can attain a 16 percent market share by year three ...

GO TO ▶
See Hours 10 through 18 for detailed information about each of these individual sections.

As you can see, the story you tell about your business maps perfectly to the typical business plan outline. Just write down your story in a bit more detail than usual, and you'll have your plan.

It's really as easy as that—and there's no reason to make the process any more complicated than it has to be. Tell your story and let that story serve as the basis for your entire business plan.

DETERMINING THE LENGTH

How big a business plan should you create? The proper answer is "as big as necessary"—although that doesn't necessarily answer your question. The reality is that it's hard to do everything you need to do in fewer than 20 pages, and if you get much above 50 to 60 pages, your audience won't read it all. Aim for a middle ground in the 30-page range and realize that shorter is probably better.

How does this length break down by section? Here's a rough sketch of how you might organize a 30-page business plan; the TOC and any appendixes would be above and beyond this page count.

Recommended Page Count by Section

Section	# Pages
Executive Summary	1
Vision	1
Mission	1
Opportunity	4
Market Strategy	6
Business Strategy	6
Organization and Operations	6
Management	1
Core Competencies and Challenges	2
Financials	2
TOTAL	**30 pages**

JUST A MINUTE

If you're operating an existing business, you will most likely need to expand the Financials section to include at least two more pages for your current and historical income statements.

VARIATIONS

There are some interesting variations on this basic business plan outline—typically influenced by the particular interests of the person or entity requesting the business plan. For example, the Small Business Administration recommends that businesses applying for loans utilize the following outline for their business plans:

- Statement of Purpose (similar to the Executive Summary section)
- Description of Business (similar to the Business Strategy section)
- Marketing (similar to the Market Strategy section)
- Competition (similar to the Competitive Advantages and Challenges section)
- Operating Procedures (similar to the Operations section)
- Personnel (similar to the Management section)
- Business Insurance (a description of the insurance you have for the business)
- Financial Data (similar to the Financials section, but with much more detail)
- Supporting Documents (including three years' worth of tax returns for your business principals, personal financial statements, resumés, franchise contracts, lease agreements, purchase agreements, licenses, legal documents, and letters of intent from suppliers)

JUST A MINUTE

The SBA recommends that you include the following financial data in your business plan: loan applications, a capital equipment and supply list, a balance sheet, a breakeven analysis, pro-forma profit and loss statements, and cash flow statements (in several different flavors, including a three-year summary, detail by month for the first year, and detail by quarters for the second and third years). Also recommended is a detailing of the assumptions on which your projections are based.

When you look at this outline, it's obvious that the SBA is especially focused on positioning the business for the loan process, which explains the unusually heavy emphasis on financial information—as well as the separate section just for business insurance (important if your business goes belly up before the loan is paid off). If you structure your business plan in this fashion, you end up with a financial section that takes up about half the plan's total page count—and that, when it's done, can pretty much serve as a standalone loan application.

FYI Find out more about what SBA has to say about business plans at their Web site, located at www.sba.gov/starting/busplan.txt.

CMGI @Ventures, a VC/incubator firm specializing in funding high-tech startups, has its own particular wants when it comes to business plans. The management team at @Ventures suggests that an interested business submit a 20-page business plan to them in the following format:

- Executive Summary (identical to the Executive Summary section)
- The Business (includes elements from the Vision, Mission, and Business Strategy sections)
- The Market (similar to the Opportunity section)
- Product Offering (similar to part of the Market Strategy section)
- Distribution (similar to another part of the Market Strategy section)
- Competition (similar to the Competitive Advantages and Challenges section)
- Management Team (identical to the Management section)
- Financials (identical to the Financials section)
- The Deal (details the amount of funding to be raised)

As you can see, @Ventures puts the business strategy information right up front; the company sees a lot of business plans each week, and likes to cut right to the chase. (Most of their cursory reads never get past the first few pages of a plan.) Note also that they require a new section, The Deal, which details the amount of money the business is asking for. Again, when you understand how a VC works, adding this section makes sense.

FYI To find out more about what @Ventures has to say about submitting a business plan, visit the company's Web site, located at www.ventures.com/contact/bizplan.html.

Although it's always good advice to follow the instructions of potential lenders or investors, these two examples, if followed exactly, could cause you to *not* present a convincing story for your business. Both of these suggested outlines place too much focus on *what* you're doing, and not enough on *why*—or on the elements that make your business unique.

Lenders and investors can't make informed judgments based merely on your company's numbers. They have to have the full story to understand where the numbers come from, and to gain confidence in your ability to hit those numbers. That's why a comprehensive business plan, one that tells the complete story of your business, is always recommended. You can still beef up particular sections of the plan for specific audiences, of course; just make sure you tell the story you need to tell to best sell your business and yourself.

MAKING YOUR BUSINESS AND YOUR PLAN FIT TOGETHER

Assuming you choose to use the business plan outline presented earlier in this chapter, how do you carve up the different parts of your business to fit within this document structure? There are two things you probably need to do—identify the relevant parts of your business and, if necessary, edit the outline.

MATCHING YOUR ORGANIZATION TO THE OUTLINE

Which parts of the plan describe which parts of your business? It's easy to tell, once you realize the goals of each section and the information contained within.

All of the high-level sections—Vision, Mission, Business Strategy, and Core Competencies and Challenges—reflect the high-level thinking of you and your senior management team. Obviously, the Management section is also related to—and describes—your company's senior management; the Business Strategy section, to some degree, also describes the activities of your product development group.

The market- and marketing-oriented sections of the plan—Opportunity and Market Strategy—are paired with your marketing department. The Market Strategy section also describes, in part, the activities of your sales and product development groups; in addition, the marketing department's activities are highlighted, to some degree, in the Core Competencies and Challenges section.

Naturally, the accounting/finance department's activities are synonymous with the Financials section of the plan. The Operations and Organization section, which describes how your company is organized and how each unit works, reflects the activities of all of your groups/units.

FINE-TUNING YOUR OUTLINE

What if your particular business doesn't quite fit into the standard outline? If you're different enough to make the outline awkward, you can always tweak the outline.

For example, if you're a business that doesn't develop any physical products and instead makes money by licensing technology or other content, you may need an additional section for licensing strategy. If your company is heavily driven by research and development, breaking out R&D or product development into its own section might make sense. If you have radically different domestic and international sales strategies, you might need a separate international opportunities or international distribution section.

There's nothing wrong with enhancing the basic outline to make it more appropriate to your specific business. However, be wary of making changes just to make changes. The vast majority of businesses can be described within the standard outline; chances are, your business isn't sufficiently unique to require radical outline revisions.

You can, of course, stick with the basic outline but change the titles of the individual sections to better reflect your industry's (or your company's) standard phraseology. A good example is the Core Competencies and Challenges section. Many businesses will simply call this section Strengths and Weaknesses; others will call it Benefits and Risks; still others will call it Marketplace Advantages and Competition. Pick the one that works best for you.

You may also, in particular circumstances, choose to rearrange the sections of the plan. Some businesspeople prefer to talk about the business (Business Strategy) before they get into the details about market opportunity and market strategy. While some feel that putting undue emphasis on internal business issues might possibly reflect the lack of a market focus on the part of senior management, others prefer to present the core business clearly at the start of the plan, rather than burying it somewhere in the middle. How you tell your story is a matter of choice—and it does reflect your personal focus—but it shouldn't make too big a difference as long as all important information is presented *somewhere* in the plan document.

JUST A MINUTE

If you construct your business plan in discrete sections, it's relatively easy to rearrange the sections at any point in the process. If you find that the document isn't flowing in the desired manner, use your word processor's cut and paste function to do some quick restructuring on the fly.

ADDING OTHER ELEMENTS

This basic outline can—and should, at your discretion—be augmented by several optional elements:

- **Cover page.** Your business plan needs to reflect the professional nature of your business, so spend some effort (or hire a graphic designer) to design a nice-looking cover page. Your cover should include your business's name and logo, the release date of the plan, and a title that reflects that this is a business plan.

- **Table of contents.** You need to provide a good roadmap to the various parts of the plan, in the form of a table of contents (TOC), which lists the page numbers of the major and minor headings in the plan.

- **Index.** If your plan is terribly long—more than 40 pages or so—readers will need a way to quickly reference items of interest. The best way to do this is through a detailed index.

- **Footnotes.** You don't have to embed all sorts of data and references in the body text of your plan; you can reference sources and other data through the use of nonintrusive footnotes and endnotes.

- **Appendixes and attachments.** Any information that needs to be included but doesn't fit within the main text—glossaries, press releases, and the like—can be added as an appendix or attachment.

GO TO ▶
See Hour 20, "Table of Contents and Index," for more information on creating a usable table of contents and index for your business plan.

GO TO ▶
See Hour 19, "Appendixes and Attachments," for detailed advice on additions to your plan.

HOMEWORK

In this hour, you learned the different elements that go into making a comprehensive business plan. In Hour 8, "Marshal Your Resources," you'll learn how to assemble the staff, information, and other resources you need to complete your business plan.

To prepare for the next hour, you may want to think about the following:

- Do you know anyone who's ever put together a business plan before?
- Do you have anyone on staff who can help you work on various parts of the business plan?
- How much time do you have to complete the plan?
- How much time can you personally spend working on the plan?
- What outside resources can you call in to assist with the writing of the plan?

HOUR 8

Marshal Your Resources

CHAPTER SUMMARY

LESSON PLAN:

In this hour, you will learn about ...

- Estimating writing time
- Who does what—and when
- Managing the project

Even though a business plan serves a simple purpose, the creation of the business plan document can be an especially complex process. All manner of individual elements need to be assembled and created, and then someone has to supply the big picture perspective, and then all the pieces and parts have to be organized, and then someone actually has to *write* the darned thing—and that's not even taking into account the work it takes to make it look professional and get it printed. For a 20-to 30-page document, a business plan represents a lot of work!

If your business is in the formative stage, all this work will probably be done by a single person—*you*. If you're running an existing business, you may be able to call on others in your organization to lend a hand, and you always have the option of calling in freelancers and consultants to help you get the job done.

However you choose to proceed, you'll be spending a lot of time over the next few weeks working on your business plan document. Even if your job is just to read the various drafts and give your okay, you'll find that the time involved is significant.

That's okay. It's worth whatever time it takes because there is little you can do that will have more impact than creating an effective business plan. If it does its job—if you obtain the funding you seek—it will be time well spent.

GETTING ORGANIZED

The first step in preparing your business plan is recognizing that you need to get prepared. You can't just sit down one morning and say, "Today I'm going to write my business plan," and then expect things to fall immediately into place. It doesn't work that way.

Putting together a comprehensive, effective business plan requires preparation, coordination, and a lot of hard work. It's a major project that, in most instances, involves multiple individuals and (in the case of larger companies) multiple departments. The process of creating the plan document is complex, with a lot of different pieces and parts that need to be worked on, many simultaneously.

How do you manage a project of this size and complexity?

First you have to realize that you probably can't do everything yourself. Even if you're a one-person startup, you'll most likely need to bring in *some* help at some point in time—even if it's just to look over the financials, proofread the text, or arrange the printing.

SPLITTING THE PROJECT INTO PARTS

The next thing to do is determine what exactly needs to get done. Here's a short list of the individual things you need to do to create your business plan:

- Manage the project
- Assemble the market data
- Generate the financials
- Supply org charts
- Supply management bios
- Obtain information about each department
- Supply the company's vision and mission statements
- Write the various sections of the plan
- Edit and format the entire document
- Proofread the draft document
- Route the various drafts of the document and obtain final management approval

- Determine the total number of copies to print—and who should receive them
- Arrange printing
- Distribute the completed plan

JUST A MINUTE

Depending on the size and scope of your individual business plan—as well as the operations of your particular business—your to-do list might look slightly different from the list presented here.

ASSIGNING A PROJECT MANAGER

Now it's time to assign specific people to specific parts of the project. The balance of this chapter will help you figure out who should do what; for now, we'll focus on the one assignment that's especially critical to making sure your business plan actually gets done. This individual is your project manager.

Your project manager will oversee the entire business plan project. This person manages all the pieces and parts of your project and makes sure everything gets done according to the schedule you've set. It's up to the project manager to track down any missing elements, to make the phone calls when a deliverable is past due, and to check everything twice to make sure all the i's are dotted and t's crossed.

If you're a small operation, this project manager might be you. However, if you're not terribly organized by nature, you're better off finding someone else who *is*. This project is important, and it has a lot of pieces and parts, and they have to be managed. Don't let your own lack of organization become the bottleneck that slows down the completion of your business plan. Recognize your own personal strengths and weaknesses and structure the management of this project around them.

DETERMINING WHAT YOU NEED—BEFORE YOU START

You're probably wondering why this hour so far has focused so much on project management skills. It's simple—there will be a lot of pieces and parts floating around as work begins on your business plan. Even if you write the entire plan yourself, you'll need to assemble a wide assortment of background documents and data, information that provides the details you need to create a comprehensive plan.

What sorts of things will you need to assemble for your plan? Here's a *short* list of data and information that needs to be gathered:

- Market data and analysis
- Vision and mission statements
- Organization charts
- Information about your company's important processes
- Information about individual departments
- Management bios
- Financial statements
- Company logo
- List of recipients for the completed document

This list is just a start. Whoever ends up writing the plan will end up with stacks and stacks (or, hopefully, files and files) of background information to refer to during the writing process.

SETTING THE SCHEDULE

How much time does it take to create a business plan? The correct answer is: longer than you think.

To be fair, a 20- to 30-page business plan can be written, after the preliminary information is assembled, in a mere matter of days. Practically, however, the actual project time is much longer. This is typically caused by one or more common factors:

- The preliminary information doesn't arrive on time. It typically dribbles in in fits and starts, with one or two departments or individuals substantially lagging the others in what they supply.
- The preliminary information isn't enough; once you get into the middle of a plan, it's not unusual to realize that you need more or different information than what you initially assembled.
- The plan—in various draft stages—needs to be circulated to one or more individuals for their comments or approval. Add at least a day—per pass—for every individual who has to vet the plan.

- Someone (probably you) decides that the original direction of the plan isn't quite right and insists on major changes. Add on at least three days for every change in direction like this.

- Someone (again, probably you) puts the plan on hold as you wait for some major development to take place. Typically, this has to do with funding; you want to hold the plan until you get a potential major investor lined up so you can either include that information in the plan or better tailor the plan for that investor.

Given these real-world complications (which, you insist, will *never* happen in your particular situation), what's a realistic time frame to complete your business plan?

The absolute minimum completion time for a 20- to 30-page business plan is two weeks. This schedule can be achieved only if the plan sticks to the planned page count, if there are a minimal number of people overseeing and commenting on the plan (one—you—is probably the right number), and if the plan proceeds exactly as planned without any interruptions or holdups for major directional changes.

The two-week plan is rare, however. Most business plans—especially those done by larger organizations and those with a lot of people providing input—take much longer to complete. Believe it or not, a good rule of thumb is to take your original estimate and change the timeframe from weeks to months. So if you think you can complete your plan in two weeks, it will probably take two months.

Really.

TIME SAVER

The most effective way to cut time out of your business plan schedule is to restrict the number of individuals who review and provide input on the plan. Not only does it take time to route drafts to multiple individuals (and for them to read the drafts and then provide formal or informal comments), you are inevitably faced with the problem of different individuals providing conflicting feedback. The bulk of your time will be spent trying to resolve these conflicts—instead of actually driving your plan to completion.

WHAT KIND OF HELP DO YOU NEED?

Okay, you're convinced that creating a business plan is a big project and that you probably can't do it all yourself. Once you decide to bring on one or more people to help you create the plan, what types of individuals should you look for?

SOMEONE WHO KNOWS YOUR BUSINESS

When it comes to creating the strategy-oriented parts of the plan—which, let's face it, will comprise the bulk of the document—you have to have someone who knows your business. It's easy enough to write words on paper (or it is for someone who specializes in it), but it's much harder to use those words to adequately describe what it is your business does and why.

The reality is that no one knows your business as well as you do—especially if you're a small or startup business. If you have someone—one of your staff members, a consultant you've been working with, or even a spouse or close friend—who does understand your business well, count yourself among a fortunate few. Use this strategic doppelganger to help you shape and review the big-picture parts of your plan—or to provide guidance to a professional writer.

SOMEONE TO MANAGE THE PIECES AND PARTS

As discussed earlier in this hour, you need a detail-oriented individual to help you organize the individual components of the project and to help keep the project on track. Don't automatically assume this is something you can do personally—although, perhaps, this is something your assistant can help you with. Better yet would be someone who specializes in managing projects of this nature and who won't be distracted by other activities during the course of the project.

PROCEED WITH CAUTION

If you hire or assign a professional writer to actually write your plan, do *not* assume that this individual can also manage the individual pieces and parts of the project. While most writers do happen to be relatively organized individuals, they might not know where to obtain all the information they need—and digging around for bits of information can be a significant distraction to the writing process. If you use a writer, let the writer write—and assign someone else to manage the other details.

SOMEONE WHO CAN WRITE—AND *SELL*

The touchiest assignment concerns the actual writing of the document's text. Many entrepreneurs assume that, since no one knows their business as they do, no one else can write the business plan. This assumption not only is incorrect, it can jeopardize the success of the plan.

The sad fact is that most Americans don't know how to write well. It's a struggle for most individuals—even those with higher levels of education—to craft a concise, impactive letter or memo. It may not be difficult to put words on paper (or on screen, in the case of e-mail and word processing), but it's a much more difficult task to choose the right words for the task and to organize those words for the greatest effect.

That's why writing is a skill taught at most major colleges and universities and why a select few individuals specialize in writing as a profession. When it comes to creating what is arguably the most important document in your company's history, do you want to trust the writing of that document to an amateur (like you) or to a professional?

JUST A MINUTE

Where do you find a professional writer for your business plan? Check with local advertising agencies as well as local marketing associations and groups. (Looking in the Yellow Pages under "Writers" can also be effective.) It also doesn't hurt to ask potential investors if they have anyone to recommend.

A professional writer will be able to take the information you assemble, supplement it with a series of interviews (with you and your key staff), and turn those pieces and parts into a well-crafted, easy-to-read document. Not only will the spelling and the grammar be correct (not always a given if you write it yourself), the sentences will flow logically from one idea to the next, and the text will read well, with a pace and a rhythm that rolls off the tongue and livens up even the most commonplace information.

A good marketing-oriented writer will also make sure that your plan *sells* your business. This writer will turn features into benefits, and add enough pizzazz to stoke the interest of potential lenders and investors. If you can write like this, then maybe you should write your own plan; if not, hire a pro to get the best results possible.

Someone Who Can Make It Look Professional

The plan isn't done when it's written; it's done when the final ink is put on paper. That means someone has to format the document to look professional and then arrange for the document to be printed.

What we're talking about here is what some call desktop publishing. Someone has to pick the fonts used, choose the page margins, decide on a color scheme (if you go four-color), pick the graphic elements, make the charts and graphs look good, and so on. In other words, you need someone to professionally design your document.

JUST A MINUTE

Many professional designers will automatically assume that you want your document published in Adobe PageMaker, Quark xPress, or some other professional desktop publishing (DTP) program. Although these programs are widely used by professional desktop publishers—and can produce fantastic results—you may be better off sticking with the desktop publishing capabilities of Microsoft Word. If you use PageMaker or similar DTP software, you'll be forced to go back to the original designer whenever you want to make any changes. If you use Microsoft Word (which can produce surprisingly similar results), you can make future changes yourself—saving you both time and money.

GO TO ▶
See Hour 21, "Format and Print," to learn more about desktop publishing and printing your business plan document.

It's possible that you have a desktop publishing expert on staff or someone who can do wonders with Microsoft Word. (You don't have to use a fancy desktop publishing program; Word can produce some great-looking business plan documents.) If so, great—you've found your designer. If not, you'll need to hire an outside firm to publish your document for you. You can choose from dedicated designers (expensive and possibly overkill for your needs), freelance desktop publishers (less expensive), or printing companies that also offer DTP services (very convenient). Look in your Yellow Pages or check with other business associates to assemble a list of prospects—and make sure you see samples of their previous work.

WHO CAN YOU USE?

Now that you know the types of skills you need, you have to determine who you know that possesses these skills.

YOU

The first place to look for any of these types of people is in the mirror—especially if you're a small business or a startup. Determine which of the tasks you're personally suited for and then decide whether or not you have the time or the inclination to do the work, according to the necessary schedule.

At the very least, you'll need to provide guidance to others who do the work and review and approve the work they do. In other words, you're going to be heavily involved in this project, even if you assign yourself a minor role.

PROCEED WITH CAUTION

Even—and especially—if you decide to do the bulk of the work yourself, you still should bring in someone else to help you with this project. At the very least, you need another set of eyes on the document to provide critical feedback and another perspective on what you've written. Consider retaining a consultant or a business associate who has prior experience with creating business plans. An experienced consultant can help provide the proper focus for your plan, and can keep you from reinventing the wheel or going down the wrong path; there's no reason *not* to learn from someone else's experience.

Your Staff

If you're in an existing business, the people who work for you can (and probably should) be tapped for some of the work required. If you have an assistant, for example, he or she might be able to handle the project management aspects of this project. If you have a copywriter or an ad writer on staff, that individual might be able to provide the writing you need. When it comes to doing the desktop publishing, check your marketing department; there's probably someone there who's up for the task. If your firm is large enough to have a separate business development or mergers and acquisition department, you can most likely hand the entire project over to them to complete.

In other words, look at all the internal resources available to you and use the ones that make the most sense.

PROCEED WITH CAUTION

If you do enlist a member of your staff to help you put the plan together, make sure that you choose someone who shares your vision for the business. Be careful not to choose someone who brings a personal agenda to the project; the plan has to reflect your business vision, not someone else's.

Outside Resources

If you're a small business or if you're an entrepreneur trying to do everything yourself, you should consider going outside for some parts of this project.

Yes, it will cost money, but if your plan is ultimately a success, it will be money well spent.

What kind of outside resources should you consider? Here's a short list:

- Consultants or consulting firms that specialize in creating business plans
- Professional writers, especially those who specialize in writing business plans, marketing plans, and marketing materials
- Editors, who can help you fine-tune your final draft—and also provide proofreading services
- Desktop publishers and designers, who can take your text and pictures and put them together in a professional-looking document
- Printers, who will professionally print and bind your final document

Finally, it never hurts to get at least one set of outside eyeballs on the final draft of your document. Find someone who has some experience with this sort of thing—a business associate or even a potential investor—and let that person have a read. Use this unbiased feedback to provide a final tweaking to your plan and don't be surprised at what you hear; sometimes you're just too close to things to see some of the issues an outsider will bring to light.

WHO DOES WHAT?

Now for the final step—deciding who does what. Use the following table to assign the various components of your business plan projects to specific individuals.

Business Plan Project Assignments

Activity	Assigned to:
Manage entire project	_____
Assemble market data	_____
Generate financials	_____
Supply organization chart	_____
Supply management bios	_____
Obtain information about each department referenced in the Operations section	_____
Supply vision and mission statements	_____

Activity	Assigned to:
Write the Opportunity section	_____
Write the Market Strategy section	_____
Write the Business Strategy section	_____
Write the Organization and Operations section	_____
Write the Management section	_____
Write the Core Competencies and Challenges section	_____
Edit and format the Financials section	_____
Write the Executive Summary	_____
Edit and format entire document	_____
Proofread the draft document	_____
Route draft documents	_____
Obtain final management approval	_____
Determine the number of copies to print	_____
Arrange printing	_____
Distribute the completed document	_____
Other:	
_____	_____
_____	_____
_____	_____
_____	_____

HOMEWORK

In this hour, you learned how to manage your business plan project. In Hour 9, "Build Your Numbers," you'll learn how to assemble the financial information you'll need to complete the plan document.

To prepare for the next hour, you may want to think about the following:

- What existing financial information do you have—and in what format does it exist?

- Who do you have—either on staff or available as a freelance resource—that can help you work up your financial projections?

- What kind of future revenue and profit numbers will potential lenders and investors expect to see—and what do you want to show?
- When planning future performance, what business assumptions have you made?
- Are you capable of performing a dispassionate logic check on all your final projections?

Hour 9

Build Your Numbers

Chapter Summary

LESSON PLAN:

In this hour, you will learn about ...

- Historical and projected income statements
- Balance sheets
- Cash flow projections
- Margin and ratio analysis

Financial statements help you set the goals and measure the success of your business. They're an essential part of any business plan—and, especially if you're borrowing money, they're every bit as important as any of the text sections.

Whether you're borrowing money or trying to attract investors, your potential lenders and investors will want to know what size business you're talking about, how profitable that business is, and how you expect to grow revenues and profits over the years. Your financial statements provide that critical information.

Although there are a few common financial statements that everyone will want to see, know that different lenders and investors will have different requirements in this regard—and different types of businesses will dictate different formats as well. You'll want to enlist the assistance of a qualified accountant or financial advisor to help you prepare these financial statements—and to prepare for any financial questions that may be asked of you.

A Quick Financial Refresher Course

Before we proceed to an examination of financial statements, let's spend a few minutes of this hour brushing up on some accounting basics.

REVENUES, EXPENSES, AND PROFITS

Three related concepts are key to the running of any business:

- **Revenues.** Revenues (also called sales) are the dollars you generate by selling your products and services. There are two types of revenues—gross revenues and net revenues. Gross revenues are the straight sales dollars you recorded; net revenues are your sales dollars less any returned or discounted sales. Revenues never have any costs or expenses deducted. It's pure sales; nothing else is included.

JUST A MINUTE

Most accounting and financial types will typically be interested in your net revenues. If a statement only lists "revenues," you can assume it's referring to net revenues.

- **Expenses.** Expenses are your costs, the money you have to pay for various goods and services. There are several different types of expenses. Cost of goods sold (COGS) are product costs directly associated with the manufacture or purchase of the goods that contribute to your revenues. Operating expenses are those nonproduct costs that reflect the day-to-day operations of your business—salaries, rent, advertising, and so on. COGS and operating expenses are typically reported in different parts of your income statement.

JUST A MINUTE

You will sometimes need to examine your costs as either fixed or variable. Fixed costs are typically those operating expenses that you have to pay no matter how many (or how few) products you sell; rent is a good example of a fixed cost. Variable costs are those costs that vary depending on your revenues; sales commissions are variable expenses.

- **Profits.** If revenues reflect how much money you take in and expenses reflect how much money you pay out, profits reflect how much money you have left after the two previous activities. (Profit is often referred to as income or earnings.)

PROFIT EQUATION

REVENUES - EXPENSES = PROFITS

Do not get these concepts confused. It's easy to slip and think of your revenues as "earnings" (since you "earned" that money!), but the word "earnings" actually refers to profits. Same with income—income is profit, not revenue. If in doubt, refer to the following table for some quick guidance:

Basic Financial Terms

Proper Names for ...		
What You Sell	*What You Spend*	*What You Get to Keep*
Revenues	Expenses	Profits
Sales	Costs	Earnings
		Income
		Bottom line

ASSETS AND LIABILITIES

Revenues, expenses, and profits are used to describe what your business does; assets and liabilities describe what your business owns—and owes. Here's how they're defined:

- **Assets.** Assets are those items that your business owns. Assets can be in the form of physical things (land, buildings, equipment, fixtures), cash or cash equivalents, or accounts receivable. In short, anything you own or that is owed to you is counted as an asset.

- **Liabilities.** Liabilities are the opposite of assets—they're things that someone else owns and for which you owe. Liabilities are typically in the form of loans, expenses, or taxes due.

If you take everything you own and subtract everything you owe, the balance represents your net worth in your business—also known as your *equity*. This equation is the core concept behind a balance sheet (discussed later in this hour).

EQUITY EQUATION

ASSETS - LIABILITIES = EQUITY

STRICTLY SPEAKING

Equity is the part of the business that is owned by its owners and investors, typically in the form of stock. Equity is calculated as assets less liabilities.

THE DIFFERENCE BETWEEN PROFITS AND CASH

You might think that the profits you make would feed the cash component of your assets. In theory, this could be the case—especially if you run a relatively small, relatively simple business. However, two factors can make these two numbers get out of whack.

First, you probably don't pay all your bills on the day you receive them. When a bill is due but you haven't paid it yet, you have created a liability, which will change your asset position. Let's use an example in which you start with zero assets and zero liabilities. You sell a widget for $5 and, after subtracting $2 COGS, generate a $3 gross profit. That $3 in your pocket is both cash and asset—until you receive a sewer bill for $2. Now you have a $2 liability—and a $2 expense. Even though you haven't paid the bill yet, you still have to figure the expense, which reduces your net profit to $1. You still have $3 in cash, but your profit is now just $1. So, for the time being, your cash doesn't equal your profit. (This will be rectified as soon as you write a check for $2 to the sewer commission, of course.)

The second way in which cash and profits differ is if you accept payment on credit. Let's say you sold that $5 widget (which generated a $3 gross profit) to Mr. Smith, who signed the invoice and promised to pay within 30 days. Now you have a $3 profit but zero dollars in cash—and you won't have the cash until Mr. Smith sends you a check later this month.

JUST A MINUTE

The $5 due from Mr. Smith becomes an asset in your books in the form of an accounts receivable.

This is all to demonstrate why you must look at your cash situation as being separate from your company's profits—as tempting as it might be to think that your monthly profits would equate to real cash on hand.

ESSENTIAL FINANCIAL STATEMENTS

There are many different ways to describe your business, but it's your financial statements that actually quantify your goals and performance.

There are dozens of different types of financial statements that you can use to describe your business. The three most common statements detail your firm's profits and losses (income statement), your firm's net worth (balance sheet), and your firm's cash on hand (cash flow projection). Other useful financial statements detail the sources of your revenues (revenue projection), project when your firm will start generating profits (breakeven analysis), and list all the "hard" assets that you own (*capital asset* inventory).

STRICTLY SPEAKING

A **capital asset** is an item you expect to own for an extended period of time—at least several years. Capital assets are typically depreciated rather than expensed.

If you're unsure just which financial statements to include with your business plan, ask your audience; your potential lenders and investors typically have very precise requirements where financial information is concerned. Lacking any specific requests, three key types of financial statements probably should be included in every business plan. The following checklist details these essential financial reports:

Essential Financial Statements

☐ Income statements (current, historical, and a three-year or five-year projection)

☐ Balance sheet (current)

☐ Cash flow projection (monthly)

JUST A MINUTE

Most financial statements can reflect a variety of different time periods. Historical financials are typically shown in one-year increments; statements for the current year are typically shown in one-month increments; and projections are typically shown in one-year increments—except for cash flow projections, which typically are shown in one-month increments.

The following sections discuss each of these three reports in more depth.

If you're unsure how to generate financial projections for a brand-new business without any history, you're not alone. Predicting how much revenue you'll generate and how much money you'll spend is part bottom-up number building, part crystal-ball gazing, and part figuring out the expectations of your potential lenders and investors. Naturally, you want to be as accurate as possible with your projections—while still delivering a set of numbers that has appeal to your audience.

For example, during the dot.com boom of the late 1990s, investors wanted to see revenue projections that went up and up and up (in a so-called "hockey stick" growth chart—so named because it resembled the sharp upward angle of a hockey stick laying on its side); they didn't particularly care about the profits (if any) associated with those revenues. In fact, if you showed a profit on your projections, you'd raise a lot of eyebrows in some quarters—it's as if the value of the investment was dependent on how big a loss you could show! In that investment environment, you had to put together a set of numbers that tracked along with the investors' expectations; you had to play the game that was being played at the time.

Of course, games change. After the dot-com bust at the turn of the millennium, investors now wanted to see financials that showed less-ambitious growth and a faster track to profitability. Now you had to put together a set of numbers that met these new expectations—or you couldn't get a VC to even talk to you on the phone.

Does this imply that you should falsify your projections just to meet the expectations of potential investors? Not necessarily. Indeed, how can you falsify *projections*? A projection is just that—something you think *might* happen. It's not a guarantee of what definitely *will* happen. (There are no guarantees in business—nor in life itself.)

Although the lawyers and certified public accountants reading this book will probably cringe at this advice, it's probably okay to fudge a little one way or another when building your financial projections. Not that you should falsify any existing financials (that would be illegal), nor should you deliberately mislead potential investors. But if you have to put on a set of rose-colored sunglasses to get the attention of a key investor, that's just the way the game is played.

Make sure, however, that you make your own private projections minus any of the BS you have to apply for potential investors. When it comes to the actual management of your business, never *ever* fall into the trap of believing your own BS!

THE INCOME STATEMENT

The income statement reflects the revenue your company generates, the expenses you pay, and the profit (or loss) that filters down. The form of the income statement is to show your revenues, subtract the cost of goods sold to show the gross profit, and then subtract all your operating expenses to show your net profit. The series of equations looks something like this:

GROSS PROFIT EQUATION

REVENUES - COST OF GOODS SOLD = GROSS PROFIT

NET PROFIT EQUATION

GROSS PROFIT - OPERATING EXPENSES = NET PROFIT

Your operating expenses are typically broken out into multiple line items. In addition, you'll see the gross profit and net profit described as percentages of net revenues. (When shown this way, they're called gross margin and net margin.)

JUST A MINUTE

An income statement is sometimes called a profit and loss statement, or a P&L (or P/L) for short.

The following figure presents the categories used in a typical income statement.

Here's a brief explanation of the most important income statement line items:

- **Gross Revenues.** This line (also called Gross Sales) reflects all of your dollar sales for the period, not counting any damaged or returned goods.

- **Returns.** Sometimes called "Returns and Allowances," this line reflects the cost of any returned or damaged merchandise as well as any allowances and markdowns.

A typical income statement.

Sample Income Statement	
Gross Sales (Gross Revenues)	A
Returns	B
Net Sales (Net Revenues)	C=A-B
Cost of Goods Sold (COGS)	D
Gross Profit	E=C-D
Gross Profit Margin (Gross Margin)	F=E/C
Operating Expenses	
Salaries (Wages)	G
Advertising	H
Marketing	I
Selling	J
Research & Development	K
General & Administrative	L
Rents and Leases	M
Utilities	N
Automobile	O
Travel & Entertainment	P
Dues/Subscriptions	Q
Loan Payments	R
Total Operating Expenses	S=sum(G...R)
EBITDA	T=E-S
EBITDA Margin	U=T/C
Interest	V
Taxes	W
Depreciation	X
Amortization	Y
Net Profit (Loss)	Z=T-sum(V...Y)
Net Margin	AA=Z/C

JUST A MINUTE

Not all income statements include the Gross Revenues and Returns lines. Many income statements start with the Net Revenues number as the first line, assuming the necessary gross-minus-returns calculation.

- **Net Revenues.** Net Revenues (also called Net Sales) reflect your Gross Revenues less your Returns and Allowances.
- **Cost of Goods Sold.** This line (also called COGS or Cost of Sales) reflects the direct costs of the products you sold for the period.

PROCEED WITH CAUTION

Do not include any indirect costs or operating expenses in the Cost of Goods Sold line. Items *not* to list would include R&D, salaries, rent, advertising, selling expense, and the like.

- **Gross Profit.** This line reflects the direct profit you made from sales during this period. It is calculated by subtracting the Cost of Goods Sold from Net Revenues.
- **Gross Margin.** This line (also called Gross Profit Margin) describes your Gross Profit as a percent of your Net Revenues. You calculate this number by dividing Gross Profit by Net Revenues.

- **Operating Expenses.** This line reflects all the indirect costs of your business. Typical line items within this overall category include Salaries, Advertising, Marketing, Selling, Research and Development (R&D), Office, Office Supplies, Rent, Leases, Utilities, Automobile, Travel and Entertainment (T&E), General and Administrative (G&A), Dues and Subscriptions, Licenses and Permits, and Training. *Not* included in this section are direct product costs (which should be reflected in the Cost of Goods Sold), loan payments, interest on loans, taxes, depreciation, and amortization.

In some simplified income statements, all operating expenses are grouped into the Sales, G&A, and R&D categories.

- **EBITDA.** EBITDA stands for earnings before interest, taxes, depreciation, and amortization. Some people refer to this line simply as Net Income Before Taxes or Net Profit Before Taxes; the words "income," "earnings," and "profit" are synonymous. This line reflects the net profit your firm generated during the period, after all actual costs have been accounted for but before you pay taxes and the interest on your loans and before you amortize or depreciate any capital assets. You calculate EBITDA by subtracting Operating Expenses from Gross Profit; a loss is notated within parentheses.
- **EBITDA Margin.** This line describes your EBITDA as a percentage of your Net Sales. You calculate this number by dividing EBITDA by Net Sales.
- **Net Profit (Loss).** This line (also called Net Earnings or Net Income) reflects your reported profit or loss after interest expenses, taxes, depreciation, and amortization costs have been factored out. You calculate this number by subtracting interest, taxes, depreciation, and amortization from EBITDA; a loss is noted within parentheses.
- **Net Margin.** This line describes your Net Profit as a percentage of your Net Sales. You calculate this number by dividing Net Profit by Net Sales.

You can present an income statement for a single period of time, or you can create an income statement that reflects a chronological impression. If you present an income statement for multiple periods (12 months, for example), you may want to include a final column that adds all the monthly numbers into a full-year number.

JUST A MINUTE

In all financial statements, a loss is typically noted by inserting the number in parentheses. So if you see ($200), you note a loss of $200. An alternative, although less accepted, method is to put a negative sign in front of any losses. If you're printing in color, you would use red (in addition to the parentheses) to notate all losses.

THE BALANCE SHEET

The balance sheet is the financial statement that describes what your company owns (assets) and what it owes (liabilities). It's called a balance sheet because it, in effect, "balances" your assets and your liabilities in a variation of the previously presented equation.

ASSETS EQUATION

LIABILITIES + EQUITY = ASSETS

The assets go on the left side of the balance sheet, and the liabilities and assets go on the right; the bottom numbers on each side must be equal.

The following figure presents the categories used in a typical balance sheet.

A typical balance sheet.

Sample Balance Sheet					
Assets			**Liabilities**		
Current Assets			**Current Liabilities**		
Cash	A		Accounts Payable	N	
Marketable Securities	B		Notes Payable	O	
Accounts Receivable	C		Interest Payable	P	
Inventories	D		**Total Current Liabilities**		Q=sum(N...P)
Short-Term Investments	E				
Total Current Assets		F=sum(A...E)	**Long-Term Liabilities**		
			Long-Term Notes Payable	R	
Long-Term Assets			Taxes Payable	S	
Building (Gross)	F		**Total Long-Term Liabilities**		T=sum(R...S)
Accumulated Depreciation	G				
Net Building	H=F-G		**Equity (Net Worth)**		U
Equipment	I				
Land	J		**Total Liabilities and Net Worth**		V=Q+R+U
Long-Term Investments	K				
Total Long-Term Assets		L=sum(H...K)			
Total Assets		M=F+L	*NOTE: M must equal V*		

Here's a brief explanation of the most important asset items on your balance sheet:

- **Current Assets.** This category includes those items that can be converted into cash within the next 12 months. Typical line items would include Cash, Accounts Receivable, Inventories, and Short-Term Investments.

- **Fixed Assets.** This category (sometimes called Long-Term Assets) includes assets that are *not* easily converted into cash, including Land, Buildings, Accumulated Depreciation (as a negative number), Improvements, Equipment, Furniture, and Vehicles.

- **Long-Term Investments.** This category includes any longer-term investments the company has made.

- **Total Assets.** This line reflects the value of everything your company owns. You calculate this number by adding together Current Assets and Fixed Assets.

The following are the key line items on the liabilities side of your balance sheet:

- **Current Liabilities.** This category includes any debts or monetary obligations payable within the next 12 months. Typical line items would include Accounts Payable, Notes Payable, Interest Payable, and Taxes Payable.

- **Long-Term Liabilities.** This category includes debts and obligations that are due to be paid over a period exceeding 12 months. Typical line items would include Long-Term Notes Payable and Deferred Taxes.

- **Equity.** This line (sometimes called Net Worth) reflects the owners' investment in the business. Depending on the type of ownership, this line may be broken into separate lines reflecting the individual equity positions of multiple partners or the company's capital stock and retained earnings.

- **Total Liabilities and Net Worth.** This line (sometimes called Total Liabilities and Equity) reflects the total amount of money due plus the owners' value. You calculate this number by adding together Current Liabilities, Long-Term Liabilities, and Equity.

JUST A MINUTE

To make your balance sheet actually balance, the Total Liabilities and Net Worth number must equal the number for Total Assets.

While an income statement can be looked at historically or projected into the future, a balance sheet is a snapshot of the present and is not shown in any chronological progression.

THE CASH FLOW PROJECTION

As discussed earlier in this hour, your usable cash is not the same as the profits you generate. Potential lenders, especially, will want to know, on a month-by-month basis, whether you'll have enough cash on hand to pay the bills incurred during that period. You figure this out by generating a financial statement called a cash flow projection.

JUST A MINUTE

Although most potential lenders will ask to see a cash flow projection, many potential investors will be less interested. Investors tend to be more interested in their potential big-time earnout than they are in the fiddly details of your monthly bill payments.

A cash flow projection might sound difficult and complex, but it's actually one of the easiest financial statements to create. You simply start each month with the amount of cash you have on hand, add the cash you expect to generate that month, and then subtract the cash you have to pay out. What you have left over is your monthly cash position.

The equation to calculate your cash flow is as follows:

CASH POSITION EQUATION

CASH ON HAND + CASH RECEIPTS - CASH PAID OUT = CASH POSITION

If your monthly cash position is positive, you have positive cash flow (meaning you paid all your bills and have some left over); if this number is negative, you have negative cash flow (meaning you didn't have enough cash on hand to pay all your bills). Your cash position at the end of one month becomes your starting cash on hand for the next month—and you keep on like this, month-by-month, over the entire projected period.

The following figure shows you how a typical cash flow projection is put together.

Here's a brief explanation of the key line items in a cash flow projection:

- **Cash On Hand.** This is the amount of cash you have available at the start of each measurement period.
- **Cash Receipts.** These reflect the cash you generate over the course of the measurement period.

- **Total Cash Available.** This is your initial cash on hand plus your cash receipts. It is the amount of cash, in total, that you have available to pay out over the course of the measurement period.
- **Cash Paid Out.** This reflects all the cash you spend over the course of the measurement period.
- **Cash Position.** This reflects your final end-of-period cash position— the amount of cash you project to have on hand at the end of the current measurement period. Your cash position at the end of one period turns into your Cash On Hand number at the beginning of the next period.

Cash Flow Projection

	Month 1	Month 2	Month 3
Cash on Hand	A1	A2=E1	A3=E2
Cash Receipts	B1	B2	B3
Total Cash Available	C1=A1+B1	C2=A2+B2	C3=A3+B3
Cash Paid Out	D1	D2	D3
Cash Position (end of month)	E1=C1-D1	E2=C2-D2	E3=C3-D3

A typical cash flow projection.

PROCEED WITH CAUTION

Lenders will probably be reluctant to advance funds if your cash flow projections reflect any extended periods of negative cash flow that aren't caused by normal sales cycles.

OTHER FINANCIAL STATEMENTS

There are instances in which you might need to supply additional financial statements to potential lenders or investors. Always ask your potential lenders/investors what financial statements they want to see and be prepared to deliver one or more of the following, just in case.

REVENUE PROJECTIONS

If your company's revenues come from a variety of different sources, you may want to break out those sources in a multiyear revenue projection statement. For example, if you generate revenue by selling widgets, leasing widget-installation machines, and putting on widget-installation training sessions, you might prepare a table that shows all three types of revenue over a multiple-year period. If you do this, you should also show the percentage of total revenue generated by each source.

Breakeven Analysis

A breakeven analysis is used to show precisely when a new business begins to show a profit. Before breakeven, the business is operating at a loss; after breakeven, the business operates profitably. (The area between the revenue and expense lines represents the profit/loss for that period.)

This topic arises because it typically takes a new business a certain amount of time to ramp up revenues to a normal run rate—even though expenses (especially fixed expenses) hit their normal rates almost immediately. You construct a breakeven analysis by taking your projected income statements and extracting the net revenues, COGS and operating expenses, and net profit numbers. The period in which your net profit turns positive is the period in which your business breaks even.

JUST A MINUTE

An alternate—and much tougher—way to analyze breakeven is to calculate cumulative profit/loss over an extended period. In this scenario, you don't actually break even until you've recovered all your previous losses from prior periods.

Capital Asset Inventory

Although investors typically won't care, many lenders will want to see a breakdown of all the capital assets your firm owns. This list would include capital items such as land, buildings, equipment, fixtures, and the like—anything physical in your asset pile.

Assumptions

Whenever you build a set of financial projections, you operate from a set of assumptions—you assume that things will work this way and not another, you assume that the economy will do this and not that, you assume that your products can be manufactured and sold for a certain price. It's wise to make note of all the assumptions you make for your own private records (so you can duplicate the financial results at a future date) and, in an abbreviated form, to include them in your business plan. Accounting types will want to know how you came up with this or that number, and having the assumptions there in black and white will ward off a lot of potential questions.

Just know that your financial assumptions are not a key sales point for your business, so you definitely want to minimize the space they take up in your plan; putting them in a series of footnotes or endnotes is perfectly appropriate.

MARGINS AND RATIOS

The numbers contained in these financial statements paint a broad picture of your business. However, a more detailed understanding can be had by analyzing various combinations of numbers and comparing them to industry averages. How your business ranks in comparison will help potential lenders and investors determine how much of a risk your business represents.

GROSS MARGIN

This number, discussed previously, describes your gross profit as a percent of net revenues. The equation is as follows:

GROSS MARGIN EQUATION

GROSS PROFIT ÷ NET REVENUES = GROSS MARGIN

This number in and of itself doesn"t tell you much. Businesses in some industries operate on high gross margins, because their cost of goods sold is very low. Businesses in other industries operate on low gross margins, because the cost of goods sold represents a high proportion of the final selling price. Saying that "XX percent is the ideal gross margin" would be pointless.

However, comparing your business's gross margin to the gross margins of other similar businesses can be a useful exercise. If all your competitors operate at 50 percent gross margin and you're squeaking along at the 40 percent level, then something is obviously wrong. (Either your costs of goods sold is too high, or your selling prices are too low.) So this type of comparison is a viable analysis.

Also viable is examining your company's gross margin over time. If, over multiple periods, your gross margin shows precipitous decline, that's a sign that something dramatic is changing in your business model. (Either your product costs are getting out of whack, or you're running too many sales, or you're offering too many discounts, or you're facing more aggressive competition ... or *something*.)

Using your gross margin to provide comparative analysis, then, makes it a very useful tool.

EBITDA MARGIN

EBITDA, as described earlier, is your profit before you have to extract the nebulous (and not always real) expenses of interest, taxes, depreciation, and amortization. Your EBITDA margin (sometimes called operating margin) is calculated by dividing EBITDA by net revenues, as in the following equation:

EBITDA MARGIN EQUATION

EBITDA ÷ NET REVENUES = EBITDA MARGIN

Obviously, you want your EBITDA margin to be a positive number; a negative EBITDA margin means that you're running an operating loss. Alas, as with your gross margin, the absolute number is next to useless. (Other than bigger is better, of course.) You need to compare your EBITDA margin with the EBITDA margin of similar businesses to determine whether you're reaching industry-average profitability. You can also analyze your EBITDA margin over time to detect any significant changes in the profitability of your business.

NET MARGIN

Net margin is similar to EBITDA margin, except it measures your profitability after interest, taxes, depreciation, and amortization have been subtracted. You calculate net margin by dividing net profits by net revenues, like this:

NET MARGIN EQUATION

NET PROFITS ÷ NET REVENUES = NET MARGIN

As with EBITDA margin, the higher your net margin, the better—especially when compared with similar businesses. A significant change in net margin over time reflects a change in the profitability of your business, and bears examination.

RETURN ON INVESTMENT (ROI)

All investors want to know what kind of return they're getting on their investments. There are actually two types of return on investment (ROI) equations that you can employ.

The first ROI equation describes the ROI of your business for a specific time period, and is based on current period net income and *tangible net worth*.

ROI EQUATION I

NET INCOME ÷ TANGIBLE NET WORTH = RETURN ON INVESMENT

STRICTLY SPEAKING

Tangible net worth reflects your equity in the company less the book value of intangible assets, such as goodwill.

The second ROI equation, shown next, measures the total return on a block investment.

ROI EQUATION II

EXIT VALUE ÷ INITIAL INVESTMENT = RETURN ON INVESTMENT

Obviously, you're always striving for a higher ROI, whichever valuation method you employ. When considering an investment, investors will estimate ROI and compare it against the ROIs represented by other investments. The investment with the higher potential ROI (and with an acceptable risk) will get the funding.

Current Ratio

Some lenders like to look at the *liquidity* of your business, as measured by the current ratio. You calculate your current ratio by dividing current assets by current liabilities, as shown in the following equation:

CURRENT RATIO EQUATION

CURRENT ASSETS ÷ CURRENT LIABILITIES = CURRENT RATIO

STRICTLY SPEAKING

Liquidity is a reflection of how quickly you can convert assets to cash. Higher liquidity is desirable; having lots of cash on hand is better than having your cash tied up in assets that may or may not be able to be quickly converted into cash.

The higher the current ratio number, the better. (A higher current ratio indicates higher liquidity.)

QUICK ASSETS RATIO

Another way to evaluate liquidity is with the quick assets ratio. This ratio is similar to the current assets ratio, except it subtracts the cost of inventory from your current assets—since inventory often can not be liquidated quickly.

QUICK ASSETS RATIO EQUATION

CURRENT ASSETS - INVENTORY ÷ CURRENT LIABILITIES = QUICK ASSETS RATIO

DEBT-TO-EQUITY RATIO

The flip side of liquidity is debt. To evaluate a company's level of debt, you use the debt-to-equity ratio, shown in the following. If your debt-to-equity ratio gets too high, it's reflective of the business taking on too much debt.

DEBT-TO-EQUITY RATIO EQUATION

LIABILITIES ÷ TANGIBLE NET WORTH = DEBT-TO-EQUITY RATIO

HOMEWORK

In this hour, you learned how to create key financial statements for your business plan. In Hour 10, "Executive Summary," you'll start to work on the business plan document itself, beginning with the one-page summary at the top of the plan.

To prepare for the next hour, you may want to think about the following:

- What is the bare minimum amount of information you need to convey about your business?
- Do you need to summarize every section in your plan?
- What do potential lenders and investors expect to find in your Executive Summary?
- Should you include your financial goals in the Executive Summary?

PART III

Plan to Write

Hour 10

Executive Summary

CHAPTER SUMMARY

LESSON PLAN:

In this hour, you will learn about ...

- Condensing your entire plan to a single page
- Determining which information to include
- Deciding which financial projections to include

The Executive Summary is a much-abbreviated version of your full business plan, located before the main body of your plan document. It should include most—but not all—of the sections that comprise your plan, with each topic condensed to a paragraph or two.

The Executive Summary functions as a brief overview of your business plan. Someone reading only the Executive Summary should be able to get a general idea of what business you're in and why, as well as learn why your business is unique and how big it's going to get.

Even though the Executive Summary should only be a single page long, it's one of the hardest parts of the plan to write. Most businesspeople find it easy to fill pages and pages with information about their business; condensing all that information to a single page is very hard work.

As Mark Twain once said, "I would have written a shorter letter, but I didn't have the time." The key to writing a successful Executive Summary is to know which information is indispensable and which isn't, and then to ruthlessly wield the red editing pencil to cut your plan down to its bare essentials.

If you do a good job on your Executive Summary, you'll have a single page that tells your entire story concisely and convincingly. If you do a bad job of it, you'll end up with a multiple-page mess that does nothing more than duplicate similar information in the body of your plan.

When it comes to Executive Summaries, shorter is definitely better.

WHY YOU NEED AN EXECUTIVE SUMMARY

If your business plan is only 20 to 30 pages long (as recommended), you have a very concise presentation of your business strategy and requirements. Why do you need a separate summary of what is, by nature, a 20-page summary? There are two reasons why.

First, as short as your business plan is, there are many people who won't read the whole thing. In the hectic world of your potential lenders and investors, the time it takes to read a full 20-page document might not always be available. Especially when a lender or investor is evaluating a large number of proposals, being able to spend five minutes vetting a summary is preferable to spending a half-hour or so reading the entire thing. If your plan is the one that doesn't include a summary, it might not get read at all.

The second reason to include an Executive Summary is because it helps set the stage for the rest of the document that follows. Think of it like a trailer for a motion picture or the back-cover blurb for the latest novel. The Executive Summary prepares the reader for the main document and—if worded properly—"teases" the reader in a way that whets his or her appetite for what follows.

A business plan *without* an Executive Summary is incomplete. Your readers will expect this overview, and they'll expect it to be exactly what its name suggests—a short (emphasis on the word *short*) summary of your plan, for busy executives.

HOW TO SUMMARIZE YOUR PLAN

How do you summarize a 20- to 30-page (or longer) plan in a single page? It's not easy, and it requires an essential grasp of what your business is all about.

In essence, you need to tell your business story as succinctly as possible. Think back to the oral story introduced at the beginning of Hour 7, "Create Your Outline." That entire seven-paragraph narrative would make an ideal

Executive Summary. It reveals the bare-bones information of your business (including your vision and mission), talks briefly about the market, and then finishes with your broad financial goals for the company—and it does all this in a length that would fit precisely in the slot allotted for the Executive Summary section of your document.

The point here is that when you boil your business down to its bare essentials, you have your Executive Summary. It's not necessary to include everything you know or want to do (that's why you have the other 20 to 30 pages); present just the basics, without a lot of flowery language, and you have your summary.

JUST A MINUTE

It's important to use short, concise sentences when writing the Executive Summary. Longer sentences not only take up excess (and valuable) space, they also defeat the purpose of enabling readers to "graze" the summary information.

Even though the Executive Summary is the first section of your business plan, you may not want to make it the first section that you write. After all, how can you summarize a plan you haven't created yet? Many business-people prefer to write the main body of the plan document first and then make the Executive Summary the last part they write. That way, they have an actual document to summarize.

However, if you've done a good job outlining your business plan—and you can easily identify the essential components of your business—then you probably can write a first draft of the Executive Summary before you start work on the rest of the business plan. Write your first draft of the Executive Summary, set it aside, and then move on to the rest of the plan. Once the rest of the plan is written, return to your draft of the Executive Summary and clean it up based on anything you've changed in the main body of the document. When you follow this procedure, you can use the Executive Summary as a guide as you're writing the details of the plan.

DIFFERENT STYLES OF SUMMARIES

There are several different ways you can present an Executive Summary to your readers. All are valid; they simply represent different styles of presentation, one of which might better suit your own personal style or the reading styles of your potential lenders or investors.

STRAIGHT NARRATIVE

The most common form of Executive Summary looks just like the balance of your business plan. In a straight narrative (see the following figure), the information is presented in complete sentences and complete paragraphs, with no subheadings or bullets to interrupt the flow of the text.

An Executive Summary presented in the straight narrative format.

Executive Summary

WidgeCo embraces the vision of enabling all college students in the U.S. with technology-based learning aids. The company's mission is to become the leading supplier of computer-based widgets to the college and higher education markets.

Analysts predict that the retail market for widgets will generate $403 million in revenues in 2002, growing to $1.3 billion by 2005. A significant factor in this growth will be the adoption of widgets for classroom use by colleges and other institutions of higher learning. It is estimated that there will be more than 10 million college-age consumers of widgets and related merchandise in the U.S. in 2005.

WidgeCo provides custom-designed widgets to the college and higher education markets. WidgeCo's primary targeted customers are the more than 10 million college students in U.S. colleges and universities, the majority of whom are now being encouraged to include widgets as part of their book purchases each semester.

WidgeCo will provide widgets in custom colors and designs to be sold through the nationwide network of college bookstores. These widgets will be marketed via a series of campus-based promotions targeted at students at the beginning of each semester.

WidgeCo's products will be manufactured in a newly constructed state-of-the-art facility in Ames, Iowa. This facility enables WidgeCo to provide highly customized products at costs below current industry averages.

As a new company in the worldwide widget market, WidgeCo will incur higher than average promotional costs, which will be more than offset by the lower than normal manufacturing enabled by the new facility. This combination of aggressive marketing and efficient manufacturing will enable WidgeCo to achieve significant market share in a short period of time.

In implementing this business model, WidgeCo anticipates generating $2.5 million in revenues by 2005, with $500K of net profit. Annual revenue growth during the 2002-2005 time frame is projected to average 25% per year.

The advantage of a straight narrative presentation is that the Executive Summary flows in the same fashion as the rest of the business plan. It doesn't draw attention to itself with a different presentation format, and (if written well) it presents the summary information in a conversational, flowing style.

There are two potential disadvantages of a straight narrative presentation: Complete sentences are relatively inefficient for presenting condensed information, and there is no formal way to draw special attention to the main points in the summary.

JUST A MINUTE

 Although a straight narrative presentation doesn't allow for subheadings or bullets, you can highlight words and phrases by using boldface, italic, or colored text.

NARRATIVE WITH SUBHEADINGS

Another way to present your summary information is to literally follow the structure of your document outline by adding subheadings between paragraphs. By using subheadings you tell the reader precisely what to expect in each section and also provide another level of "grazing" for those who don't want to read the entire Executive Summary (see the following figure). The primary downside of using subheadings is that it leaves even less room for your text; it's the least efficient presentation you can use.

NARRATIVE WITH A FINANCIAL TABLE

Some businesspeople want to draw special attention to the financial goals in their Executive Summary. (Others prefer not to mention financials in the summary; this objection is discussed in the "What *Not* to Include in the Executive Summary" section later in this hour.) Describing your financials in the body of a paragraph tends to bury the numbers, so you may want to pull the numbers out and present them separately.

An Executive Summary that uses subheadings along with narrative text.

Executive Summary

Vision and Mission

WidgeCo embraces the vision of enabling all college students in the U.S. with technology-based learning aids. The company's mission is to become the leading supplier of computer-based widgets to the college and higher education markets.

Opportunity

Analysts predict that the retail market for widgets will generate $403 million in revenues in 2002, growing to $1.3 billion by 2005. A significant factor in this growth will be the adoption of widgets for classroom use by colleges and other institutions of higher learning. It is estimated that there will be more than 10 million college-age consumers of widgets and related merchandise in the U.S. in 2005.

Market Strategy

WidgeCo provides custom-designed widgets to the college and higher education markets. WidgeCo's primary targeted customers are the more than 10 million college students in U.S. colleges and universities, the majority of whom are now being encouraged to include widgets as part of their book purchases each semester.

WidgeCo will provide widgets in custom colors and designs to be sold through the nationwide network of college bookstores. These widgets will be marketed via a series of campus-based promotions targeted at students at the beginning of each semester.

Business Strategy

WidgeCo's products will be manufactured in a newly constructed state-of-the-art facility in Ames, Iowa. This facility enables WidgeCo to provide highly customized products at costs below current industry averages.

As a new company in the worldwide widget market, WidgeCo will incur higher than average promotional costs, which will be more than offset by the lower than normal manufacturing enabled by the new facility. This combination of aggressive marketing and efficient manufacturing will enable WidgeCo to achieve significant market share in a short period of time.

Financial Goals

In implementing this business model, WidgeCo anticipates generating $2.5 million in revenues by 2005, with $500K of net profit. Annual revenue growth during the 2002-2005 time frame is projected to average 25% per year.

The best way to present numbers separate from your text is to add a financial table at the bottom of your Executive Summary page. This financial table doesn't distract from the narrative, even though it does draw your eye to the key projections (see the following figure).

Executive Summary

WidgeCo embraces the vision of enabling all college students in the U.S. with technology based learning aids. The company's mission is to become the leading supplier of computer-based widgets to the college and higher-education markets.

Analysts predict that the retail market for widgets will generate $403 million in revenues in 2002, growing to $1.3 billion by 2005. A significant factor in this growth will be the adoption of widgets for classroom use by colleges and other institutions of higher learning. It is estimated that there will be more than 10 million college-age consumers of widgets and related merchandise in the U.S. in 2005.

WidgeCo provides custom-designed widgets to the college and higher-education markets. WidgeCo's primary targeted customers are the more than 10 million college students at U.S. colleges and universities, the majority of which are now being encouraged to include widgets as part of their book purchases each semester.

WidgeCo will provide widgets in custom colors and designs to be sold through the nationwide network of college bookstores. These widgets will be marketed via a series of campus-based promotions targeted at students at the beginning of each semester.

WidgeCo's products will be manufactured in a newly constructed state-of-the-art facility in Ames, Iowa. This facility enables WidgeCo to provide highly customized products at costs below current industry averages.

As a new company in the worldwide widget market, WidgeCo will incur higher-than average promotional costs, which will be more than offset by the lower-then-normal manufacturing costs enabled by the new facility. This combination of aggressive marketing and efficient manufacturing will enable WidgeCo to achieve significant market share in a short period of time.

	2002	2003	2004	2005
Revenues	$1,250,000	$1,600,000	$2,000,000	$2,500,000
Net Profits	(400,000)	$10,250	$250,000	$500,000
Net Margin	-32.0%	6.0%	12.5%	20.0%

An Executive Summary with a financial table added to the bottom of the narrative text.

Bulleted Outline

Knowing that many readers will "graze" the information in the Executive Summary (rather than reading it straight through), some businesspeople prefer to present that information in a very "grazeable" format. The preferred way to do this is to present the key information in short, bulleted phrases and organize it into an outline format. The disadvantage to using this type of format is that it permits no narrative whatsoever. Although the key information is presented, there is context for that information, and the Executive Summary starts to function more like a second table of contents (but without the page-number references).

This type of format isn't for everyone (see the following figure), but don't be afraid to use it if you think it will improve the readership from your target audience.

Narrative/Bulleted Blend

If none of these formats is perfect for your particular situation, go for a blend. In this type of blend, you use bullets to convey data and narrative text to provide context and flow.

What to Include in the Executive Summary

When creating your Executive Summary, you have a single page to work with (see the following figures). What should go on that page?

Vision

GO TO ▶
See Hour 11, "Vision and Mission," to learn more about writing the Vision and Mission sections of your business plan.

It's good to start your Executive Summary the same way you start the main part of your business plan—with a statement of why you're in this particular business. That means including your single-sentence vision statement, in most cases exactly as written in the Vision section of your plan.

Mission

Next up is your mission statement, from the Mission section of your business plan. Assuming your mission statement has been held to a single sentence, you can cut and paste this exactly as presented in the Mission section.

Executive Summary

Vision

- Enabling all college students in the U.S. with technology based learning aids

Mission

- Become the leading supplier of computer-based widgets to the college and higher-education markets

Opportunity

- $403 million U.S. retail widget market in 2002
- $1.3 billion U.S. retail widget market in 2005
- More than 10 million U.S. college-age consumers of widgets in 2005.

Market Strategy

- Provide custom-designed widgets to the college and higher-education markets
- Primary targeted customers: U.S. college students
- Provide widgets in custom colors and designs to be sold through college bookstores
- Market product via a series of campus-based promotions targeted at students

Business Strategy

- Manufacture products in newly constructed state-of-the-art facility in Ames, Iowa
- Provide highly customized products at costs below current industry averages
- Combination of aggressive marketing and efficient manufacturing will enable WidgeCo to achieve significant market share in a short period of time.

Financial Goals

- 2005 revenues: $2.5 million
- 2005 net profit: $500K of net profit
- Average annual revenue growth 2002-2005: 25% per year

An Executive Summary presented in a bulleted outline format.

JUST A MINUTE

 You can save space—and improve the narrative flow—by combining the Vision and Mission sections into a single paragraph.

An Executive Summary presented with a blend of narrative and bulleted information.

Executive Summary

Vision and Mission

WidgeCo embraces the vision of enabling all college students in the U.S. with technology based learning aids. The company's mission is to become the leading supplier of computer-based widgets to the college and higher-education markets.

Opportunity

- $403 million U.S. retail widget market in 2002
- $1.3 billion U.S. retail widget market in 2005
- More than 10 million U.S. college-age consumers of widgets in 2005.

Market Strategy

WidgeCo provides custom-designed widgets to the college and higher-education markets. WidgeCo's primary targeted customers are the more than 10 million college students at U.S. colleges and universities, the majority of which are now being encouraged to include widgets as part of their book purchases each semester.

WidgeCo will provide widgets in custom colors and designs to be sold through the nationwide network of college bookstores. These widgets will be marketed via a series of campus-based promotions targeted at students at the beginning of each semester.

Business Strategy

WidgeCo's products will be manufactured in a newly constructed state-of-the-art facility in Ames, Iowa. This facility enables WidgeCo to provide highly customized products at costs below current industry averages.

As a new company in the worldwide widget market, WidgeCo will incur higher-than average promotional costs, which will be more than offset by the lower-then-normal manufacturing costs enabled by the new facility. This combination of aggressive marketing and efficient manufacturing will enable WidgeCo to achieve significant market share in a short period of time.

Financial Goals

	2002	2003	2004	2005
Revenues	$1,250,000	$1,600,000	$2,000,000	$2,500,000
Net Profits	(400,000)	$10,250	$250,000	$500,000
Net Margin	-32.0%	6.0%	12.5%	20.0%

OPPORTUNITY

Now the editing begins. The next part of your Executive Summary should be a single paragraph describing the market opportunity offered to your business. This paragraph will summarize the key data presented in the Opportunity section of your plan.

PROCEED WITH CAUTION

You don't have to—and probably shouldn't—present every scrap of market data from your Opportunity section in the Executive Summary. Definitely avoid using any charts or graphs in the Executive Summary; this section should be all text, no graphics.

You need to boil down the market information to the bare essentials necessary to paint a compelling picture of market opportunity. Include market size and growth, the number of potential customers (if available), and a basic explanation of why the market is sized or growing the way it is.

Here's an example of a short, succinct, single-paragraph market opportunities summary:

> Analysts predict that the retail market for widgets will generate $403 million in revenues in 2002, growing to $1.3 billion by 2005. A significant factor in this growth will be the adoption of widgets for classroom use by colleges and other institutions of higher learning. It is estimated that there will be more than 10 million college-age consumers of widgets and related merchandise in the United States in 2005.

GO TO ▶
See Hour 12, "Opportunity," to learn more about writing the Opportunity section of your business plan.

MARKET STRATEGY

Next up are one or two paragraphs that describe how your business is responding to this market opportunity. This part of the summary abridges the complete Market Summary section of your business plan, with an emphasis on the products and services you'll be offering.

Unless your business is a sales- or channel-driven business (such as a cataloging or direct-mail marketer, for example), there is probably no need to present the details of your marketing and sales plans in the Executive Summary. If distribution channels are important or unusual, present them in a single-sentence list, as in: "We will distribute our products through specialty retailing and direct-mail channels."

GO TO ▶
See Hour 13, "Market Strategy," to learn more about writing the Market Strategy section of your business plan.

This part of the Executive Summary will require *extreme* editing from the full Market Opportunity section of the business plan. You should only present information necessary to describe your business and products; you probably don't need to talk about competitors, advertising, packaging, distribution, and the like. Keep your focus on the products and services you'll be offering and leave the rest of the marketing and sales details to the Market Opportunity section.

BUSINESS STRATEGY

GO TO ▶
See Hour 14, "Business Strategy," to learn more about writing the Business Strategy section of your business plan.

The business strategy part of your Executive Summary abridges the Business Strategy section of the main plan document. You should be able to present the key information in no more than two paragraphs.

Use this part of the summary to tell the reader about your business—what business you're in, what business model you employ, how you're going to generate revenues and profits, and what sets you apart from the competition. Do *not* include information about specific departments in your organization, and don't get too wrapped up in the details of what you do present.

The key to this short section is being able to convey your company's *unique business proposition*. Convey—either directly or indirectly—the one important thing you do that gives you a leg up on competitors. Your unique business proposition should be the reason investors invest in your company rather than in a competitor; if they're sold on the market opportunity, they have to choose which firm to back, and that choice is greatly influenced by each company's unique business proposition. Identify yours straight away in the Executive Summary and draw attention to it.

FINANCIAL GOALS

Businesspeople are divided on the topic of what financial information to include in the Executive Summary. The numbers-oriented crowd (accountants, financial analysts, bankers, and so on) will argue that as complete a set of financials as possible should be included in the front of the plan. (This is most likely because this crowd is only interested in the numbers and will probably pass over the narrative part of the document to get right to the spreadsheets.) Other, more marketing-focused businesspeople will opt for including little or no financial information in the summary. (This is most likely because this crowd believes that the real story is with the opportunity and the business; the numbers are secondary.) The right numbers to include probably fall between these two camps.

STRICTLY SPEAKING

Your company's **unique business proposition** is the one thing that sets your business apart from its competition. It's the reason for your business to exist and the key element that will lead to its success. Your unique business proposition might be the product or service you offer, the price you charge, your ability to contain costs, your skill for keeping ahead of market trends, or some other thing your business does that your competitors don't.

GO TO ▶
See Hour 18, "Financials," to learn more about writing the Financials section of your business plan.

Despite the protestations of accountants everywhere, there is unlikely to be any real value in providing a full set of numbers on the Executive Summary page. Anyone who wants to see the full financials can easily flip to the back of the plan to access the Financials section.

That doesn't mean there is no value in presenting *any* financial information. On the contrary, presenting an out-year financial goal helps put the entire business plan in context and helps the reader size the opportunity before delving into the details.

The right financials to include will differ depending on your circumstances, but they most commonly include revenues and profits for your "out" year—and nothing more. There is no reason to include financials for each year in the projection; you need to tell the reader where you aim to go, not how you intend to get there. (That's what the body of the document is for.) Including anything more than your top and bottom line is also unnecessarily detailed; the Executive Summary is not the place to present or discuss line-item expenses. Just present your top- and bottom-line goals, perhaps along with a simple percentage or two (net margin is good, as is an average yearly growth number), and you've achieved your purpose.

Here's an example of a good one-paragraph financial summary:

> In implementing this business model, WidgeCo anticipates generating $2.5 million in revenues by 2005, with $500,000 of net profit. Annual revenue growth during the 2002–2005 timeframe is projected to average 25 percent per year.

JUST A MINUTE

You should not include any assumptions, background detail, references, or footnotes /endnotes in your Executive Summary. That information will be provided in the main body of the plan document and does not have to be represented here.

WHAT *NOT* TO INCLUDE IN THE EXECUTIVE SUMMARY

When you're struggling to decide what to include in the Executive Summary section, you'll have to make many sacrifices. Some individuals will insist that their particular part of the business is so vital that it must be part of the single-page summary; you'll have to make hard choices about what information just isn't important enough to make the cut.

ORGANIZATION AND OPERATIONS

GO TO ▶
See Hour 15, "Organization and Operations," to learn more about writing the Organization and Operations section of your business plan.

In general, all the information in your plan's Organization and Operations section isn't essential enough to include in the Executive Summary. This section of your plan provides interesting detail about how your business is run and organized, but it doesn't tell *why* you're pursuing the opportunity at hand.

Unless your business has some unique operational advantage that is key to its success, you can probably leave out this entire section.

MANAGEMENT

GO TO ▶
See Hour 16, "Management," to learn more about writing the Management section of your business plan.

Likewise, information about who is managing your business is seldom essential to describing why you're doing what you're doing. The exception to this is if you or one of your staff is extremely well known within your industry and therefore becomes part of your company's unique business proposition.

In most cases, however, any managerial fame exists purely internally and does not warrant space in the Executive Summary.

Core Competencies and Challenges

The entire Executive Summary section should sell the strengths of your business. To that end, including a separate Core Competencies paragraph is, to a degree, redundant. Not that you shouldn't push those items that your business does exceedingly well. If there's a way to weave particular competencies into the Executive Summary, do it. Especially focus on your company's unique business proposition, which by definition is one of your core competencies. However, you probably won't have space to include a list of separate strengths in a one-page summary.

GO TO ▶
See Hour 17, "Core Competencies and Challenges," to learn more about writing the Core Competencies and Challenges section of your business plan.

JUST A MINUTE

The careful use of descriptive adjectives is a good way to insert core competencies into the text of your Executive Summary. For example, the phrases "the world's largest," "the market's highest-quality," "the industry's most experienced," and "the fastest-to-market" all introduce unique competitive advantages as part of the text, without the need for a space-consuming separate section.

Along the same lines, the Executive Summary is not the place to discuss your competitors—or your weaknesses. Think of the Executive Summary like the trailer for a film; you don't see too many trailers that present the movie's weakest moments. The Executive Summary is the place to put your best foot forward, with no obligation to present any counterbalancing risks or challenges.

Detailed Financials

As discussed previously, you don't need to present detailed, year-by-year (or month-by-month) income statement, balance sheet, and cash flow information in the Executive Summary. Since this is a summary of important information, presenting your year-three revenue and profit goals is adequate in most cases. Any other financial information detracts from the main points you're trying to make; besides, readers obsessed with financial information know how to flip directly to your book's final pages, where they're used to seeing the full financial statements.

Charts and Graphs

It goes without saying that all information in the Executive Summary must be presented in the most efficient format possible. That precludes the use of charts and graphs, which are actually fairly inefficient. For example, you can say that "the market is growing 15 percent each year and will reach $10 million in revenues by the year 2005" in a single sentence; graphing that data could take up to a quarter page of space.

Leave the graphs and charts for the body of the document; present what data is necessary in either narrative or bulleted format in your text.

Alternate Approaches

So far in this hour, you've learned one approach to writing an Executive Summary. As with all things business plan–related, there are several alternate approaches, recommended by this expert or that consultant, that you can adopt.

JUST A MINUTE

When deciding on a style, format, or approach, make sure you choose the option that best suits your particular business and that will be best received by your specific potential lenders or investors.

Describe the Business Up Front

As with the structure of the business plan itself, some consultants advise describing your business and business model at the very beginning of the Executive Summary, instead of "burying" it in the middle of the page. The thinking is that some readers will only get as far as the first paragraph or two, so you'd better describe your business right up front.

Be aware, however, that separating out this descriptive information can interrupt the flow of the story you're trying to tell and can make it difficult to segue into the rest of the recommended outline. If you take this approach, you may want to visually separate this descriptive information, either by making the text of this paragraph bold or in color or by putting a box around the descriptive text.

ASK FOR THE MONEY

Some potential lenders and investors like to get straight to the point. They want to know what you're asking for before they even know what kind of business you're in.

For lenders and investors of this type, creating an initial paragraph summarizing your funding needs is the way to go. One possible approach is to combine your business description with your funding request, as follows:

> WidgeCo is a distributor of high-quality widgets to the college and higher education markets. To realize its goal of achieving a 15 percent market share by 2005, WidgeCo is seeking equity funding of $10 million to be completed by December 31st.

SIDEBAR THE DETAILS

Even the most abridged Executive Summary will contain a plethora of data. Rather than burying that data within the narrative, it may make more of an impact to separate the data out in a sidebar, outside the normal summary text. If you follow this approach, consider putting all your market data and financial goals in the sidebar (see the following figure).

WHAT TO DO IF YOUR SUMMARY RUNS LONG

The ideal length for an Executive Summary is one page. Not two pages, not one and a half—one.

Keeping an Executive Summary to a single page, as you'll no doubt discover, is quite a challenge. Your first pass at writing an Executive Summary will probably result in a summary that goes two or three or even four pages in length. That's because you're including information that you think is essential to tell your story, even though it really isn't.

The challenge, then, is to edit your initial pass into a single-page document. That means slashing and cutting; you'll find yourself removing whole ideas that aren't necessary, as well as trimming a word or two here or there to tighten the language and edit the section down to size, line by painful line.

In some instances, no matter how hard you try, you still end up with something in excess of a single page. (This often happens when you're writing a plan for someone else who *insists* that the summary include this and this and this and this—until the summary is almost as long as the main document itself!) What are your options then?

Executive Summary

WidgeCo embraces the vision of enabling all college students in the U.S. with technology based learning aids. The company's mission is to become the leading supplier of computer-based widgets to the college and higher-education markets.

Analysts predict that the retail market for widgets will generate $403 million in revenues in 2002, growing to $1.3 billion by 2005. A significant factor in this growth will be the adoption of widgets for classroom use by colleges and other institutions of higher learning. It is estimated that there will be more than 10 million college-age consumers of widgets and related merchandise in the U.S. in 2005.

WidgeCo provides custom-designed widgets to the college and higher-education markets. WidgeCo's primary targeted customers are the more than 10 million college students at U.S. colleges and universities, the majority of which are now being encouraged to include widgets as part of their book purchases each semester.

WidgeCo will provide widgets in custom colors and designs to be sold through the nationwide network of college bookstores. These widgets will be marketed via a series of campus-based promotions targeted at students at the beginning of each semester.

WidgeCo's products will be manufactured in a newly constructed state-of-the-art facility in Ames, Iowa. This facility enables WidgeCo to provide highly customized products at costs below current industry averages.

As a new company in the worldwide widget market, WidgeCo will incur higher-than average promotional costs, which will be more than offset by the lower-then-normal manufacturing costs enabled by the new facility. This combination of aggressive marketing and efficient manufacturing will enable WidgeCo to achieve significant market share in a short period of time.

In implementing this business model, WidgeCo anticipates generating $2.5 million in revenues by 2005, with $500K of net profit. Annual revenue growth during the 2002-2005 time frame is projected to average 25% per year.

Market Data

- U.S. retail widget market: $403 million (2002)

- U.S. retail widget market: $1.3 billion (2005)

- College-age widget consumers: 10 million

WidgeCo Financial Goals

- 2005 revenues: $2.5 million

- 2005 net profit: $500K

- Average annual growth 2002-2005: 25%

If worst comes to worst and there is *nothing* more to cut (which isn't true, of course, but there's no arguing that point here), you end up with a long Executive Summary. There's no law that says the summary *has* to be a single page; no one will go to jail if your Executive Summary slops over onto a second or (heaven forbid!) third page. If that's the way it is, that's the way it is.

If your Executive Summary just *barely* exceeds a single page (by a sentence or a paragraph), you may want to try some formatting tricks to squeeze the excess text back onto the first page. Here are some of the most common tricks to employ:

- Reduce the font size (of the Executive Summary only—*not* of your entire document!).
- Reduce the spacing between paragraphs.
- Reduce the line spacing.
- Shrink the page margins—going from 1-inch to 0.9-inch margins is barely noticeable and may be just enough to squeeze an extra word in per line.

JUST A MINUTE

A better way to squeeze excess text onto a single page is to edit the text. Pore over your Executive Summary sentence by sentence and word by word, excising any words or phrases that aren't absolutely necessary. Look especially for ways to rephrase wordy sections; isn't there a better (and shorter) way to say something than what was originally written?

One last thing: Consider the use of abbreviations and contractions throughout the Executive Summary text. Writing "COGS" instead of "cost of goods sold" might give you the extra space you need to meet your single-page goal.

EXECUTIVE SUMMARY CHECKLIST

When preparing the Executive Summary for your business plan, work through the following checklist of items to include:

Executive Summary Checklist

☐ Vision statement (1 sentence)

☐ Mission statement (1 sentence)

continues

Executive Summary Checklist   (continued)

☐ Market opportunity (1 paragraph)

☐ Market strategy (1 to 2 paragraphs)

☐ Business strategy (1 to 2 paragraphs)

☐ Financial goals (1 paragraph)

HOMEWORK

In this hour, you learned how to create the Executive Summary section of your business plan. In Hour 11, "Vision and Mission," you'll learn how to write the Vision and Mission sections of the plan.

To prepare for the next hour, please do the following:

- Reread Hour 5, "Analyze Your Strategy."
- Write a one-sentence statement of your vision for your business.
- Write a one-sentence mission statement for your business.

HOUR 11

Vision and Mission

CHAPTER SUMMARY

LESSON PLAN:

In this hour, you will learn about …

- Creating a compelling vision
- Writing a powerful mission statement
- Concisely presenting your vision and mission

As you learned back in Hour 5, "Analyze Your Strategy," every business starts with a vision and a mission. The vision describes how you see the world, and the mission describes your business purpose. Together, these two statements define why you're in business and what reason this particular business has to exist.

Your vision and mission are presented in the Vision and Mission sections of your business plan. Although these are the shortest sections of your plan (no more than a paragraph each), they may be among the most difficult sections to write. That's because many businesspeople find it difficult to articulate the reasons why they do what they do.

"I just make widgets," you might respond if asked why you're in business. But in reality, you make widgets because you have some sort of vision for widgets' role in the world at large, and you've set for yourself a mission to help achieve that vision.

It's getting to that core rationale—the overriding idea that drives everything you do—that is key to creating compelling vision and mission statements.

THE VISION STATEMENT

The vision statement you write for the business plan should express your ultimate dream for the market or consumers your company targets. You are guided by your dreams, and your company should be driven by your vision. Anyone reading the Vision section of your business plan should immediately know why you do what you do and should get a sense of what it is that your company is trying to accomplish.

In other words, the Vision section describes why your company exists—which is why it's the very first section (after the Executive Summary, of course) of your plan. An effective Vision section sets the tone for the entire business plan and provides the sense of purpose that has driven you to seek funding from the people reading the plan.

PROCEED WITH CAUTION

 Don't confuse your vision with your mission. Your vision should be broad and somewhat grandiose; your mission should be narrower, focusing on one particular aspect of your vision.

CRITERIA FOR AN EFFECTIVE VISION STATEMENT

The Vision section of your plan should consist of a simple statement of vision, ideally no longer than a single sentence. (That's right—the entire section is just a sentence long!)

The vision statement should be a somewhat broad, somewhat vague declaration. Remember, your vision statement doesn't describe your mission (that's what the mission statement is for) or define your goals; your vision statement expresses your dreams.

The ideal vision statement should meet these criteria:

- It must be short—one sentence, ideally, and no more than a paragraph at the longest.
- It must be to the point; it shouldn't ramble.
- It must be focused on a single thought or topic.
- It must be sufficiently farsighted and "big" in concept as to be virtually unquantifiable.
- It must provide a distinct focus and direction for the business to follow.

If you can't describe your vision in a paragraph or less, you're either describing too broad a vision or defining multiple missions or goals.

EXAMPLES OF VISION

If you're having trouble coming up with just the right vision statement, remember that—in its own somewhat vague and universal way—the vision statement should provide a clear sense of direction for your business. Think about what you're really trying to achieve, what broad goal you're working toward, and turn that general direction into your vision.

As an example, until recently, Microsoft Corporation was driven by the vision of a computer on every desktop. That's a very clear idea, easily visualized, and it's easy to see how that vision drove every product and service that Microsoft developed over its first decade and a half of existence. To put a computer on every desktop, you have to have a usable operating system and practical applications—both of which Microsoft supplied. The vision also helped focus the company; you didn't see Microsoft (until recently, anyway) producing operating systems for intelligent toasters and kids' toys. The vision was about computers on desktops, and that's where Microsoft focused its attention. Microsoft's vision drove its business.

Here are some more examples of effective business statements:

WidgeCo embraces the vision of enabling all college students in the United States with technology-based learning aids.

Working Girl Fashions envisions a world in which the accepted dress code for women in the workplace is defined by affordable casual clothing.

Phones4Less embraces the vision of universal cellular phone availability and use.

ChampionshipVinyl.com envisions the one-stop availability of a broadly diverse and enriched selection of entertainment products and services to the online entertainment consumer.

As you can see, each of these vision statements is short (one sentence), to the point, and relatively far-reaching in scope. Yet each statement also provides a distinct direction for the business; it would be hard to misconstrue what each of these businesses is trying to achieve.

THE MISSION STATEMENT

Where your vision statement defines the *why* behind your business, your mission statement describes the *what*—what it is that your business does and what it is that you're trying to achieve.

The Mission section of your plan directly follows the Vision section and is also a single-sentence (or single-paragraph) section. It has a narrower focus than the Vision section and truly defines the type of business you're in. Someone reading your Mission section should know immediately what your business does—and what you *don't* do.

For example, if your mission statement says you want to become the largest U.S. retailer of fishing equipment, you would expect the business to have a chain of stores across America that sells fishing poles, lures, and sonar detectors—and maybe even fishing boats and rubber boots. You would *not* expect the company to have stores in Europe, nor to sell baseball bats and handbags. (Unless, of course, these were special baseball bats designed specially for bashing fish ... but that would be pushing it.)

JUST A MINUTE

You can easily determine when a company has lost focus by comparing its real-world activities with its mission statement; activities outside the parameters of the mission statement indicate an unfocused and possibly diluted business.

CRITERIA FOR AN EFFECTIVE MISSION STATEMENT

An effective mission statement provides a focus for the company's vision. Like the vision statement, it should be concise, to-the-point, and devoid of unnecessary verbiage.

PROCEED WITH CAUTION

Make sure your mission statement doesn't just restate your vision statement. Your mission should have a narrower focus than your vision and—at least in very general terms—define a situation that is achievable.

The ideal mission statement should meet these criteria:

- It must be short—one sentence, ideally, and no more than a paragraph at the longest.
- It must define a clear direction for the business.

- It must define specific parameters for the business.
- It must be achievable.
- It must be measurable in general terms—you either achieve your mission or you don't.

EXAMPLES OF MISSIONS

If you're having trouble coming up with the just the right mission statement, think of it in terms of your ultimate goal for your business. Try to complete this sentence: "I want to be the ..."

Depending on your specific business, your answer might start with "I want to be the *largest* ..." or "I want to be the *best* ..." or "I want to be the *lowest-priced* ..." or even "I want to *provide the largest variety of* ..." or "I want to *have the most* ..." However you complete this sentence is most likely a good start on your mission statement.

Returning to Microsoft, remember that the company's vision was a computer on every desktop. Now, there are many ways to embrace that vision; you can build computer hardware, you can design and manufacture microprocessor chips, you can open a computer retail chain, you can establish a charity to provide PCs to the poor, or you can develop and sell computer software and operating systems. Microsoft chose the later course and set for itself the mission of becoming the world's largest provider of PC operating systems, software, and programming tools. (It's also a mission that proved to be achievable.)

Here are some more examples of effective mission statements, matched to the vision statements presented earlier:

WidgeCo intends to become the leading supplier of computer-based widgets to the college and higher-education markets.

Working Girl Fashions will become North America's largest manufacturer of affordable casual clothing for working women.

Phones4Less will become the world's largest online retailer of wireless products and services.

ChampionshipVinyl.com seeks to create the largest and most profitable vertical entertainment portal for purchasing entertainment products and services over the Internet.

Note that all of these mission statements are short, focused, achievable, and measurable. Reading each mission statement, you know exactly what it is that each company does.

Presenting Your Vision and Mission

You have a few options available to you when presenting the Vision and Mission sections of your plan.

The most common approach is to present Vision and Mission as separate sections, each occupying a separate page. This isn't a terribly efficient use of paper (each section is only a paragraph long), but it does reinforce the importance of each section.

Another common approach is to format your document so that both sections appear on the same page—as separate sections. This approach means you have to put two section headings on the same page, which might require some reformatting of your heading styles in Microsoft Word. The advantage of this approach is that it saves space while still presenting Vision and Mission as separate—and equally important—sections.

An alternate approach is to combine the vision and mission statements into a single "Vision and Mission" section. Again, this approach saves space, although it does tend to diminish slightly each of the individual sections. If you take this approach, make sure you edit the text of the vision and mission statements to make them flow together.

Finally, some business plans simply skip the Vision section completely and start with Mission (sometimes labeled "Mission Statement"). This might be the preferable approach if you're having difficulties coming up with a clear vision statement or if your vision and mission statements sound too similar.

Vision and Mission Checklist

When preparing the Vision and Mission sections of your business plan, work through the following checklist:

Vision and Mission Checklist

Is your vision statement

- ☐ Short?
- ☐ Focused on a single thought?
- ☐ Farsighted?
- ☐ Reflective of your real dreams for this particular industry or market segment?

Is your mission statement

- ☐ Short?
- ☐ Achievable?
- ☐ Measurable (in big-picture terms)?
- ☐ Clear in the direction and parameters it defines for your business?

HOMEWORK

In this hour, you learned how to create the Vision and Mission sections of your business plan. In Hour 12, "Opportunity," you'll learn how to write the Opportunity section of the plan.

To prepare for the next hour, please do the following:

- Reread Hour 3, "Analyze Your Market."
- Collect any analyst reports or research regarding your industry.
- Search for any newspaper or magazine articles that feature your industry or any of your competitors.
- Retrieve the most recent 10-K filings or annual reports from any of your competitors that are public companies.
- Gather the following data, if available: industry revenues, industry profits, industry growth, the number of potential customers in your industry, and any other pertinent data regarding the size and potential of your company's market.

HOUR 12
Opportunity

LESSON PLAN:

In this hour, you will learn about ...

- Which market data to include
- Finding market data online
- Displaying data with charts and graphs

The Opportunity section of your plan (sometimes called Market Opportunity, Market Dynamics, or just The Market) is the first meaty section you need to prepare. This goal of this section is to describe the market opportunity you seek to pursue and convince potential investors that it's a significant enough opportunity to be worth pursuing.

As such, this section will include substantial narrative text (you have to tell a story about the market) and a large amount of numerical data. Which data you choose to present, how you choose to present it, and how you weave it into your narrative will determine the effectiveness of this section.

When the Opportunity section is complete, you should have four pages or so of compelling market information. The reader should understand the basic nature of the market, the size of the market, the market's growth rate, the types of customers who comprise the market, and the key competitors in the market. Potential lenders and investors don't have to (and don't *want* to) absorb trivial details about how the market works, but they should be left with a top-level understanding of the issues that will drive your business decisions.

Choosing the Data You Need

As you learned back in Hour 3, "Analyze Your Market," there is most likely a substantial amount of public information available about your particular market—if you know where to look. Once you find the data, you'll need to determine which data is important enough to include in the plan and which is essential enough to highlight in some fashion.

Let's start by examining the type of data that will help you create the most effective plan.

What You Need, If You Can Get It

Why do you need to present market data in your business plan, anyway? The answer is simple—to help you sell prospective lenders and investors on your specific business strategy. If a particular market metric helps convince your readers of the significant opportunity available, then it's worth including in your plan.

What kind of information should you be looking for? Here's a short list of hard data that would be great to include in your plan, if it's available:

- Current, historical, and projected market size (typically in revenue dollars)
- Historical or projected industry revenue growth
- Number of industry customers
- Market *penetration*

STRICTLY SPEAKING

Penetration measures what percentage of potential customers is currently using a specific type of product or service. You calculate penetration by dividing the number of current customers by the number of potential customers. For example, if there are currently 100,000 customers of a particular service, and it's estimated that 1 million customers might potentially be interested in the service, the penetration currently sits at 10 percent (100,000 divided by 1 million).

- Average expenditures by customer type
- Average purchase price for key product types
- Market share, revenues, and profits of the largest industry players

- Average industry profit margins
- Any information describing the industry itself, its customers, its key businesses, and its history and trends

Depending on your industry, other types of data might also be relevant. For example, if you're in a dot.com business, not only is the size of the industry (measured by the number of Internet users) useful, you might also want to include data on page views for specific sites, the number of hours per day spent online, where users spend their time when online (at what sites or types of sites), and total consumer dollars spent purchasing at online merchants. If your market is segmented regionally, you might want to include data detailing market size per region or average customer purchases per region.

As you can see, any data that advances your case is worth considering for inclusion in your plan.

WHERE TO LOOK FOR DATA

As discussed in Hour 3, there are many potential sources for the market data you need. Good data sources for your industry might include the following:

- Industry research reports
- Financial analyst reports
- Trade organizations
- Trade newspapers and magazines
- Annual reports and SEC filings by public companies in the industry
- Competitors' Web sites
- Internet search sites

This last source warrants some discussion. Although you can use any Internet search site to look for the information you need, some sites are better suited than others when you're looking for industry or business-related information. For example, Yahoo! is the most popular search site, but it contains a relatively small amount of business-related information. You'll have better luck at sites that offer larger search indexes or that specialize in business-type information.

When you're searching for market-related data for your business plan, check out these Web sites:

- **Annual Reports Library** (www.annualreportslibrary.com), a collection of more than a half million annual reports from public companies and institutions

- **Company Sleuth** (www.companysleuth.com), a free service that searches the Internet for inside information on the public companies you select—including new patents and trademarks, SEC filings, press releases, and so on

- **Corporate Information** (www.corporateinformation.com), a site that specializes in corporate research on both publicly traded and privately held companies; also includes links to market research reports for particular industries

- **CompaniesOnline** (www.companiesonline.com), a comprehensive listing (from Dun & Bradstreet) of more than 500,000 private and public companies; sometimes contains information about private companies not available elsewhere

- **FreeEDGAR** (www.freeedgar.com), a source of publicly filed SEC documents in an easy-to-use format

- **Google** (www.google.com), a general search engine that uses one of the Internet's largest indexes—it's big and fast and gives great results

- **Hoover's Online** (www.hoovers.com), a site that specializes in both general (free) and detailed (for a fee) reports on public businesses

- **Multex** (www.multexnet.com), a fee-based site that offers analyst reports on individual companies and entire industries

- **NewsTrawler** (www.newstrawler.com), a fee-based search engine for news articles; great for finding articles about your industry and competitors

- **Northern Light** (www.northernlight.com), a general search site that offers both free and paid searches; the paid search includes access to a Special Collection of documents not available elsewhere

- **PR Newswire** (www.prnewswire.com), a site that archives press releases from both public and private companies—*the* place to look for company-released press releases

- **SEC EDGAR Database** (www.sec.gov/edgar.shtml), the official source of all public company filings, including S-1s and 10-Ks

- **U.S. Census Bureau** (www.census.gov), the official site of the U.S. Census—chock full of useful demographic and business data

 FYI To learn more about effective Internet searching, read *The Complete Idiot's Guide to Online Search Secrets* (Alpha, 1999), also by the author of this book.

What If You Can't Find the Data You Want?

Prepare yourself for the inevitable—no matter how hard you look, there will be some vital information that you simply can't locate. Perhaps this information doesn't even exist; perhaps it exists but you don't know where to find it.

Whatever the reason, what do you do if you can't find a particular piece of data?

The short answer is that you work around it. Here's how:

- You may be able to simply ignore that particular market metric and not have your plan suffer for it. For example, if you can't find any indication of average industry profit margin, the success of your plan won't be jeopardized. Chances are, if you can't find the data, no one else can either—which means you're not competitively disadvantaged by the missing metrics.

- You may be able to find a piece of related information that you can use in its place. For example, if you can't find the total number of current customers, use the market penetration number instead.

- You may be able to use data from a previous period. For example, if you can't find last year's industry revenues but you do have data from the year before, just use the older data—and make sure you label it properly.

- You may be able to estimate the missing data from other available data. If you're missing a single year of revenues and you have the surrounding years, for example, use a trend to fill in the missing year. As another example, if you know the total number of customers and the total revenues for a specific period, you can easily calculate average expenditures per customer by dividing the second number by the first.

- You may be able to imply the missing data by using an expert quote. For example, if you can't dig up any hard data on market growth, you can make do with a quote from a named industry analyst that says, in effect, that the market is experiencing rapid growth. (In other words, if you can't show it, have someone say it.)

PROCEED WITH CAUTION

 Some potential lenders and investors—and any lawyer who gets hold of your plan— will want to know where every piece of information came from. Make sure you clearly label any data you've extrapolated or estimated as coming from "company estimates" or "internal analysis."

The bottom line is that you have to work with the data you have—so don't spend too much time pining for what you don't.

How Much Data Is Enough?

If you're fortunate, you'll end up with several large piles of market data that you can use in your business plan. If you include every last scrap of data, the Opportunity section will be about 40 pages long all by itself! How do you choose what to include—and what to leave out?

PROCEED WITH CAUTION

 Don't let your own personal interests and biases get in the way of choosing the most effective information for your plan. Select the data that best supports and advances your chosen strategy, not the data you find personally interesting.

The first thing to look at is the overall relevance of the data. Does this piece of data directly pertain to your market or industry? If not, it's just an interesting fact and is probably not worth including.

Next, look at the data's relevance to your plan. Does this piece of data relate directly to the business you're building? If not, lose it.

Now examine the magnitude and universality of the data. Does this data point describe the entire market, or is it more limited or anecdotal? Always choose bigger-picture data over the finer details.

Finally, look at the age of the data. Especially if you have multiple data points, always choose the freshest data. In fact, depending on your particular industry, you may want to automatically discard data that's more than a few years old.

The data that remains after you perform this triage should be very persuasive data. If you still feel as if you have too many numbers to include, you need to dispassionately select the data that best fits into the story you're telling and that best demonstrates the potential of the market you're choosing. A few major points will be more persuasive than a lot of minor ones; as with the rest of the plan, shorter is almost always better.

PROCEED WITH CAUTION

It's not uncommon to dig up two or more conflicting pieces of data. For example, two different research firms might give two different numbers for the size of your industry. If you find yourself in this situation, you can pick the data point that comes from the more trustworthy or experienced source, pick the data point that "feels" right to you, or pick the data point that best helps sell your business strategy. Most businesses will choose the more aggressive numbers.

DON'T FORGET THE SOURCE

When you're gathering your market data, make sure to keep track of precisely where each data point came from. It's important to attribute sources to each point of data you use in your plan—in the text, in a footnote or endnote, or at the bottom of or in a caption for a chart or graphic.

When attributing sources, make sure you attribute the true original source. It's not uncommon to see an industry number quoted in a newspaper or magazine. In most cases, the number didn't come from the publication itself; it came from another source and was simply quoted for publication. In this type of instance, do *not* quote the newspaper or magazine as the source; attribute the data to the source quoted in the publication.

JUST A MINUTE

In the case of second-hand data, you may want to dig up the original source document, which is probably available on the Web—especially if the source was a research firm or analyst. (Quoting from a firm's press release, if that's all you have access to, is perfectly acceptable—and is preferable to quoting from a newspaper that quoted from the same press release.)

There are many different ways to attribute sources. If you want to flow the attribution into the text of your document, you would use a phrase like this:

"According to the Gartner Group's *Research in America* report ..."

If you want to use a footnote or endnote for attribution, use the full name and date of the source, like this:

[1]Gartner Group, *Research in America* (June, 2001)

You should use the same type of attribution within all charts and graphs in your report.

What do you do if you can't find the source for a particular piece of data? Maybe you found a magazine article that said something along the lines of "Industry analysts claim that revenues will double over the next five years." The first thing to do, of course, is to hunt for the true source of that information. If the unattributed magazine article is the *only* source of data, then you have a choice. You can use the data and attribute the magazine as the source (which some might find uncomfortably fuzzy), or you can choose not to use the data at all. Let your own comfort level be your guide.

JUST A MINUTE

If, at some later date, you decide to repurpose your business plan into a private placement memorandum or S-1 document (see Hour 24, "Create a Private Placement Memorandum [PPM]"), the lawyers involved will question you on every piece of data that you've used. They'll want to know *precisely* where each number and quote came from—down to the issue and page number, if you have it. If you don't have supporting documentation, you may be asked to remove that data point from the new document. All of this is a good reason to fully document all your data from the start.

WRITING THE OPPORTUNITY SECTION

The Opportunity section of your plan needs to be about four pages long—less if your market is relatively small and easy to understand, more if it's a complex market with a lot of different submarkets. This section needs to not only describe the market, but also lay out the business opportunity that you want your company to pursue.

After you've gathered your market data, you need to create a detailed outline for the Opportunity section. As you write the section, you'll need to "chunk" the text into easily digestible parts, each part with its own heading (or subheading). The individual points in your outline should become your section heads and subheads.

As a general rule, you don't want to go more than four or five paragraphs without having a head of some sort. This helps the reader visually find key topics and enables you to create a very detailed table of contents based on the section heads and subheads.

How detailed should your outline be? Here's an example of a detailed Opportunity section outline for a business focusing on the mobile phone market:

Opportunity

    Wireless Market Size and Growth

        U.S. Market

        Global Market

    Emerging Products and Services

        Data and Paging Services

        Wireless Internet

        3G Services

        Bluetooth

    Industry Trends

        Replacement Handset Sales

        Decreasing Service Plan Pricing

        Carrier Competition

        Wireline Replacement

    Competitive Dynamics

        Handset Manufacturers

        Service Providers

        Retailers

The Opportunity section that follows this outline will be divided into four major sections: Wireless Market Size and Growth, Emerging Products and Services, Industry Trends, and Competitive Dynamics. Within each of these sections will be multiple subsections; for example, the Wireless Market Size and Growth section will contain two subheads—U.S. Market and Global Market. Some of these subheads will contain a half-page or more of information; others will only be a single paragraph long.

The key point is to outline your market in a logical fashion and make the information flow to tell your story. You want to tell the reader what the industry is all about, how big it is, how much it's growing, and what new things are happening that make it even more attractive. You can also use this section to talk about key industry players, although that information can also go in the Market Strategy section—it's your call.

Presenting Data in Alternate Formats

As you tell the story of your market, there are several different ways to present your key points. Much of your information will be presented in narrative text, of course, but some key data will be numeric—market size, growth, the number of customers, and so on.

PROCEED WITH CAUTION

Don't assume that you can tell your market story *without* numbers. At the very least, you'll need numeric metrics to describe the market's size (in revenues) and growth rate.

You can choose to present numeric data within the textual narrative, you can bullet the data, you can break it out into tables, or you can present it in a graph format. All four options have their advantages and disadvantages, and you may want to present some key pieces of information in multiple formats. For example, you may want to break out historical revenue data into a bar graph but then repeat the key data points in the text.

Bullets

If you're afraid of "burying" key data within a long text paragraph, considering breaking out the data into a bulleted list. As you can see here, a bulleted list does the following:

- Draws the reader's attention
- Helps "chunk" the information into easily grazed bits

- Enables you to efficiently highlight key information without the use of large charts and graphics

When presenting numbers within text, keep the numbers simple—limit the detail to a single decimal point whenever possible. Also, it's common to describe "1,000,000" as "1 million" or "one million" and to abbreviate "thousands" as "K"—as in "500K" for "500,000."

TABLES

When you're presenting data that spans multiple time periods or that compares the attributes of two or more items (such as competitors), that data is often best presented in tabular format.

For example, you could present the following information in a standard paragraph:

The number of U.S. wireless telephone subscribers was 69.2 million in 1998, 85.7 million in 1999, 103.7 million in 2000, and grew to 120.2 million in 2001.

It's a long, awkward sentence, and it does a good job of both burying the data and making it difficult to grasp.

A better way to present this same data would be in a table, like this:

U.S. Wireless Telephone Subscribers (Millions)

1998	1999	2000	2001
69.2	85.7	103.7	120.2

If you're using Microsoft Word to write and format your document, you can create some very sophisticated table formats—including tables with shaded backgrounds and shadowed borders—to match other graphical elements in your plan document. You can also format your table with a different font from your body text; using a smaller, simpler font (such as Arial) will enable you to conserve space on the page. See the following figure for an example of how to incorporate a sophisticated table within the text of your Opportunity section.

Using a fancy table to present complex market data.

Opportunity
Wireless Communications

The market for wireless services constitutes a significant and rapidly growing part of total consumer spending on telecom services. While local telephone service and long distance services represent 46% and 29% of total U.S. consumer telecommunications spending, respectively, wireless ranks third in total expenditures with 15% of total dollars spent.[1]

The number of U.S. wireless subscribers is projected to grow from 69 million at the end of 1998 to almost 149 million in 2003.[2] The net addition of 16.5 million subscribers in 1999 will be an all-time high that will be surpassed in 2000 when 18 millions new subscribers are added. Gross activations—which reflect both new subscribers switching services or purchasing replacement handsets—are expected to increase from an estimated 25.2 millions in 1999 to 30 million in 2002.

Wireless service revenues are projected to remain steady at approximately $25 billion/year,[3] as the larger subscriber base is factored against lower airtime rates. Handset revenues will decline slightly from 2000 forward as increased competition drives prices downward. The market for wireless data services will increase from its current sub-$1 billion level to $4 billion by the end of 2001—when data services revenues will for the first time, surpass handset revenues.

The following table details the number of U.S. wireless subscribers, in millions:

1998	1999	2000	2001
69.2	85.7	103.7	120.2

Current (year-end 1999) U.S. wireless penetration is estimated at 31.6% (up from 25.7% in 1998), and is projected to increase to 53.3% by 2003. Analysts predict that U.S. wireless penetration will hit the 70% level by the end of 2008—with a subscriber base of 201 million.

Factors contributing to this projected growth in U.S. wireless subscribers include:
- Declining airtime costs
- Simplified pricing plans and reduction(or elimination) of roaming and long distance fees
- Shift to digital service (PCS—a subset of the total digital market—currently represents 21% of all wireless subscribers, projected to increase to 40% by 2003)
- Improved wireless coverage
- Increasing availability of and demand for Internet-based wireless data applications

---

[1] The Yankee Group National Tele-Trend Data
[2] Donaldson, Lufkin, and Jennette, The Global Wireless Communications Industry (Summer 1999)
[3] Strategy Analytics

CHARTS AND GRAPHS

For the most important and most complex data in your Opportunity section, consider presenting it in chart or graph format. A graph lets you present multiple layers of information in a single space and definitely attracts the reader's eye.

For example, the wireless telephone data presented in the previous table makes even more of an impact when presented as a bar chart, as shown in the following figure.

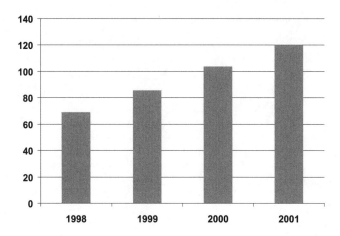

Using a bar chart to present tabular data.

CHOOSE YOUR CHART TYPE

When you start using charts and graphs, you have several important choices to make. The first choice is what kind of graph to use. When you're graphing data over time, for example, you can use a simple line chart, a vertical bar chart (such as the one shown previously), or an area chart. As you can see in the following figures, each different chart type gives a different feel to the numbers.

What are the best types of charts to use for various types of information? Here are some basic guidelines:

- If you're presenting data for various parts that add up to a whole (region by region sales, for example), use either a pie chart or a horizontal bar chart.

- If you're presenting data for various parts that *don't* add up to a whole (market share of the top five competitors, for example), use a horizontal bar chart.

- If you're presenting data over several periods that are separate for each period (yearly revenue for a multiple-year period, for example), use a vertical bar chart.

- If you're presenting multiple-period data that builds on each previous period (installed base over a multiple-year period, for example), use an area chart.

- If you're showing trends (market share increasing over a multiple-year period, for example), use a line chart, as in the following figure.

- If you're presenting data for multiple items on the same chart, use a 3D bar or area chart, as in the following figure.

Data presented as a line chart.

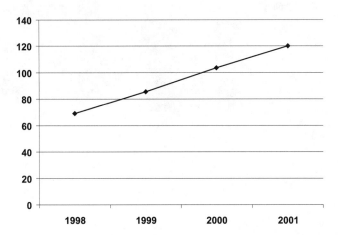

Choose Your Formatting

Another way to put a spin on your numbers is to change the chart formatting. For example, the growth numbers shown in the previous area chart have a more powerful impact when you use a 3D chart type, add some *perspective*, and then rotate the chart to a substantial degree.

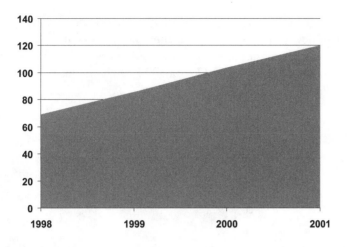

Data presented as an area chart.

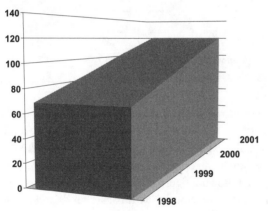

Data presented as a 3D area chart with perspective added.

STRICTLY SPEAKING

In terms of charts and graphs, **perspective** changes the relationship between the front of the chart and the rear. Increasing perspective adds the illusion of depth to the chart, although too much perspective can distort the visual effect.

PROCEED WITH CAUTION

 Sometimes you can get so fancy with chart rotation and perspective that you can obfuscate your basic data. You don't want to confuse your audience by presenting charts that are too complex to figure out!

When you're presenting key data in graph format, your audience may want to know the precise numbers behind the bars and lines. If the exact data is important, consider displaying the data values for each bar or point on your graph or adding a data table below the graph, as illustrated in the following figure.

Using a data table to display key numeric values.

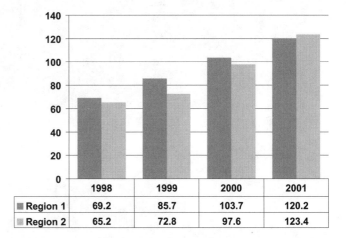

	1998	1999	2000	2001
Region 1	69.2	85.7	103.7	120.2
Region 2	65.2	72.8	97.6	123.4

The biggest mistake most novices make is using Word's default graph types and formatting. You want your business plan to have a professional look, and Word's default graphs just don't cut it. When you take the time to utilize all of Word's formatting options, you can create some very impressive-looking graphs. The following figure show how you can spruce up the simple vertical bar chart (shown previously) with backgrounds and gradients for a much more professional look.

 FYI To learn more about creating sophisticated graphs in Microsoft Word, read *Mastering Microsoft Word 2000, Premium Edition* (Sybex, 2000), also by the author of this book.

PICTURES AND GRAPHICS

If you're looking to add visual interest to your plan document, consider adding a few photographs or drawings, as appropriate. For example, you can use photographs to accompany descriptions of key products or use drawings to illustrate important processes or concepts.

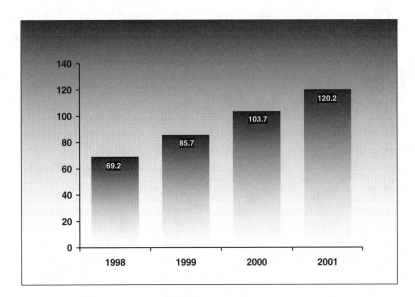

A horizontal bar chart formatted with gradient background and fills.

The following figure shows how you might build a typical page in your Opportunity section. The chart at the top of the page is used to present key market data, while the product photo at the bottom is used to illustrate a key product category.

JUST A MINUTE

If you use pictures in your document, make sure they reproduce well. Be especially wary when using color photographs in black and white documents and make sure, in all cases, that the photograph is of high enough resolution to print without pixelation or jagged edges.

Using photographs to present key products or concepts.

Opportunity

Wireless Communications

The market for wireless services constitutes a significant and rapidly-growing part of total consumer spending on telecom services. While local telephone service and long distance services represent 46% and 29% of total U.S. consumer telecommunications spending, respectively, wireless ranks third in total expenditures with 15% of total dollars spent.[4]

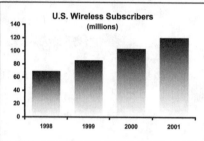

U.S. Wireless Subscribers (millions)

The number of U.S. wireless subscribers is projected to grow from 69 million at the end of 1998 to almost 149 million in 2003.[5] The net addition of 16.5 million subscribers in 1999 will be an all-time high that will be surpassed in 2000 when 18 million new subscribers are added. Gross activations—which reflect both new subscribers and subscribers switching services or purchasing replacement handsets—are expected to increase from an estimated 25.2 million in 1999 to 30 million in 2002.

Wireless service revenues are projected to remain steady at approximately $25 billion/year,[6] as the larger subscriber base is factored against lower airtime rates. Handset revenues will decline slightly from 2000 forward as increased competition drives prices downward. The market for wireless data services will increase from its current sub-$1 billion level to $4 billion by the end of 2001—when data services revenues will, for the first time, surpass handset revenues.

Current (year-end 1999) U.S. wireless penetration is estimated at 31.6% (up from 25.7% in 1998), and is projected to increase to 53.3% by 2003. Analysts predict that U.S. wireless penetration will hit the 70% level by the end of 2008—with a subscriber base of 201 million.

Factors contributing to this projected growth in U.S. wireless subscribers include:

- Declining airtime costs

- Simplified pricing plans and reduction (or elimination) of roaming and long-distance fees

- Shift to digital service (PCS—a subset of the total digital market—currently represents 21% of all wireless subscribers, projected to increase to 40% by 2003)

---

[4] The Yankee Group National Tele-Trend Data
[5] Donaldson, Lufkin & Jenrette, *The Global Wireless Communications Industry* (Summer, 1999)
[6] Strategy Analytics

OPPORTUNITY CHECKLIST

Use the following checklist to help you prepare for and write your business plan's Opportunity section:

Opportunity Checklist

- ☐ Assemble key market data
- ☐ Description of your market (include growth factors and emerging trends)
- ☐ Description of customers in the market (demographics, psychographics, and so on)
- ☐ Total number of industry customers
- ☐ Market penetration
- ☐ Total industry revenues
- ☐ Market growth
- ☐ Market profitability
- ☐ Major competitors (with accompanying revenue and market share data, if available)
- ☐ Other market metrics: _____
- ☐ Other market metrics: _____
- ☐ Other market metrics: _____
- ☐ Determine which data to include in the plan
- ☐ Create a detailed section outline
- ☐ Determine how to present key data (text, bullets, graphs)
- ☐ Write the narrative text
- ☐ Add appropriate charts, graphs, and pictures

HOMEWORK

In this hour, you learned how to create the Opportunity section of your business plan. In Hour 13, "Market Strategy," you'll learn how to write the Market Strategy section of the plan.

To prepare for the next hour, please do the following:

- Describe your target customer base.
- Gather all the marketing information and internal documents available that describe the products/services your company offers.
- Gather all the marketing and sales materials your company has produced in the past 12 months—catalogs, brochures, spec sheets, press releases, and so on.
- Prepare a detailed description of how you bring your products and/or services to market—how you sell your products, what distribution channels you utilize, who your major accounts/customers are, and so on.
- Assemble all available information about your largest competitors and their key products.

Hour 13
Market Strategy

Chapter Summary

LESSON PLAN:

In this hour, you will learn about ...

- Introducing product and market strategies
- Presenting sales and marketing plans
- Addressing the competition

If you did a good job writing the Opportunity section of your plan (discussed in Hour 12, "Opportunity"), you've left your reader with one very important question: How does your company plan to take advantage of this enormous opportunity?

The answer to this question is presented in the business plan's Market Strategy section. This section walks the reader through the products and services you intend to bring to market, describes *how* you intend to bring them to market (in terms of both sales and marketing), and discusses the competition you'll face in the marketplace.

The Market Strategy section, more than any other section of your business plan, describes what your business does—from an external perspective. You don't go into how your products are developed or manufactured (that's for the Business Strategy section) or even how you intend to make money from your activities (also in the Business Strategy section); you focus on what you're doing, in terms of products and services, to take advantage of the large market opportunity before you.

Building Your Market Strategy

The Market Strategy of your plan describes how your company intends to pursue the opportunity presented in the previous section. Typically, you will pursue an opportunity by executing the following activities:

- Develop one or more new products or services to offer to the market.
- Price, package, and position the product(s)/service(s) in a unique and competitive fashion.
- Place the product(s)/service(s) in one or more channels of distribution that best reach the target consumer. This may involve selling directly to the consumer or through two- or three-step distribution.
- Promote the product(s)/service(s) to the target consumer.

When you describe how your firm will execute these four activities, you've described your market strategy.

WRITING THE MARKET STRATEGY SECTION

Your first step in writing the Market Strategy section of your plan is to create an outline of the major subsections within the section. A good course of action is to use a three- or four-part outline, incorporating the three main components of your market strategy plus an optional fourth section that discusses how your product(s)/service(s) stacks up against competing product(s)/service(s). Your outline should incorporate further subsections, as necessary, to deal with issues specific to your particular market strategy.

Your outline should follow the flow of your basic story, which starts with the big market opportunity you discussed in the Opportunity section. You now tell the reader that you're going to take advantage of the opportunity by producing one or more new products, and you tell how they're positioned, priced, and packaged (the Product section in your Market Strategy outline); you describe how and where you're going to sell the products (the Sales and Distribution section); you discuss how you'll market and promote the products (the Marketing section); and you end by discussing how your products will compete with other products already on the market (the Competitive Comparison section).

Following this approach, here is a sample outline, complete with subheads, which can serve as a starting point for your own outline:

Market Strategy

    Product

        Positioning

> Pricing
>
> Packaging
>
> Sales and Distribution
>
>> Targeted Channels
>>
>> Sales Strategy
>
> Marketing
>
>> Advertising and Promotion
>>
>> Public Relations and Trade Shows
>
> Competitive Comparison

JUST A MINUTE

The subheads you use in your own plan should reflect your own individual market strategy. For example, if you do both trade and consumer advertising but *don't* attend trade shows, you might want to include the following subheads in your Marketing Plan section: Trade Advertising, Consumer Advertising, Promotion, and Public Relations.

The balance of this hour discusses each of these sections.

If your entire business plan is set to run about 20 pages in length, you should expect the Market Strategy section to be about 6 pages long. If your products are few and simple, fewer pages are acceptable; if your products are many and complex, you might need a higher page count.

PRODUCT

The product you sell or the service you offer *is* your business. To have an effective business plan, you have to do a really good job of presenting your product—not only what it is and what it does, but also how it compares to other similar products on the market.

This is why the first part of your response to the aforementioned market opportunity should present—in appropriate detail—your company's key products or services.

DEFINING PRODUCT

The Product part of the Market Strategy section should focus on the most important products and services offered by your company—your flagship products, as it were. Don't include *every* product or service you offer; focus on the one or two products—or product categories—that define your company.

For example, Microsoft wouldn't list the hundreds of products it offers in a Product section of its business plan. Microsoft would most likely define its product as "software" (*not* "Excel" or "Word" or "Windows") and describe, in general terms, its strategy for developing, selling, and marketing its software. Along the same lines, Honda might define its product as "automotive vehicles," and Paramount might define its product as "movies." None of these companies would focus on individual products, only on the overall category of product that it offers.

It's important to note that, in some cases, your "product" is actually your entire business. This is especially true of retail and wholesale businesses, in which you provide a service to customers by offering them a variety of products to purchase. So you don't want to discuss all the products you sell in the Product section; you want to discuss your entire business as a single product/service. For example, if you're Office Max, your product is a chain of office-supply superstores that exploits an opportunity in the market for office supplies; if you're a local video store, your product is your store, and it exploits an opportunity in the market for video entertainment.

THREE Ps: POSITIONING, PRICING, AND PACKAGING

When you start writing the Product part of your Market Strategy section, begin by introducing each product; present the name of the product and its general function (what it does). Then, in separate subsections, you should discuss the following three Ps:

- **Positioning.** This describes your product's unique features that make it different from other products or uniquely suited to exploit the market opportunity. (If you're a retailer offering a variety of products, use this point to discuss how you're positioning your store vs. competing stores.)

- **Pricing.** This is a straightforward presentation of the product's pricing strategy—the product's suggested price and why you chose it. If you sell a variety of products, you can discuss the strategy behind the range of prices you've selected (good-better-best, for example), or you can discuss your overall pricing philosophy (always offer the lowest prices, for example).

- **Packaging.** If you sell your product at retail, discuss any unique aspects to the product's packaging, such as size or color or shape. (If you don't sell at retail, ignore this point.)

JUST A MINUTE

Most standalone marketing plans focus on what some call the six Ps: product, packaging, pricing, positioning, placement (sales), and promotion. To better fit within the structure of an effective business plan, the six Ps have been spread throughout the Market Strategy section.

JUST A MINUTE

This is probably a good place in your business plan to include a photograph or two. Not only does a photo help the reader to visualize your key product, it also serves to break up the monotony of several pages of nothing but plain text.

Particular focus should be placed on the first point—positioning. It's all well and good to say that you're coming out with a new product called DynoBlast that unclogs stopped-up sinks. Until you present the product's positioning, however, your reader will wonder why he or she should invest money in what sounds like a generic competitor to Draino. You have to convince your readers that DynoBlast is different enough—and superior enough, in some fashion—to warrant their investment. When you engage in this discussion, you're discussing how the product is positioned, relevant to other products on the market.

What contributes to a unique positioning? It may be something the product does, or it may be something about the product's form factor, or its price, or its colors and options, or the way it's distributed. You need to highlight the things that make your product stand out from other similar products and point them out to the readers of your business plan.

PROCEED WITH CAUTION

If you can't identify any unique features of your product, either you're too close to the process to see what is obvious to others or there *isn't* anything unique. If the latter is true, you should seriously reconsider your chances for success in the marketplace.

Sales and Distribution

Once you've presented your product, you can discuss how you intend to present that product to potential consumers. If you sell directly to your customers, you should discuss how you reach those customers and how you execute a typical sale. If you sell to customers via the Internet, you should discuss your Web site strategy. If you sell via telemarketing, you should discuss where you get your lists and the kind of close rates you project. If you sell via retail, you should discuss what types of retailers stock your product and how you get your product to them (either direct or through distributors).

This section is where you can and should go into some detail about your company's distribution model. For example, if you're a book publisher, you would describe how you sell your books directly to some large accounts but use independent distributors to reach most smaller accounts. Describing your distribution model in words might suffice, but you also may want to include some sort of diagram to illustrate the process.

When you're describing your distribution model, it's okay to name names—that is, to mention by name the major distributors and retailers that carry your product. If you're in an existing business, putting some numbers behind the names might also be a good idea. List the top five accounts or retailers or distributors (or whatever), along with their market share, total revenues, total units shipped, or other relevant data. (A table is a good way to present this information.)

If you employ one or more sales forces to sell your product, use the Sales and Distribution section to provide a brief description of each sales force. For example, if you use different sales forces to sell your products into mass merchants and direct to government agencies, devote separate subheads to your mass merchant and government sales forces. Use a paragraph or two to describe the size and shape of each sales force, without going into undue detail about commissions and structure and the like.

Note that the Sales and Distribution section is *not* the place to discuss how you intend to compensate your salespeople (that can go in the Operations section if you feel it's important enough to include the plan). It is also *not* the place to discuss the painful details of your discount schedule—although you might want to mention an average discount, a range of discounts, or anything that investors might perceive as being out of the ordinary about the way you discount.

PROCEED WITH CAUTION

Customer discount schedules represent a level of detail that is too fine to include in most business plans. At this stage of the game, potential lenders and investors don't need (or want) to know precisely what prices you're charging each of your customers for each of your products. Defining an average discount or a discount range will most likely be sufficient.

MARKETING

Now that you've presented your product and described how you get it to your customers, you should spend a page or so discussing how you intend to get the product noticed—in other words, how you intend to market your product.

JUST A MINUTE

You can get most of the information you need for the Marketing section from your marketing department's standalone marketing plan, if it exists.

The marketing of your product can take several forms and comprise many different types of activities. Depending on your individual business, you may want to discuss some or all of the following activities (under separate subheads) in the Marketing section:

- **Advertising.** Advertising is just that—the paid advertising you undertake for your product or business, in whatever media you use. Your advertising might consist of print advertisements, radio spots, television ads, or online banner advertisements. You may want to segment your advertising by type of media, by national vs. local, by region, by audience (consumer vs. trade), by intent (product focused vs. corporate), or by whatever factors are relevant in your particular situation.

Some businesses tend to lump a variety of marketing activities under a single heading, which is a practice you should avoid. Do *not* include items such as promotion or trade shows under the advertising subhead; keep these activities separate to better inform your audience.

- **Promotion.** Promotion is a separate activity from advertising. Promotion involves sales, discounts, coupons, special deals, and big campaigns, all designed to move more product. Certain types of advertising (*not* image advertising!) can be a component of a promotion but not vice versa. If you're not sure what to include here, ask yourself this question: "What are we doing to promote our product?"

- **Public relations.** P.R. is often characterized as free advertising, even though it's not free and it's not advertising. It's often difficult to describe specific P.R. activities in a business plan, so this section is typically short and somewhat generic.

- **Trade shows.** Attendance at trade shows and conferences is crucial to the success of some types of businesses. If this describes your business, you'll want to devote a subhead to your planned activities in this regard.

- **Catalogs.** If your business is catalog based, you'll need to discuss in detail how you execute this part of your operation—how many catalogs a year you send out, to how many customers, and what kind of response rate you get.

- **Direct mail.** The same detail is needed here as was needed for catalog-based businesses. Discuss how many mailings a year you intend to do, how many pieces you intend to mail, your projected response rate, the average cost of each mailing, and so on.

- **Marketing materials.** If your business produces large numbers of brochures, point-of-purchase displays, and other assorted marketing materials, spend a paragraph or so discussing the types of materials you produce, how the materials are used, and how much money you spend on them over the course of a year.

- **Online marketing.** Many businesses today devote a part of their marketing budget to Internet-based marketing. Describe your online activities—your Web site, the advertising you do on other Web sites, and any other online marketing activities you engage in.

The Marketing section is another good place to include some graphic elements. Consider including a small reproduction of an advertisement, the cover of a catalog, or a screenshot of your Web site's home page; it will help illustrate your marketing activities and will add some visual appeal to your plan document.

COMPETITIVE COMPARISON

This last part of your Marketing section is optional. Some companies prefer to leave any discussion of competitors in the Opportunity section or throw it under the Core Competencies and Challenges section later in the plan. However, because any true market strategy should address how a business will compete against other players, it's fitting to devote a part of your Market Strategy section to your major competition.

A good way to focus this section is to present the most directly competitive products or companies, introduce a few key competitive points (price, size, number of stores, availability of colors, and so on), and then produce a table that shows how you stack up against your competitors. This sort of comparison chart enables you to present a lot of data in a compact space and to highlight those areas where your product or company excels (typically through boldfacing, use of color, or use of shading). You can also downplay any competitive *disadvantages* of your company or product by simply not including those points in your comparison table or by presenting them in such a way as to minimize their importance.

You don't need to devote a lot of space to this particular part of your plan. A half page is probably sufficient, especially if you take the comparative table approach.

When you're putting together a competitive comparison, make sure you choose the largest and most direct competitors. You don't want to draw undue attention to smaller competitors, so leave them out. Pick two or three (no more!) competitors and show how your product stacks up against—and hopefully outperforms—these important players.

For example, if you're Honda and you're putting together a competitive comparison for the Honda Civic, you probably want to include the Toyota Corolla, the Ford Focus, and the Nissan Sentra. You probably *don't* want to include the Mazda Protegé or the Hyundai Elantra; even though they may be fine cars, in terms of sales they're too unimportant to bother with. Along the same lines, you don't want to include the Ford Taurus because it isn't a direct competitor. Keep the comparison focused and keep it relatively small.

What types of attributes should you compare? It's going to differ from product to product, but price is always good, as is distribution—especially if you're in a channel or outlet that your competitors aren't. Also consider comparing size, value (price per ounce, for example), warranty, expected life, available colors or options, performance, and other similar features. If available, a unit or dollar sales comparison is also good.

Going back to the Honda Civic example, your comparison table might include comparisons of engine size, horsepower, interior volume, warranty, price, and prior-year unit sales. You could include more items, but then the simple table starts to look more like a detailed product brochure, which this part of your business plan is *not*. (The point here isn't to sell your product; it's to sell your audience on the viability of your market strategy.)

PROCEED WITH CAUTION

If you do a company or product comparison, make sure all your data is accurate; you don't want to be accused of lying about the data to prove your point. To that end, make sure you include sources for all competitive data you use. These sources can be noted in a footnote or endnote or within the table itself.

MARKET STRATEGY CHECKLIST

Use the following checklist to make sure you include all necessary information in the Market Strategy section of your business plan:

Market Strategy Checklist

- ☐ Product information (what your product is and what it does; include product photos, if appropriate)
- ☐ Market positioning information (how you'll price, package, and position your product)
- ☐ Sales and distribution information (how and where you'll sell your product; include a chart of your distribution model, if appropriate)

☐ Marketing information (how you'll market your product, including advertising, promotion, P.R., direct mail, and Internet-based marketing; include pictures of ads, Web sites, catalogs, and other materials, if appropriate)

☐ Competitive comparison (how your product compares to competitive product; use a comparative table whenever possible)

☐ Other: _____

☐ Other: _____

☐ Other: _____

HOMEWORK

In this hour, you learned how to create the Market Strategy section of your business plan. In Hour 14, "Business Strategy," you'll learn how to write the Business Strategy section of the plan.

To prepare for the next hour, please do the following:

- Describe your company's business model—how you intend to produce revenues, what kind of margins you expect to generate, and how much market share you expect to attain over the next three years.

- Describe any large strategic initiatives (acquisitions, expansion, and so on) that you expect to undertake over the next three years.

- Plot out a timeline of key milestones you need to achieve to accomplish your business objectives.

HOUR 14
Business Strategy

CHAPTER SUMMARY

LESSON PLAN:

In this hour, you will learn about …

- Defining your business model
- Discussing major strategic initiatives
- Presenting a timeline for your goals

The Opportunity section of your business plan (discussed in Hour 12, "Opportunity") told your readers about the big-market opportunity you've identified; the Market Strategy section (discussed in Hour 13, "Market Strategy") told them how you were going to pursue that opportunity. Now the Business Strategy section will tell your readers how you'll implement your market strategy and how you'll make money doing it.

Key to the Business Strategy section is the presentation of your business model—exactly how you intend to generate revenues and profits. It is this section that will convey both your business savvy and your overall goals for what your business will become.

BUILDING YOUR BUSINESS STRATEGY

The Business Strategy section of your business plan describes how you will build your business and how that business will make money. You'll start, of course, by creating a detailed outline and then filling in the blanks for the necessary sections and subsections.

Business Strategy

    Business Model

        Revenue Streams

        Profit Margins

        Market Share

        Growth

    Strategic Initiatives

        Acquisitions

        Expansion

    Timeline

JUST A MINUTE

As with other outlines for your business plan, the specific headings and subheadings you use to describe your business may differ somewhat than the headings suggested here.

There are three major parts to this outline:

- **Business Model.** This is the key part of the Business Strategy section, and it should describe how you'll generate revenues, what kind of profit margins you expect to produce, how much market share you intend to gather, and how much growth you intend to achieve over the plan period.

- **Strategic Initiatives.** This part should discuss any major initiatives, outside the day-to-day running of your business, that are vital to the success of your business model. These initiatives might include acquisitions, physical expansion, international development, and the like.

- **Timeline.** This final part should present the major milestones you face in successfully implementing your chosen business model—through either narrative text or a graphical timeline.

The introduction of new products and the exploration of new accounts or channels are not typically considered strategic initiatives. A true strategic initiative is a one-time event that changes the shape of your business. An acquisition or merger, for example, is a strategic initiative, whereas the release of a new product line is not.

These major topics will be discussed in the following sections. Expect to write anywhere from four to six pages to create a comprehensive Business Strategy section.

DEFINING YOUR BUSINESS MODEL

For many potential investors, your business model is *the* key part of your business plan. Your business model describes how you intend to build your business, and it represents what is unique about your business. Different companies can (and will) approach the same opportunities with similar products and services; it's how you bring those products to life, how you intend to profit from that activity, and how you intend to get from here to there that makes your business unique. Investors will analyze your business model and come to some sort of conclusion about whether you've picked the right model and whether you can actually accomplish what it will take to implement that business model. If your model and your plans pass muster, you'll most likely get the money you need.

Your business model describes your approach to four different issues: revenue, profit, market share, and growth. You should treat each of these issues as separate subheads underneath the main Business Model head in your plan document.

REVENUE STREAMS

The first component of your business model is revenue. In this part of the section, then, you need to describe precisely where your revenues will come from.

The Revenue Streams section is sometimes called the Revenue Model. The "Revenue Streams" heading is recommended, however, to avoid confusion between the terms *business* model and *revenue* model in the same section of the plan.

If your company produces only one product or offers only one service, this section has the potential to be relatively simple. "One hundred percent of all company revenues are generated by Product A" would be a valid approach—unless, of course, there were other defining parameters. For example, you might sell only one product or service, but you might sell it into multiple channels or regions. In this scenario, you'd want to describe the revenues generated from each channel or region.

Obviously, if you produce multiple products or product lines, or if your revenues are split between different products and services, you need to describe each major source of revenue. The defining parameters for each revenue stream should be noted in your text; important characteristics might include any or all of the following:

- Product
- Price
- Discount rate
- Sales cost
- Type of sales force or sales vehicle employed
- Amount of marketing and advertising necessary
- Intensity of competition
- Length of sales cycle

In short, you need to point out any important differences between your revenue streams.

As an example, consider a business that sells lawn care services and equipment. For this business, revenue comes from selling lawn care equipment (lawn mowers and the like) and from providing lawn maintenance services (mowing, seeding, weeding, and so on). When describing the first revenue stream (equipment sales), the business plan would note that the equipment revenue stream has an average revenue per sale of $750, that sales generate a 20 percent gross margin, that sales are made by a team of six commissioned in-store salespeople, and that each equipment sale generates $50, on average, in add-on sales. When describing the second revenue stream (maintenance services), the business plan would note that these services are billed on a monthly basis, that the average monthly cost to each account is $120, that sales are made via in-house telemarketers, and that your firm employs a force of 30 lawn maintenance specialists to provide these services.

Again, provide enough detail about each revenue stream so that the reader gains a basic understanding of how you're generating your revenues.

JUST A MINUTE

Unless you only sell a handful of products, you probably want to group your revenues by product line or product type instead of by individual product. Also, if a particular product, line, or type represents a small percent of your revenues—less than 10 percent, let's say—you might want to group all the smaller revenue streams into a single "Other" category.

Not only do you need to describe each revenue stream, you also need to quantify it. For the purposes of the Business Strategy section, describing each stream in terms of percentage of total revenues (as opposed to showing actual revenues by stream) is the preferred method. This way, potential lenders and investors can apply this revenue mix (on a percentage basis) to different total revenue numbers. (For example, if you say that revenue stream A represents 20 percent of total revenues, the reader can do his or her own math to size this stream against different projected total revenue numbers, by multiplying the total revenue by the 20-percent share.)

A good way to present your revenue mix is with a pie chart (see the following figure). The visual nature of a pie chart very quickly imparts the comparative size information that is key to the revenue stream mixture. Use the narrative text to describe each revenue stream and a pie chart to show its relative size.

PROFIT MARGINS

Now that you've shown where your revenues will be coming from, it's time to discuss just how profitable you expect each revenue stream to be.

PROCEED WITH CAUTION

If you break your business into more than one revenue stream, you *must* break down your profit margin by revenue stream. Once you've segmented your business like this, reverting to a single overall margin number will do nothing but raise questions from potential lenders and investors; if you don't show the breakout by revenue stream, they'll assume you're trying to hide a lower-profit part of your business.

Using a pie chart to show the different components of your revenue stream.

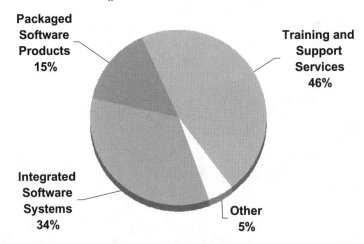

Revenue Streams
(percent of total revenues)

Packaged Software Products 15%

Training and Support Services 46%

Integrated Software Systems 34%

Other 5%

This part of the Business Model section can be relatively short. The first thing you need to do is list the projected gross margin for each revenue stream. You use gross margin (which represents your profit after cost of goods sold but before operating expenses) because it represents the direct costs of a particular product or service. Operating expenses include some amount of fixed costs, as well as costs (such as corporate overhead) that are shared between different revenue streams and thus don't accurately represent the true costs of an individual product or service.

JUST A MINUTE

Some businesses prefer to calculate an operating margin, by applying all relevant direct operating expenses to each revenue stream. You should only do this if you can accurately break out operating expenses—including sales, product development, and advertising costs—for each individual revenue stream. In this type of presentation, G&A and other nonproduct-specific costs are left out of the equation.

You can present these gross margins in your text, in a table, or in a horizontal bar chart (see the following figure). (Don't use a vertical bar chart; bars aligned from left to right imply the passage of time, which is not what you're presenting.) You should also devote some narrative text (a paragraph per revenue stream perhaps) to describing why one revenue stream has higher or lower gross margins than another.

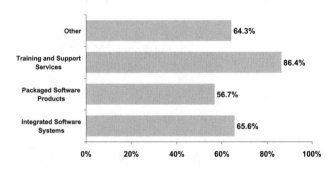

Using a horizontal bar chart to show gross margin for each revenue stream.

At the very end of this section, you should present and discuss your projected net margin for your entire business. If this number will change over time—as your company gets up to speed, for example—you may want to show a vertical bar chart showing projected net margin over the plan period (see the following figure).

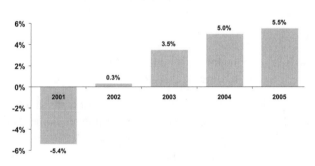

Using a vertical bar chart to show how your company's net margin is projected to change over time.

MARKET SHARE

In most cases, your company's revenues are directly related to your market share. To achieve a projected revenue number, you'll have to achieve a specific share of your market—or you'll have to somehow generate revenues from outside your market, which is really difficult to plan for and explain.

This short section, then, should project your market share over the plan period. The best way to do this is with either an area chart or a vertical bar chart, accompanied by a short piece of narrative text. At this point, it is not necessary to present competitors' market share, although you may need to describe (in your text) from which competitors you expect to take share (see the following figure).

Using an area chart to show your company's projected market share over the plan period.

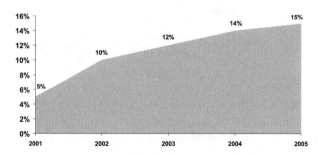

Market Share 2001-2005 (projected)

JUST A MINUTE

Remember that your market share is calculated by dividing your net revenues by the industry's total net revenues. Profit numbers are never used to determine market share; a company can have a commanding market share and still be unprofitable.

GROWTH

The final component of the Business Model section is about growth—the growth of your business and the growth of the underlying industry.

This should be a relatively short section (just a paragraph or two) that should start out with a reiteration of the industry growth numbers (in terms of average yearly growth percentages) that you first stated back in the Opportunity section. This should be followed by your own average yearly growth number (in percent) and (if you want to go into this much detail) a table or vertical bar chart that displays your year-over-year growth (in percent) over the plan period. In most cases, however, a single *compound annual growth rate* (CAGR) number is sufficient.

Along with your CAGR number, this section is also a good place to show your yearly revenue projections for the balance of the plan period. Although these numbers will be presented in detail in the Financials section (discussed in Hour 18, "Financials"), displaying an overview of these numbers is entirely appropriate at this point in your plan document. If you do decide to show revenues here, use a vertical bar chart (see the following figure), provide a short paragraph of accompanying text, and refer readers to the Financials section for more detail.

STRICTLY SPEAKING

Compound annual growth rate (CAGR) is the year-over-year rate of growth for a specified period of years. You need three figures to calculate CAGR—the revenues for the starting year, the revenues for the ending year, and the number of years for which you're calculating. Then you calculate CAGR by applying these numbers to the following equation:

([Final year/First year] raised to the [1/total number of years] power) - 1

If this seems like fairly complex math (and it is!), most sophisticated business and financial calculators provide automatic CAGR calculation.

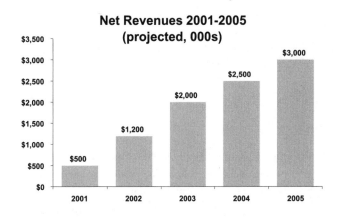

Using a vertical bar chart to display projected revenues for the plan period.

IDENTIFYING NECESSARY STRATEGIC INITIATIVES

In some instances, achievement of your plan numbers depends on undertaking one or more major strategic initiatives. These would be activities that fall outside the normal day-to-day operation of your business and that significantly change the dynamics of your business. Examples of this type of strategic initiative include mergers, acquisitions, physical expansion, international expansion, strategic partnerships, and the like.

Use this section to describe the *type* of strategic initiatives you plan to undertake. You do not have to provide explicit goals here (such as "In 2003, we intend to acquire the Dog 'n' Suds chain for $500 million"); simply indicate the type of activity planned, why you want to undertake that activity, and the benefit that activity will bring to your business. You should also indicate a rough date for accomplishing each initiative.

Here's an example of how a strategic initiative might be discussed in your plan:

> By 2003, it will be necessary to establish an international presence for our business. To facilitate an international expansion in that timeframe, we intend to acquire or partner with existing players in the European, Latin American, and Asian markets to ensure effective distribution of our products in those regions.

Yes, it's a little vague, but that's okay. You've stated your intentions and have provided enough guidance so that management at that time will know, generally, how to proceed.

JUST A MINUTE

If you've already made any key acquisitions, you should go ahead and list them in this section. This will demonstrate that you're serious about taking the steps you need to take to grow your business.

PREPARING A TIMELINE

Now that your business model is out of the way, you need to discuss just what you need to do, over time, to put everything into place. This is typically done through the use of some sort of timeline. The subhead for this section can be titled either Timeline or Key Milestones.

There are four basic types of timeline you can present:

- **Narrative.** A narrative (text-based) timeline, in which you discuss key milestones in the context of a normal paragraph, is the least popular type of timeline because you force the reader to read the entire paragraph to pick up key data that would be better absorbed through browsing.
- **Bulleted.** Making a bulleted list of key milestones is better than burying the dates in the text. Create a separate bullet for each milestone

and make sure the completion dates are duly highlighted, either in bold or in color.

- **Tabular.** A table-based timeline functions much like a bulleted timeline. Create a two-column table with one column for the date and another column for the task; each task (milestone) should then be assigned a separate row within the table.

- **Graphical.** If you have the expertise to pull it off, presenting your timeline in a graphical fashion is the best way to impart this important information. One approach is to draw a line (or an arrow, as in the following figure) and mark each milestone at its appropriate place along the timeline. Another approach is to create a vertical bar chart displaying quarter-by-quarter revenues and then place each milestone under the appropriate quarter. (This last approach has the advantage of tying activities to revenues.)

2001	2002	2003	2004	2005
Introduce WidgiWiz 1.0	Introduce custom school products	Introduce WidgiWiz 2.0	Introduce first companion products	European expansion
Establish bookstore distribution	Launch Web site	Achieve profitability	Open West coast distribution center	

Using a custom timeline graphic to display key milestones for your business.

What types of milestones should you display? Big ones, naturally—and those that are key to the achievement of your plan. Consider displaying milestones for key management hires, new product introductions, key acquisitions or physical expansions, or key business events—such as achievement of breakeven. Do *not* clutter your timeline with too many milestones; you shouldn't list more than two or three events per time period.

PROCEED WITH CAUTION

When you list a milestone in your timeline, make sure the milestone can actually be achieved. Investors *will* check back to see if you've delivered on your promises, so you may want to pad your dates a little to ensure their successful completion.

BUSINESS STRATEGY CHECKLIST

Use the following checklist to make sure you include all necessary information in the Business Strategy section of your business plan:

Business Strategy Checklist

- ☐ Information about major revenue streams, including the percentage of total revenues represented by each stream
- ☐ Projected gross profit margins for each revenue stream, along with accompanying narrative
- ☐ Your projected market share over the plan period, on a year-by-year basis
- ☐ Compound annual growth rate for total company revenues over the plan period
- ☐ Projected total company revenues for each year of the plan period
- ☐ Information about any major strategic initiatives anticipated over the plan period
- ☐ A timeline of key accomplishments to be achieved over the plan period
- ☐ Other: _____
- ☐ Other: _____
- ☐ Other: _____

HOMEWORK

In this hour, you learned how to create the Business Strategy section of your business plan. In Hour 15, "Organization and Operations," you'll learn how to write the Organization and Operations section of the plan.

To prepare for the next hour, please do the following:

- Obtain a top-level org chart for your company.
- Obtain department-level org charts for all the units or departments in your company.
- Obtain brief descriptions of operations for each department or division in your company.

- Have your MIS or IT department compile a list of key computer equipment and systems used in your business.
- Have your legal department compile a list of key patents and copyrights held by your company.
- Prepare flow charts of the key processes incorporated within your business.
- Obtain any other important schedules or information pertaining to the operation of your business—including lease agreements, franchise agreements, and so on.

HOUR 15

Organization and Operations

CHAPTER SUMMARY

LESSON PLAN:

In this hour, you will learn about …

- Presenting your structure
- Discussing core operations
- Listing intangible assets

So far, your business plan has discussed why you're in business (the Vision and Mission sections), has defined the market opportunity you want to pursue (Opportunity), has described how you intend to pursue that opportunity (Market Strategy), and has presented the business model you'll use to implement your market strategy (Business Strategy). Now, in the Organization and Operations section, you get to discuss, from an operational perspective, just how you'll go about executing your business strategy.

In short, the Organization and Operations section of your business plan is where you detail how your business is structured and how each part of your business (each department or business unit) works. Most businesses can present this information in six pages or less, although the larger your business, the more space you'll need to devote to this section.

OUTLINING AND PREPARATION

You attack the Organization and Operations section the same way you attack the rest of your business plan document—by building a detailed outline and by assembling the key information you need to flesh it out.

Organization and operations information is sometimes lumped together into a single Organization and Operations section (sometimes called The Company), and sometimes it is split into two separate sections. Use whichever structure works best for your business.

BUILDING YOUR OUTLINE

The outline for your Organization and Operations section splits into two obvious parts: Organization and Operations. The Organization section describes your company's structure (typically in the form of an organization chart), and the Operations section is divided into separate sections for each major department or operating unit of your business.

Here's a sample outline, geared to a typical multiple-department corporation:

Organization and Operations

    Organization Structure

    Key Operations

        Product Development

        Manufacturing

        Warehousing and Distribution

        Sales

        Marketing

        Information Technology

        Finance and Accounting

        Human Resources

        Facilities

        Copyrights and Patents

Naturally, you should adjust this outline based on the structure and specifics of your own organization. The more important a particular function is to your business, the higher up it should go in the outline. For example, if you're a franchise retailer, you'll want to add a section called Franchise and put it near the top of the Operations section; you'll also want to move the Facilities section up higher and add a section for Purchasing. If you're an Internet-based business, you'll want to move the IT section up higher—and possibility give it a more "important" title, such as Technical Infrastructure or Web Site Management. And if you're a smaller company, you may only need a few sections to cover your entire business.

In fact, if a particular part of your business is key to the implementation of your specific plan, you may want to elevate that department into its own section on level with the Organization and Operations section. Just follow the simple rule that more important functions deserve more coverage, and you'll be on the right track.

ASSEMBLING THE DETAILS

What kind of detail do you need to write your plan's Organization and Operations section?

For the Organization section, you'll need a high-level org chart—show the top level (president or owner or CEO), the next level of direct reports, and maybe (in less detail) the next level below that. While you're creating the main org chart, however, you should consider including departmental org charts for each subsection of the Organization section; you may need to get this detail from the individual departments.

An org chart isn't the only thing you need to get from each of your key departments. Since each department or operating unit gets its own subhead, you'll need to collect detailed information from each department—what it does, how it does it, how it's organized, and so on. It's not uncommon to devote a half page or more to each department, which is a lot of space to fill—especially if you don't know much about what's really going on there.

A good approach is to assign the writing of each department's section to the departments themselves. Ask each department for a three- to four-page overview and then have the business plan's main writer use those overviews to create the actual sections for the plan document. This approach helps involve your key managers in the business plan process, provides information you might have trouble coming up with yourself, and then leaves the final editing to a real writer.

You should know that the Operations section is the least-read section of most business plans; many investors just aren't interested in the detailed operations of your IT or HR departments. Perversely, it's because this section is seldom read that you can include more insignificant detail than you can in other parts of your plan; this is the one section where mind-numbing detail doesn't detract from the plan's effectiveness, and it may actually serve to impress your audience. (They won't read the detail, but the sheer bulk may be comforting!)

Presenting Your Organization

The Organization part of this section is relatively easy to write. All you need is a brief introductory paragraph and an org chart.

How you approach the org chart, however, is important. You have to determine how many levels to include on the chart and how much detail to provide about each level. You also have to decide whether you want to include only departments and titles on the chart or also include the names of key managers.

Here are some of the approaches you should consider:

- **Two-level, minimal detail.** This is the minimalist approach. You include the CEO/president level, the next level of direct reports, and that's all—no departmental detail, no names, no nothing. The advantages to this approach are its simplicity, the way it focuses attention on key units or activities, and the fact that it removes all focus from individuals. This last point may be important if you don't yet have your entire management team in place or if you expect the makeup of your team to change over the next six months or so. As you can see in the following figure, when you leave the names off, readers will focus on the departments only.

- **Two-level, personal detail.** This approach adds the title and names of key individuals to your basic two-level org chart. As shown in the following figure, this helps personalize your structure and provides a clear link to the information in the Management section of your plan (discussed in Hour 16, "Management"). Note that when you add titles and names, it's okay to not include the name of the department, which is typically redundant with each individual's title.

A two-level org chart with minimal detail.

A two-level org chart with names and titles.

- **Two-level, departmental detail.** If it's unclear just what each department or business unit does, consider adding detail about each department to the org chart. You should be able to describe the function of each department in a single sentence, which can fit either inside or below the department box (see the following figure).

A two-level org chart with departmental detail.

- **Three-level.** For larger or more complex organizations, you may want to include a third level in your org chart. When you do this, you should decrease the size of the third-level boxes and text; you'll probably need to do this anyway to make everything fit. You should also consider aligning the third-level boxes vertically instead of horizontally (see the following figure); if you try to run *everything* horizontally, you'll most likely end up reducing box and text size to an unacceptable level.

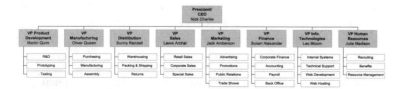

A three-level org chart; note the small text and boxes (and the vertical alignment) for the third level.

Whichever approach you take for your org chart, make sure you customize the chart in an attractive and professional fashion. If you include org charts for each of your departments, you should ensure that those charts match the formatting of your main org chart.

PROCEED WITH CAUTION

When assigning titles to your key managers, know that some potential investors expect to see "high-level" titles. While you may have a personal preference for titles like Manager and Director, some investors will expect all of a president's direct reports to have the title of vice president (VP of operations, VP of marketing, etc.). Titles below VP might signify weak management that needs to be replaced—or, even worse, a weak president/CEO who isn't hiring a strong enough supporting staff.

DISCUSSING YOUR OPERATIONS

The Operations part of your plan (sometimes called Infrastructure) is where you describe what each piece and part of your company does. This section is mainly here to show potential lenders and investors that you actually do have a depth of organization and that someone who knows what he or she is doing is watching over the company at that level of detail.

You should create subheads within this section for each major department, group, or operating unit. A solid strategy is that if a department or unit shows up on the second level of your corporate org chart, it needs its own subhead. (Conversely, if it's important enough for it's own subhead, it had *better* show up as a direct report to the CEO/president, or something's seriously wrong with your company's structure!)

For example, most larger companies would have subheads for Product Development, Manufacturing, Sales, Human Relations, and the like. Within each subhead should be a description of what the department does (including key processes), how big it is (the number of employees), where it's located (if it's not housed within corporate headquarters), and any other important details. You may want to include a departmental org chart as well as a flow chart for any key processes. (For example, a flow chart illustrating the product development process would be a valuable addition to the Product Development section.)

Of course, if you're running a small business with a half-dozen or so employees, you don't need to create separate subheads for each member of your staff. For small businesses, the Operations section can be short and without subheads—since your operations should be relatively simple to describe.

The following sections discuss the information that a larger business may want to include for specific departments. Naturally, the nature of your own business will dictate the specific information you include in your plan document—as well as which departments you break out for discussion.

PRODUCT DEVELOPMENT

Whether you make or buy your products, Product Development (or whatever you call it at your company) is a fairly important part of your Operations section. Not only will you want to describe your product development department, you'll also want to describe your product development *process*. You'll want to describe how you obtain new products, from conception to manufacturing; illustrating this process with a flow chart of some sort would be a good idea. You should also include data relating to the cost of development either for an average product or for your most important products.

MANUFACTURING

If you make your own products, this is the place to discuss that process. Include a flow chart if appropriate, as well as descriptions of all your manufacturing facilities. (If you want to include a picture of some high-tech assembly line or manufacturing apparatus, it would at least serve to break up a long chunk of text.) You should also discuss product costs here, as well as any unique processes you utilize to control or reduce those costs.

WAREHOUSE AND DISTRIBUTION

If you do your own warehousing and distribution, talk about that department here. Make sure to include all pertinent data, including the size of your warehouse(s), the average number of days of inventory on hand, the time it takes to process a typical order, and the like.

Sales

You should have already presented your sales strategy and sales forces back in the Market Strategy section, so all you need to discuss here is the structure of the sales department itself. If you want to include a commission schedule or a discussion of compensation plans, this is the place to do it—although that might be too much detail, even here.

Marketing

You've already presented your marketing strategy and activities (back in the Market Strategy section), so all you need to discuss here is the structure of your marketing department. You may want to present projected yearly marketing/advertising expenses, if those weren't included earlier in the plan.

Information Technology

Whether you call it IT or MIS or something else, this is where you discuss the technical backbone of your company. If your company is reliant on technology, go into some detail here and include a list of the servers, software, and systems you employ. This section is especially important if you're in a high-tech industry; potential investors might actually examine this section to see if you have a strong enough technical infrastructure to execute the components of your plan.

JUST A MINUTE

A good way to present your key systems and software is in a bulleted list or table. You don't have to list every desktop PC in the company, but you should include the key hardware and software you use to manage your various customer transactions. If this list is too intrusive in the text, include it as an appendix at the end of the plan document.

In this era of high-tech corporate attacks, make sure you include information about the security of your computer systems. Also consider adding a sentence or paragraph relating to system redundancy (in case your main system crashes or gets hacked) and expansion (in case your business grows faster than expected). You should also include a sentence or paragraph regarding your company's privacy policy, especially if you manage large amounts of customer data.

If you're running an Internet-based business, this section takes on even more importance—and might need a different title, such as Technical Infrastructure. Any discussion of Web site development should also go in this section, and you may want to either place this section nearer the top of the Operations section or elevate it into its own separate section.

FINANCE AND ACCOUNTING

You don't have to say much about your finance, accounting, accounts receivable/payable, and similar departments. Include a list of functions and an org chart, and you have it covered.

JUST A MINUTE

Depending on how your company is structured, you may want to combine some of these individual sections into a single Back Office section. This section could also include other backend operations, such as payroll, accounts receivable, and the like.

FACILITIES

If you operate out of a single office, this section should be short and sweet—just describe your location, list the total space, and tell the rent you pay (either in total or in terms of dollars per square foot). If you own several different facilities, you should list and describe each one, including the core functions at each location.

If you're a retailer, this becomes a much more important section of your plan. You'll need to describe your facility management strategy—how you locate new locations, how much (on average) you pay to build or rent, what kind of expense goes into getting a new location ready for operation, and so on. In fact, if you're a retailer, you may want to place this section closer to the top of the Operations section and include appropriate tables and graphs to provide the kind of detail a potential lender or investor might be looking for.

HUMAN RELATIONS

HR is similar to finance/accounting in that it doesn't provide a unique competitive advantage to your business. (Some HR people would disagree, of course—although the reality is that few if any business strategies revolve around the company's HR department.) Include a list of basic functions and an org chart, and you've provided more than enough information.

JUST A MINUTE

If your company provides any unique employee programs or benefits—such as stock options, management training, telecommuting, and so on—the place to mention them is in the Human Relations section.

COPYRIGHTS AND PATENTS

If applicable, you should include a separate section detailing the intellectual property, copyrights, and patents that your company owns. You can choose to list all of these assets (if it's a manageable list), list just the major ones, or simply describe the fact that you do own various intellectual assets and that you have a process for protecting them. Depending on your business, you may want to call this section Intellectual Property, Intellectual Assets, Copyrights and Patents, or just Legal.

FRANCHISE

If your company is a franchise of a larger organization, you need to have a section within the Operations section describing both your franchise agreement and the franchising firm. You should include detailed information regarding your franchise payments and the structure and requirements of the franchise. If you're using your business plan to ask for a loan, make sure you include full contact information for the franchising organization. If the franchise arrangement is a key component of your business plan, you should place the Franchise section at the beginning of the Operations section—or even give it it's own separate section.

ORGANIZATION AND OPERATIONS CHECKLIST

Use the following checklist to make sure you include all necessary information in the Organization and Operations section of your business plan:

Organization and Operations Checklist

- ☐ Upper-level org chart showing the CEO/president level and the next level of departments and direct reports
- ☐ Org charts for each major department or operating unit
- ☐ Descriptions of each department or operating unit
- ☐ Employee count for each department or operating unit
- ☐ Flow charts of key processes within each department—especially as they relate to product development and manufacturing
- ☐ Detailed list of key information systems hardware and software
- ☐ Detailed information about each of your locations—core functions, rent, length of leases, and so on
- ☐ If appropriate, detailed information about your franchise agreement
- ☐ Detailed list of all intellectual property, copyrights, and patents that your company owns—as well as the processes you employ to register and protect these assets
- ☐ Other: _____
- ☐ Other: _____
- ☐ Other: _____

HOMEWORK

In this hour, you learned how to create the Organization and Operations section of your business plan. In Hour 16, "Management," you'll learn how to write the Management section of the plan.

To prepare for the next hour, please do the following:

- Obtain bios of all the members of your senior management team—including yourself.
- Obtain bios of all the members of your board of directors.
- Obtain background information about any major strategic or institutional investors.

HOUR 16

Management

CHAPTER SUMMARY

LESSON PLAN:

In this hour, you will learn about ...

- Who to include in the Management section
- Writing a compelling bio
- Determining other people to mention

As you've progressed through the sections of your business plan, you've answered the key "why," "what," and "how" questions—*why* you're in business, *what* opportunity you're pursuing, and *how* you're pursuing it. The next section, Management, answers the "who" question—*who* are the people you've chosen to help you achieve your goals.

In other words, the Management section—sometimes called Management Team or Management Background— is where you get to show off the management talent in your company. This short (typically one- or two-page) section presents each of your key managers in a fashion that shows what strengths he or she brings to your business.

PROVIDING A STRONG LEAD-IN

The Management section of your business plan has a simple structure. All you have to do is provide an introductory sentence or two and then write a short one-paragraph bio for each member of your core management team.

The introductory paragraph should stress the breadth and depth of experience that your team possesses. A good way to do this is to discuss the overall background of the team and the number of years of "combined experience" that everyone brings to the table. (Just add up each manager's individual number of years in the workplace.)

Here's an example of a strong introductory paragraph:

> The Gadget Company has assembled an experienced multidiscipline management team, with executives from the retail, consumer electronics, and Internet industries. Together, the Gadget Company team has more than 150 years of combined experience in consumer electronics retailing.

WRITING A COMPELLING BIO

Once you're past the introduction, you face the task of writing bios for each of the key individuals on your management team. Each bio should be relatively short (no more than a paragraph in length) and should include a handful of key information points.

JUST A MINUTE

Some businesses prefer to de-emphasize the Management section by moving it to an appendix at the end of the business plan document. This could improve the flow of the document and might be worth considering, especially if your management team is small or unproven.

The bios you write for each manager should focus on information relevant to your business and to his or her assigned duties. You don't need or want to include all the information that might be included in personal resumés; think about what might impress your potential lenders and investors and focus on those points.

For example, you definitely want to mention previous job experience that relates to a person's current position in your company. You *don't* want to mention hobbies, clubs, or other outside activities that have no bearing on what the person tries to accomplish during the day.

What does a good bio look like? Consider this example:

> **Lewis Archer**, *Vice President of Retail Sales*. With nearly 20 years of experience in electronics retailing, Lew Archer brings a proven track record of sales success to The Gadget Store, where he is responsible for hiring, training, and managing the sales staff for the entire chain. Prior to joining The Gadget Store, Mr. Archer was Vice President of Sales at

Gadget.net, one of the first online retailers of consumer electronics products. Previously, he spent 12 years in various positions at Best Buy City, the nation's largest retail chain specializing in consumer electronics equipment. While at Best Buy City, Mr. Archer managed the largest single store in the chain (San Jose, Calif.) and served as Sales Director for the West Coast region, increasing revenues for that region by more than 20 percent over a three-year period. Mr. Archer received a Masters of Business Administration from Northwestern University and a Bachelor's degree in English from James Madison University.

As you can see from this example, the bio starts with the individual's name and title followed by a single-sentence overview—which also serves to "sell" the individual by tying his or her past experience with the responsibilities of his or her current position. From there, we move to a recap of prior job experience, going back one or two positions and pointing out any relevant accomplishments. The bio finishes up with the individual's educational background, if relevant.

JUST A MINUTE

While accepted style is to present all titles in lower case (vice president of marketing, director of information services, and so on), many businesspeople feel that this tends to bury the titles in the text. It's perfectly acceptable to buck convention and capitalize titles in your text, as shown in this example.

Not all of this information needs to be included in every bio. You may, for example, choose to not include the job overview sentence—especially if the job title is fairly self-explanatory. You may also decide not to include educational background if that background isn't totally relevant to the individual's current position (if your IT guy has a philosophy degree, for example). The thing to remember is to include only directly relevant information and then spin that information in a way that shows how much value that person brings to his or her job at your company.

When writing this section of your plan, know that not all bios need to be the same length. It's perfectly acceptable—and a pretty good idea—to include a longer bio for the owner/president/CEO than for the rest of the management team. (After all, investors are investing in part because of their faith in the person on top, so it makes sense to elaborate on that person's strengths.) As you move down to less important managers—or younger managers with less history—it's okay to shrink the bio down to two or three key sentences.

JUST A MINUTE

Most bios are relatively formal in style ("Mr. Archer"). If your company is smaller or less formal, you may want to use first names or nicknames instead ("Lew"). Note also that you should boldface the first appearance of the individual's name and put his or her title in italics. Alternately, you could present each individual as part of a bulleted list or use a subhead to present his or her name and title—although this last approach really interrupts the document's flow and elevates each individual to a relatively high level within your document's outline and TOC.

MAKING THE LIST

You have six direct reports, each of which has at least three direct reports. Plus you have a board of directors, a "kitchen cabinet" of key advisors, and some important strategic investors. How many of these individuals do you want to include in the Management section of your plan?

DEFINING KEY MANAGEMENT

There are no hard-and-fast rules about who gets into the plan and who doesn't. Just because an individual is a direct report to the president doesn't mean he or she should necessarily be included; just because someone *isn't* a direct report doesn't exclude him or her either.

In general, you should include bios for individuals who meet the following criteria:

- Have a strategic impact on the business
- Are crucial to the day-to-day management of the company
- Have daily interaction with the owner/president/CEO
- Are likely to have contact with investors or the board of directors

In most companies, this means that the owner/president/CEO and all direct reports get included. Key high-level staff members might also make the list, as might selected middle management. You will most likely end up with 6 to 10 bios from your management team.

INCLUDING THE BOARD OF DIRECTORS

If your company has a board of directors, you may want to include a list of board members in your Management section. If you do so, you probably want to list the board separate from your management team.

JUST A MINUTE

An alternate approach is to list the entire board (name and title only) in a sidebar or text box. If you do this, you may want to include a full bio for the chairman directly underneath the president's bio in the main Management section.

If you include bios of your board members, structure them similarly to the bios of your management team. Start with the individual's name, followed by his or her current firm and position. Since most people at this level have relatively self-descriptive titles, you don't need to include a description of their current duties, although you might want to list any other boards on which they serve.

UTILIZING LARGE AND STRATEGIC INVESTORS

If you've already attracted some investors to your business, you may be able to leverage those investors to attract new investment. If you have "name" venture capital, well-known individuals, or strategic companies on your list of current investors, you can add a Strategic Investors subhead to your Management section. If you do list an existing investor, include the name of the investor or investment firm, along with a brief overview emphasizing that investor's importance in the industry, in your local community, or to your business.

PROCEED WITH CAUTION

Some investors might not want their names publicized in this manner. You might want to check with your key investors before you play them up in this manner in your business plan.

MAKING THE MOST OF ADVISORS

Finally, you may have a formal or informal board of advisors that plays a key strategic function in how you run your business. If this group includes well-known individuals or individuals whose titles or connections can lend credibility-by-association to your business, you may want to mention them in your plan. If you do so, create a separate subhead within the Management section and call it Board of Advisors or Key Advisors or something similar. Create bios similar to those you'd use in a board of directors section—and remember to ask for these individuals' permission before you continue!

ORDERING THE LIST

Once you've assembled all your bios, it's time to decide who goes first—and who brings up the rear.

First, remember to keep bios for your management team separate from bios for your board of directors, strategic investors, and key advisors. (It's a good idea to put these other bios under separate subheads.)

Within your management section, you always—*always*—start with the bio for your owner/president/CEO. This is the leader of your business and the person in which potential lenders and investors are most interested.

Next you have a choice. You can list the other managers by order of importance or by their appearance on your org chart. More common, however, is a simple alphabetical listing (by last name, not by title). If you're listing staff from two different levels of your organization, you may want to list the first-level managers first (alphabetized, of course) and the second-level managers second.

JUST A MINUTE

The depth of history in the bios might also influence your ordering of individuals. For example, if you have an individual with a very short and unimpressive bio (typical of younger and less-experienced managers), you probably don't want to put that bio right under the owner/president/CEO—and ahead of more impressive, more important managers. Feel free to break the alphabetical rule to hide the weaker bios in your list.

MANAGEMENT SECTION CHECKLIST

Use the following checklist to make sure each bio in the Management section of your business plan includes the key information:

Management Section Checklist

- ☐ Full name (nicknames at your discretion)
- ☐ Title
- ☐ One-sentence overview, tying previous experience to current position
- ☐ Title and function of immediately previous position(s); include key accomplishments if relevant
- ☐ College attended and degree received (at your discretion)
- ☐ One-sentence job description
- ☐ Other: _____
- ☐ Other: _____
- ☐ Other: _____

HOMEWORK

In this hour, you learned how to create the Management section of your business plan. In Hour 17, "Core Competencies and Challenges," you'll learn how to write the Core Competencies and Challenges section of the plan.

To prepare for the next hour, please do the following:

- Reread Hour 4, "Analyze Your Strengths."
- Make a list of your company's key strengths and unique competitive advantages.
- Make a list of your company's most critical weaknesses.
- Make a list of the major potential obstacles that could keep your company from achieving its plan.

HOUR 17

Core Competencies and Challenges

CHAPTER SUMMARY

LESSON PLAN:
In this hour, you will learn about …

- Highlighting your key strengths
- Identifying potential obstacles
- Positively presenting your weaknesses

Now that you've shown potential lenders and investors how your business works, your business plan is almost complete. All that's left is to present your detailed financial goals (see Hour 18, "Financials") and provide a brief wrap-up. This hour addresses the wrap-up, otherwise known as the Core Competencies and Challenges section.

Back in Hour 4, "Analyze Your Strengths," you did a preliminary assessment of your company's strengths and weaknesses. It's time to revisit the list you made in that hour because it can serve as the foundation of this final text portion of your business plan document.

PRESENTING YOUR STRENGTHS AND WEAKNESSES

There are several reasons to incorporate a Core Competencies and Challenges section in your business plan document:

- Summarizing your unique competitive advantages in a single section serves to highlight and remind readers about those unique aspects of your business strategy.
- Ending the text part of your plan with a list of your strengths is a great way to end your plan; you leave your readers with a summary of the key points you want them to remember.

- By bringing up potential objections before your audience does (in the Challenges section), you preempt some tough questions and are able to address these issues on your own terms.

- When you answer potential challenges with distinct strategies, you turn your weaknesses into strengths—and present yourself as being both realistic and proactive.

In other words, including a Core Competencies and Challenges section permits you to focus the reader's attention on the issues that you deem most important.

JUST A MINUTE

Including a Core Competencies and Challenges section in your plan isn't mandatory; many businesspeople prefer not to draw attention to their company's weaknesses or feel that their core competencies are covered adequately elsewhere in the plan. If you would rather leave this section out, you won't be breaking any hard and fast rules; constructing your plan without this section is a perfectly viable option.

If you decide to include the Core Competencies and Challenges section in your business plan document, there are several options to choose from in terms of the presentation of information. These options are discussed next.

One Section or Two?

Most often, Core Competencies and Challenges is a single section with two subheads ("Core Competencies" and "Challenges"). However, you may choose to present this information as two separate sections, which would elevate the presentation of your strengths to section-level importance. (This also elevates your weaknesses to a similar level, of course.)

You may also want to change the order of presentation. Although it's very logical to talk about your unique advantages and then answer that with a discussion of potential issues, if you switch the order (to present Challenges first and then the Core Competencies section), you end the text portion of your document on an extremely high note.

Alternate Titles

"Core competencies" is a modest way to say strengths, and "challenges" is a polite way to say weaknesses. That said, there are any number of alternate titles you can use for this section, as you can see in the following table.

Alternate Titles

Core Competencies	Challenges
Strengths	Weaknesses
Competitive Advantages	Potential Weaknesses
Unique Advantages	Risks
Unique Competitive Advantages	Risk Factors
Market Strengths	Market Challenges

TEXT, BULLETS, OR TABLE

What is the best format for presenting your strengths and weaknesses? Here are some options to consider:

- **Narrative text.** The easiest way to present this information is in standard narrative text format. The disadvantage of this approach is that it can bury your unique competitive advantages in text-heavy paragraphs; the advantage is that it can bury your potential weaknesses in text-heavy paragraphs.

- **Bulleted list.** If you want to draw more attention to your specific strengths (and weaknesses, of course), separate them out into a bulleted list. This is a particularly good approach when you consider that this entire section is meant as an unofficial summary of your entire business proposition; summaries (and previews) are meant to be grazed, not read, and bullets provide one of the best formats for grazing.

- **Simple table.** Listing your strengths in a simple table (and your weaknesses in a separate table) serves a similar purpose to the bulleted list; you make the information eminently grazable for the time-constrained reader.

- **Comparative table.** A more radical approach is to use a single table for both strengths and weaknesses, with your strengths in one column and your weaknesses in another. As shown in the following figure, this sets up a kind of "call and response" format, in which each strength is paired with a similar potential weakness. This is most certainly a balanced approach, but it may inadvertently diminish the impact of your competitive advantages—and put undue emphasis on your potential weaknesses.

Matching strengths with weaknesses in a comparative table.

Competitive Advantages	Marketplace Challenges
Speed to market. Thanks to its entirely in-house and proprietary assembly operations, CompuWedge can deliver a completed product in just 5 days from the initial order.	**Higher delivery and installation costs.** CompuWedge's focus on timely delivery results in delivery/installation costs that are approximately 10% higher than some slower competitors. CompuWedge intends to convince customers of the value of this trade-off via a topic-specific advertising campaign.
No need for third-party support. From day one, CompuWedge intends to make available all necessary add-ons and peripherals for its key product line, direct from the factory. No other competitor offers this type of integrated add-on support.	**Lack of third-party support.** All major competitors are supported by a variety of add-ons and peripherals from various third-party suppliers. As a new entry in this marketplace, CompuWedge lacks this support—but minimizes its impact by supplying its own self-branded line of add-on and peripheral products through its own distribution.
New player in established market. CompuWedge intends to leverage its late entry into the marketplace by embracing state-of-the-art manufacturing techniques not available to entrenched companies with older manufacturing plants.	**New player in established market.** Because CompuWidge's brand is not as well-known as those of more established competitors, the company will have to engage in an intense advertising and promotional campaign to increase brand visibility.

PROCEED WITH CAUTION

A comparative table is often difficult to create, as a company's strengths seldom match directly with its weaknesses.

When all is said and done, however, the bulleted list is the most-used approach. It probably does the best job of summarizing and highlighting your strengths without overly emphasizing your potential weaknesses.

THE QUESTION OF CHALLENGES

Presenting the challenges to your business is a real challenge. You want to preempt any negative questions or comments from your audience, and you want (or may be required) to list any real risks to success, but you don't want to draw undue attention to the weak links in the chain of your business strategy. What challenges you ultimately choose to present should reflect, to a degree, your personal convictions and should support the thrust of your business strategy.

In general, you have three options when it comes to presenting challenges:

- Present a reasonable number of true challenges, focusing on areas in which you possess some degree of competitive disadvantage in the marketplace.

- Present a long laundry list of potential challenges, weaknesses, and risks—much like the Risk Factors section you'd be forced to include in a PPM or S-1 filing.
- Leave out the Challenges section completely.

The first option is the most popular approach—you include real issues but only the big ones. This approach shows that you're on top of your business and that you're realistic as to your company's prospects.

The second option is probably overkill for this type of business plan. Listing every conceivable risk (the economic market could collapse, your product might be recalled, the earth could get hit by a wayward comet, and so on) is a requirement for more formal documents, but it is seldom necessary for a standard business plan. A complete laundry list of risks will draw attention away from your main strategy and your competitive strengths and will reflect a lack of priorities on your part.

JUST A MINUTE

If you've sought legal assistance to help you create your business plan, you will likely be pressured to include a lengthy laundry list of risk factors. You need to know that, unless you're using this document to explicitly solicit the sale of stock (in which case, you're actually preparing a private placement memorandum, as discussed in Hour 24, "Create a Private Placement Memorandum [PPM]"), you are under zero obligation to point out any potential risks. At this point, you can resist the legal advice—although the lawyers will be correct in demanding such a section if and when you issue a formal PPM.

The third option—to not include the section at all—is actually a viable option. There is nothing that requires you to talk about the challenges you face, and no one will question its absence if the section isn't there. Excising this section also creates a greater emphasis on the Core Competencies section, which can be a plus. The primary disadvantage is that if you don't address your challenges, your readers will; you won't have the opportunity to preempt their concerns and present issues on your own terms. Still, going without a Challenges section is a definite option for your specific business plan.

PRESENTING CORE COMPETENCIES

If you think of the Core Competencies section as a summary of your business's unique competitive advantages, you'll agree that this section should be no more than one page in length and include a half-dozen or so separate points. Approach this section as you would a summary, and you'll start off on the right track.

CHOOSING YOUR STRENGTHS

Which strengths should you choose to include in the Core Competencies section? Here are some tips:

- The strengths should be of major import to the success of your business strategy. Being able to negotiate terrific pricing on pens and paper is a good thing, but it won't impact the success of your strategy one iota.

- The strengths should be immediately visible. This means you're most likely looking at marketplace or external strengths rather than internal operational strengths. This isn't a hard and fast rule though; if you have internal operations that enable you to reduce the cost and selling price of your product or to bring your product to market faster, then that internal strength should be noted.

- The strengths should be unique. If you note that you can bring a product to market in five days, but all your competitors also have a five-day delivery, then your strength isn't unique—and shouldn't be included in this section.

- The strengths should be real. In no instance should you claim an advantage you don't actually possess. Above all else, your business plan document should be truthful; even the littlest of white lies can come back to haunt you big time.

JUST A MINUTE

You will most likely be tempted to list your management team as a core strength of your business. That's okay; *every* company lists their management team as a strength. In reality, of course, this is an extremely subjective strength, unless you've just wooed Bill Gates away from Microsoft to run your product development department. If you insist on including the management team point, then, at least have the good judgment to list it as the final (and least important) bullet point.

WRITING ABOUT YOUR STRENGTHS

How do you write about your company's strengths without it sounding like unmitigated bragging? Here are some points to keep in mind:

- **Turn your features into benefits.** It's always tempting to talk about what you do rather than what you do *for the customer*. You need to go beyond presenting the key features of your business to discuss how those features benefit your customers.

- **State the facts, but don't brag.** There's no need to exaggerate the facts. State what it is you offer without undue embellishment; avoid the temptation to brag about your strengths, and allow your readers to draw their own conclusions.

- **Be concise.** At this point in the business plan document, your readers are ready to call it a day and don't want to be bombarded with yet another long and detailed section. Make each advantage fit within a single paragraph or bullet point and keep it short enough to be easily grazable by your readers.

- **Highlight the key point.** You can enhance grazability by stating the specific advantage in the first sentence of the paragraph and then boldfacing that sentence.

- **Compare to competitors.** For your competitive advantage to be unique, you must compare it to what your competitors offer. If you do X, spend a sentence pointing out that your competitors do Y—and that customers definitely prefer X to Y.

If you follow this advice, you end up with a bullet point that probably looks something like the following example:

Fast, expert installation. From day one, The LightHouse will offer timely and professional distribution and installation services. While most competitors contract with less-reliable third parties to install their lighting products, The LightHouse will utilize a team of professionally trained in-house installers will ensure total control over delivery schedules and installation quality.

Note how this example presents a fundamental competitive advantage. The advantage is stated in the first sentence, simply and in boldface text. The advantage is presented both as a feature (in-house installers) and a benefit (fast, expert, reliable installation). The reason for the benefit is presented (we use in-house installers) and is compared to competitive practices (they use third-party installers). It's all there in a short, easily grazable, *powerful* paragraph.

JUST A MINUTE

Another, more modest way to present your strengths is to let somebody else do it for you. Customer or third-party testimonials can be very persuasive when sprinkled throughout your business plan document. You can include the testimonials within the narrative text, of course, but they might have more impact if separated out into individual sidebars or text boxes.

Presenting Challenges

The challenges to your business are very real and extremely important—which is why they need to be addressed in your business plan document. However, you need to present these challenges in a fashion that doesn't scare away potential lenders and investors; if at all possible, you need to present these challenges in a way that inspires additional confidence in your management abilities.

PROCEED WITH CAUTION

Comparative length is important. The worst business plans devote more space to their challenges than to their strengths. Dwelling on the negative will cast doubts on the viability of your strategy and will make it appear as if your business doesn't have much of a chance to succeed. If anything, your weaknesses should take up *less* space than your strengths and should be presented in a fashion that diminishes their apparent importance.

Choosing Your Challenges

If you want your Challenges section to be no more than a page in length (and shorter is probably better), then you can only include four or five distinct points. Your criteria for deciding which challenges to include should be the mirror image of your criteria for choosing strengths:

- The challenges should have major potential impact on the success of your business strategy. The fact that your chief competitor offers free soft drinks to all its employees might be interesting, but it's not strategically significant.

- The challenges should be immediately visible. This means that you're most likely looking at marketplace challenges, such as higher-quality or lower-cost products, rather than your competitors' internal operational strengths.

- The challenges should be unique. If your competitors all offer special pricing to certain accounts—and you do, too—then it's a competitive wash.

- The challenges should have real impact. Sometimes it looks as if a competitor is doing something truly unique in the marketplace—but unless that activity results in additional revenues or profits, it really doesn't count.

In short, you need to identify four or five things that your competitors are doing better than you are and that have measurable impact on marketplace performance. These are your true competitive challenges and need to be addressed.

JUST A MINUTE

 Sometimes your challenges can be internal. If there is some *thing* that is keeping your company from competing sufficiently in the marketplace—a negative brand image, outmoded processes, or an inexperienced management team—that *thing* should also be identified as a potential challenge to your success.

Turning Challenges into Strengths

Just listing your challenges isn't enough; you need to tell your readers how you're going to respond to those challenges. If all you do is list your problems—without solutions—you come off as both problematic and ineffectual.

Here is some advice to follow when writing about your company's challenges:

- **Identify the challenge.** Don't beat around the bush; get everything out in the open from the start by identifying the problem in the first sentence.

- **Quantify the problem.** If you can quantify the potential impact of the problem (in terms of revenues, profits, customer counts, market share, or whatever), then you should include that number in the text.

- **Get to the root of the problem.** Once you've identified and quantified the problem, discuss what factors are contributing to the issue. Maybe it's something you're doing that you shouldn't be; maybe it's something you should be doing that you're not; maybe it's something your competitors are doing that you can't. Whatever it is, get it out into the open—quickly.

- **Strategize a solution.** Once the challenge is identified, tell the reader how you intend to respond to it. You can try to minimize the impact; you can try to equalize the playing field; you can pledge to improve your own performance. Whatever it is, after you've set up the problem, present your solution—positively and succinctly.

This last point is the most important point. You not only have to identify potential challenges, you have to convince your readers that you have a plan to do something about them. Raise an issue and then address an issue; identify a problem and then propose a solution. That's the key to shifting the Challenges section from a painful listing of problems into a reassuring reflection of your management savvy.

JUST A MINUTE

What do you do if you identify a problem that you can't solve? You have two choices. First, you could choose not to list that issue in the Challenges section of your plan. (That kind of issue avoidance, however, can backfire on you—especially if potential investors subsequently question an issue you've avoided.) Second, you can present the issue without a solution, but with a spin that minimizes its impact. ("Yes, this is a problem—but because we're already doing X, Y, and Z, the impact of this problem is minimal.")

CORE COMPETENCIES AND CHALLENGES CHECKLIST

Use the following checklist to make sure you include the appropriate information in the Core Competencies and Challenges section of your business plan:

Core Competencies and Challenges Checklist

☐ Five to six unique competitive advantages that your firm possesses, in the form of a bulleted list

☐ Four to five potential challenges that your company faces, in the form of a bulleted list

☐ One-sentence solutions to the challenges you identify

☐ Other: _____

☐ Other: _____

☐ Other: _____

HOMEWORK

In this hour, you learned how to create the Core Competencies and Challenges section of your business plan. In Hour 18, "Financials," you'll learn how to write the final section of your business plan, the Financials section.

To prepare for the next hour, please do the following:

- Reread Hour 9, "Build Your Numbers."

- Assemble all available income statements for at least the past three years.

- Have your finance/accounting department prepare a current-period income statement and balance sheet.

- If you've prepared multiple-year revenue and income statement projections, make sure you have a copy; if not, get ready to plan your business performance out over at least a three-year period.

HOUR 18
Financials

CHAPTER SUMMARY

LESSON PLAN:

In this hour, you will learn about ...

- Which financials to include
- Preparing forecasts
- Making your numbers look better

The final section of your business plan document is the Financials section. This is where you present the past, present, and future financial statements of your business.

In a way, the Financials section defines the goals you have for your business. The revenues and profits you project for future years *are* your company's financial goals—they're the yardstick with which you'll measure the success of your business strategy over the next several years.

Even though this section of your plan is only a few pages long, it's important enough to warrant significant attention on your part. Not only must the historical numbers be accurate, the future financials should be believable, achievable, and in synch with the rest of the story you're telling through the business plan. Given this importance, it takes time to get the numbers just right—and to present them in a fashion that has the most impact on your audience.

WHAT FINANCIALS TO INCLUDE

When preparing the Financials section of your plan, the first thing to decide is *which* financial statements to include. If you include too much information, you'll overwhelm the readers and dilute the impact of your most important financial goals. If you include too little information, you'll raise more questions than you answer and possibly inspire doubt on the part of potential lenders and investors. What information you include, then, has to be addressed from a strategic perspective.

CORE FINANCIAL STATEMENTS

GO TO ▶
Refer to Hour 9, "Build Your Numbers," to learn more about creating key financial statements.

Although every business is different, there are a handful of basic financial statements that you should consider including in the Financials section of your business plan document. While you should consult with potential lenders and investors to find out what numbers they expect to see, chances are the list will include some or all of the following:

- **Revenue projection.** Not all businesses need to include a revenue projection separate from that in the pro forma income statements, but if your business generates revenues from a complex assortment of sources, breaking down your projections by type of revenue might be a good idea.

- **Income statements.** One or more income statements are virtual requirements for the vast majority of business plans. A pro forma income statement projecting forward at least three years is a necessity for both old and new businesses, and if you're running an existing business, you should also include current and historical (going back at least three years) income statements.

JUST A MINUTE

If you've adequately condensed your projected income statement, as discussed later in this hour, you can probably fit the multiple-year revenue projection and projected income statement together on a single page.

- **Balance sheet.** If you're just starting up your business, you obviously won't need to include a balance sheet, but if you're running an existing business—and especially if you're presenting to bankers or other lenders—a current balance sheet should be included. (In some rare occasions a projected balance sheet might also be necessary, especially if you're asking for asset-based financing.)

- **Cash flow projection.** Larger investors might not be interested in your cash flow requirements, but lenders will be—as will some smaller investors.

In what order should these financial statements flow? As always, you can control the order to best fit the demands of your audience and your business. However, the normally accepted order for these documents would be as follows:

1. Revenue projection (if included)
2. Income statement projection
3. Income statement current (if included)
4. Income statement historical (if included)
5. Balance sheet (if included)
6. Cash flow projection (if included)

All projected financial statements should be accompanied by a list of the assumptions used to construct the numbers. These assumptions can be in the form of footnotes or endnotes and can (and probably should) be presented in an extremely low-key fashion—this means smaller type without a lot of fancy formatting.

JUST A MINUTE

There is one school of thought that recommends not including *any* financials in your business plan document. The thinking is that the business plan and the financials should be kept separate, so as not to dilute the importance of your business strategy. In this scenario, you present the balance of the business plan document as usual, but after you prepare the financials, you include them in a separate handout.

There are other types of financial statements that, though less-frequently used, you may need to include in your particular business plan. These could include a breakeven analysis, a listing of your capital assets, and other similar documents. Include these if specifically requested to by a potential lender or investor.

How Much Detail?

If you ask your CFO or accountant to prepare your financial statements, he or she is likely to come back with some very detailed documents. It's not unusual for financial folks to prepare income statements, for example, that include every single expense line item you've established on your books. These overly detailed statements will include separate lines for *everything*—even those items that register single-digit amounts!

The reality is that while you might want to see that kind of detail when managing your business on a day-to-day basis, potential lenders and (especially) investors do *not* want or need to see that kind of detail. When people evaluate a potential investment, they want to know that the detail is there, but they only want to see the big picture. Too much detail can overwhelm your audience members and cause them to either lose interest or focus on unimportant particulars.

A better approach is to condense some of the detail into a shorter, easier-to-read format. For example, instead of listing a dozen different line items for paper, toner, staples, pens, and pencils, you can combine all these items into a single office expense category. In fact, some businesses condense all their operating expenses into three major categories—Selling, Research and Development (R&D), and General and Administrative (G&A).

The following figures show the same income statement presented in both detailed and condensed formats; if you work the combinations right, you can fit an entire income statement on just a half page of your business plan document!

If you create condensed financial statements for the business plan document, however, you probably want to carry around copies of the fully detailed financials in your briefcase—to refer to or to hand out *just in case* someone asks for more detail than what's presented in the plan. Along the same lines, if there are certain financial statements that you choose not to include in your plan document—such as a cash flow projection—you should still prepare those documents and include copies in your briefcase in case anyone asks for them when you make your presentation.

Income Statement

Gross Revenues	$	**50,000**
Returns		1,000
Net Revenues		**49,000**
Cost of Goods Sold		25,000
Gross Profit		**24,000**
Gross Margin		49.0%
Operating Expenses		
Advertising		3,000
Trade Shows		1,000
Public Relations		800
Catalogs		1,200
Direct Mail		1,450
Marketing Salaries		3,750
Marketing (other)		1,000
Research		35
Research & Development		1,200
Product Development		800
Testing		350
Prototyping		200
R&D Salaries		2,500
R&D Other		290
General & Administrative		500
Copier Supplies		20
Paper		11
Forms and Literature		8
Furniture		275
Books and reports		40
Computer Software		100
Computer Hardware		1,200
Telephone		75
Rents and Leases		1,000
Electricity		100
Gas		45
Water		120
Utilities (other)		175
Automobile		250
Travel & Entertainment		500
Dues/Subscriptions		100
Total Operating Expenses		**22,094**
Net Profit (Loss)		**1,906**
Net Margin		3.9%

An overly detailed income statement— it's not only hard to read, it's hard to focus on the important numbers!

Income Statement

Gross Revenues	$	**50,000**
Returns		1,000
Net Revenues		**49,000**
Cost of Goods Sold		25,000
Gross Profit		**24,000**
Gross Margin		49.0%
Operating Expenses		
Advertising		12,235
Research & Development		5,340
General & Administrative		4,519
Total Operating Expenses		**22,094**
Net Profit (Loss)		**1,906**
Net Margin		3.9%

The same income statement, with much of the detail condensed into key line items.

PREPARING PROJECTIONS

The key financial statement for most business plans is the projected income statement, sometimes called a pro forma income statement. This is a standard income statement projected forward for a specified period, normally three years. (Note that the three-year period isn't set in stone; some businesses will project forward as far as five years.)

However far ahead you project, you should make sure that the numbers you forecast actually make sense. Is there a logic to the revenue buildup over the period? Do the projected expenses make sense in relation to the projected revenues? Are these numbers realistic? Are they achievable? Are they *comfortable*—to you and to your investors? Bottom line, do the numbers feel right?

JUST A MINUTE

Don't let this discourage you, but many potential lenders and (especially) investors won't look too closely at your financial projections—they'll actually perform their own projections and use them for their analysis. The reason for this is that far too many business plans include totally unrealistic pie-in-the-sky growth projections; an experienced analyst or investor will discount such improbable projections and instead apply his or her own analysis and logic to your business expected performance over time.

There are two basic approaches you can take when preparing a projected income statement—you can build the income statement from the bottom up, or you can build it from the top down.

BOTTOM-UP FORECASTING

A traditional bottom-up forecast requires each department to create future budgets based on their expected expenditures (and, in the case of the sales department, their expected sales) for the designated time period.

For example, instead of saying that you typically spend 1 percent of your total budget on travel and entertainment expenses, you make each manager plan out what trips his or her department will be taking in that time period—and then cost out the individual trips as precisely as possible. You work up your entire expense budget in this fashion and have the sales department work up its revenues on a month-by-month, account-by-account, customer-by-customer basis. The end result, theoretically, is the most accurate projection possible.

There are numerous problems with pure bottom-up forecasting:

- Nobody can really predict the future, so to say with certainty that two people in the HR department will be traveling to Houston in March two years from now is a tad disingenuous.

- The farther out you project, the less accurate your projections will be. This is a problem with *any* forecasting but particularly so with bottom-up planning, which is based on an assumption of total accuracy.

- In a rapidly growing business, you have no idea what will be happening at a fine level of detail in the future; the best you can do is "broad stroke" guessing—which is *not* bottom-up forecasting.

- Bottom-up sales forecasting assumes a precise knowledge of your revenue mix; this is seldom possible with new and growing businesses.

- It's highly unlikely that the numbers you come up with from a bottom-up forecast are the numbers you really want to present to potential investors (this is especially true with revenue projections); chances are, you're going to end up dictating the final numbers anyway, so why even bother with the charade of bottom-up planning?

- The detail involved with bottom-up forecasting will not be appreciated—or even seen—by most people reading the plan document; most investors want to see only rough detail, not the highly granular detail you get with bottom-up budgets.

In short, as nice as bottom-up forecasting might appear on paper, in reality, it's not an efficient method for creating three-year projections for rapidly growing businesses. This means, then, that you need to turn to an alternate method of planning—top-down forecasting.

JUST A MINUTE

The one situation in which bottom-up forecasting might be recommended is if an established, relatively stable business was applying for a loan. Bankers and other lenders tend to be more receptive to (and desirous of) the bottom-up detail and may even want to see a detailed buildup for some of the larger line items.

TOP-DOWN FORECASTING

As much as the strict financial folks like bottom-up planning, that approach doesn't always get you to where you want to go—at least not without a lot of reforecasting. Sometimes a better approach is to start with where you want to go (in terms of total revenues) and then work your way down through the rest of the income statement from there.

Actually, true top-down forecasting starts with a projection of total industry revenues. (Refer to Hour 3, "Analyze Your Market," to learn more about making industry-wide projections.) With this number in hand, you next turn your attention to your market share goal. Multiply the projected industry revenues by your desired market share (expressed as a percent, of course), and the result is the projected revenue number you have to hit to achieve that market share.

Now that you have the top line of your pro forma income statement, you work your way down through the remaining line items on the income statement, applying percentages for those items that are directly linked to sales and plugging in firm numbers for your fixed-cost items. For example, if you know that COGS is always 52 percent of net revenues and your net revenue number was $1 million, then you can pencil in $520,000 as your COGS number for the plan year.

After you've applied and plugged, you should end up with your projected net income for the year.

The main variable expense in any income statement projection is the advertising/marketing/promotions line. In essence, you have to ask the question, "How much money do I have to spend on advertising to achieve the desired market share?" The answer, of course, will have to be a guess. If you're new to a particular industry, you'll have to spend more than industry averages to make your presence known. If you're attempting to gain significant share in a specific year, you'll also have to spend more than industry averages. If all you need to do is maintain your current share, however—and if no new competitors are expected to join the fray in that year—then you can pick an advertising number that's close to your industry's average. Seldom should you forecast a lower-than-average number for advertising—unless you plan to lose market share in that period. Experience dictates that no matter what advertising number you forecast, it's likely that your real spending will exceed it.

The other main benefit of top-down forecasting is that it allows the head of the company to dictate the numbers that he or she wants to present. Accountants and lawyers may want to believe otherwise, but all projections (especially revenue projections) are manipulated to some degree, based on the story that the owner or president wants to tell—and on what he or she personally feels comfortable presenting. If you assume that the boss will dictate the revenue number, you're automatically in a top-down planning mode; you work backward from that dictated top-line number to fill in the rest of the income statement and produce the desired net profit number (also typically dictated by the president).

FORMATTING FOR IMPACT

The way in which numbers are typically integrated into business plan documents is a travesty.

Far too many business plans contain 20 or 30 pages of well-thought-out, professionally formatted, great-looking text—until they come to the Financials section. Then the great-looking document gets pretty ugly, with rows and columns of small, unreadable numbers in a typeface that's different from that used previously, with none of the professional formatting the reader has come to expect. The worst of these disastrous documents feature financial statements formatted in landscape mode, so the reader has to turn the document sideways to read the numbers.

If your business plan looks like this, you've just jeopardized your ability not only to attract funding but also to successfully implement your business strategy.

WHY NUMBERS LOOK BAD

Why does the Financials section of the average business plan look so bad? Well ... there are several potential reasons why a great-looking business plan might have an ugly Financials section—none of which are insurmountable. Here are the most common excuses:

- **"Someone else prepared the financials."** If you're the person responsible for creating the final business plan document, you're abrogating your responsibility if you let anyone supply information that you just plug into the document, sight unseen. It's okay for the financial folks to put together the numbers, but then it's your job to make them look good and to make them fit in with the rest of the document.

- **"The financial people didn't provide an electronic file—all I could do was copy the printouts they gave me."** This isn't a good excuse at all for several reasons. First, you know that the financial folks used a spreadsheet program (probably Excel) to create the numbers, so the numbers definitely exist electronically. Second, if the financial people won't give you the electronic file—probably because they're afraid you'll mess with their numbers—you have to convince them that you're part of the same team and that they have to trust you, even if you don't have an accounting degree. Third, even if you didn't get the numbers electronically, you can still hand-key them into a Microsoft Word table or into your own Excel spreadsheet. Ask the financial folks what is worse—you formatting their electronic spreadsheet or them risking the possibility that you might incorrectly enter a number or two while you're doing it by hand.

- **"We had to shrink it to fit it all on a single page."** One response to this situation is to split the spreadsheet in two (between the revenue and expense sections of an income statement, for example), but a better solution is to simplify the spreadsheet. When a large spreadsheet won't fit on a page, it's typically because the numbers people have included way too much detail—especially for the intended audience. You don't need or want to show two dozen lines of expense items, for example; combining all the minor expenses into major categories not only shrinks the spreadsheet, it also makes it easier to read from the 10,000-foot level.

JUST A MINUTE

If you do decide to combine categories, make sure you do it with the help of one of the financial people—just to make sure you combine things into the correct categories.

- **"The financial people didn't give me the numbers until the very last minute, so I didn't have time to format them."** This excuse reeks of bad project management. Yes, it's common for the numbers to be the very last part of the plan to get finalized; senior management (is that you?) has a tendency to tweak the numbers until the last possible moment. However, this last-minute playing around with the numbers should not impact your ability to create an impactive, successful business plan. Establish a cutoff time for changes and enforce it. If changes come in after that point, delay the plan to effect the changes properly.
- **"That's the way the numbers people expect financial statements to look."** This is the only excuse that has some validity; there is a theory that the uglier the numbers (in terms of style, not in how they add up!), the more likely it is that the financial people will trust them.

However, you're probably not handing this document over to a group of accountants. The people who make decisions about investments are seldom pure numbers people; if they were, you wouldn't have taken the time and trouble to write the 20-odd pages of text in front of the Financials section.

Everyone involved with the creation of the business plan needs to understand that it's a sales and marketing document and that *everything* in the document has to be presented as if it were appearing in a really big sales brochure or annual report. There is zero harm in creating an attractive-looking Financials section; there is much risk in not doing so.

The bottom line is that there is no excuse for including an unattractive Financials section in your business plan. Do whatever you have to do to ensure that you have the time and the resources to make the numbers look as attractive as possible—at least from a style standpoint!

CHOOSING A STYLE

The worst way to present a financial statement in your business plan is to Xerox a copy of a report originally output on greenbar paper run through a dot-matrix printer. Compared to that, any formatting you do will represent significant improvement.

There are several things you can do to improve the looks of your financial statements:

- **Use an appropriate font.** The first thing to do is to present the numbers in a readable fashion. This means picking an appropriate and readable font—either the same font you use in the main text of your document, or a clean sans serif font, such as Arial or Helvetica, that looks good at smaller sizes.

- **Shrink the type.** To fit a multiple-column spreadsheet onto a single page, you'll probably need to reduce the type size you use in your financial statements. If you use an 11- or 12-point type for your main text, try an 8-, 9-, or (at most) 10-point type for your numbers.

- **Use dollar signs sparingly.** You should include dollar signs for the very first row of numbers and maybe the very last row, but leave all the other numbers plain. Make sure you're using a standard comma format for your numbers but make minimal use of the dollar sign—it's assumed.

- **Present in 000s.** If you're running a very large business, consider dropping the thousands from your numbers—so that ten thousand is represented as just 10 instead of 10,000. If you do this, make sure you note "in 000s" somewhere on each page. If you're running a smaller business, don't worry about this; just present your numbers as normal. (Along the same lines, you should *never* include cents in your financials—it's not significant, and it clutters the page.)

- **Indent appropriately.** If you're including a level or two of detail in your income statement, remember to indent those items that are combined into a larger number. For example, you may list several components that add up to a total advertising number; as shown in the following figure, you would indent the individual line items, and leave the total Advertising line flush left.

Indenting items that contribute to a category total or subtotal—and underlining the final row in the series to be totaled.

Income Statement

Gross Revenues	**$ 50,000**
Returns	1,000
Net Revenues	**49,000**
Cost of Goods Sold	25,000
Gross Profit	**24,000**
Gross Margin	49.0%
Operating Expenses	
Advertising	3,000
Trade Shows	1,000
Public Relations	800
Catalogs	1,200
Direct Mail	1,450
Marketing Salaries	3,750
Marketing (other)	1,000
Total Advertising	**12,200**

- **Underline the columns to total.** An income statement is nothing more than a series of additions and subtractions. Whenever you get to a line that totals several preceding rows, make sure you place a line underneath the last row to be totaled.

- **Highlight important line items.** You need to draw the reader's eyes to the most important line items in your income statement—in particular, the Gross Profit, Total Operating Expenses, Net Profit (or EBITDA) lines. There are a number of ways to do this. You can boldface those line items, apply borders above or below them, display them in a different color, apply shading, or use any combination of these effects (see the following figure). (Note, however, that while shading looks good on an original copy of your document, it doesn't photocopy well—and can make it difficult to read the numbers if your readers make their own copies of your plan.)

Income Statement

	2002	2003	2004
Net Revenues	$ 50,000	$ 65,000	$ 80,000
Cost of Goods Sold	25,000	32,500	40,000
Gross Profit	**25,000**	**32,500**	**40,000**
Gross Margin	50.0%	50.0%	50.0%
Operating Expenses			
Salaries	8,000	9,000	10,000
Advertising	3,000	4,000	5,000
Marketing	2,500	3,000	4,000
Selling	2,500	3,000	3,500
Research & Development	2,000	2,500	3,000
General & Administrative	500	600	700
Rents and Leases	1,000	1,000	1,000
Utilities	500	550	600
Automobile	250	300	350
Travel & Entertainment	500	650	750
Dues/Subscriptions	100	120	150
Loan Payments	400	400	400
Total Operating Expenses	**21,250**	**25,120**	**29,450**
Net Profit (Loss)	**3,750**	**7,380**	**10,550**
Net Margin	7.5%	11.4%	13.2%

Using boldfacing and other effects to highlight key lines.

- **Use fancy headings.** To create a more professional appearance for your financial statements, apply various types of formatting effects to your column headings. You can use boldface, italics, different typefaces and type sizes, shading, and other formatting effects. The following figure shows the yearly columns formatted with black background and reverse white type.

Income Statement

	2002	2003	2004
Net Revenues	$ 50,000	$ 65,000	$ 80,000
Cost of Goods Sold	25,000	32,500	40,000
Gross Profit	**25,000**	**32,500**	**40,000**
Gross Margin	50.0%	50.0%	50.0%
Operating Expenses			
Salaries	8,000	9,000	10,000
Advertising	3,000	4,000	5,000
Marketing	2,500	3,000	4,000
Selling	2,500	3,000	3,500
Research & Development	2,000	2,500	3,000
General & Administrative	500	600	700
Rents and Leases	1,000	1,000	1,000
Utilities	500	550	600
Automobile	250	300	350
Travel & Entertainment	500	650	750
Dues/Subscriptions	100	120	150
Loan Payments	400	400	400
Total Operating Expenses	**21,250**	**25,120**	**29,450**
Net Profit (Loss)	**3,750**	**7,380**	**10,550**
Net Margin	7.5%	11.4%	13.2%

Applying formatting effects to column headers for a more professional look.

JUST A MINUTE

You can also apply formatting effects to section headers within your financial statement. For example, you can format your income statement to highlight headings for the Revenues, Cost of Sales, and Operating Expenses sections.

- **Use color.** Even though the numbers people might be shocked, it's okay to use different colors throughout your financial statements. The most common use of color, of course, is to present any losses in red. You can also use color for your column and section headers and for your major line items such as Gross Profit and Net Income.

- **Highlight the total column.** When you're presenting a three- or five-year projection, you might also want to present a final column that totals the numbers for that time period. This Total Period column should then be set off from the normal yearly columns; you can do this by changing color or applying shading (see the following figure).

Adding a Total Period column (to show total revenue and expenses over a multiple-year period) and setting it off with light shading.

Income Statement

	2002	2003	2004	3-Year Period
Net Revenues	$ 50,000	$ 65,000	$ 80,000	$ 195,000
Cost of Goods Sold	25,000	32,500	40,000	97,500
Gross Profit	25,000	32,500	40,000	97,500
Gross Margin	50.0%	50.0%	50.0%	50.0%
Operating Expenses				
Salaries	8,000	9,000	10,000	27,000
Advertising	3,000	4,000	5,000	12,000
Marketing	2,500	3,000	4,000	9,500
Selling	2,500	3,000	3,500	9,000
Research & Development	2,000	2,500	3,000	7,500
General & Administrative	500	600	700	1,800
Rents and Leases	1,000	1,000	1,000	3,000
Utilities	500	550	600	1,650
Automobile	250	300	350	900
Travel & Entertainment	500	650	750	1,900
Dues/Subscriptions	100	120	150	370
Loan Payments	400	400	400	1,200
Total Operating Expenses	**21,250**	**25,120**	**29,450**	**75,820**
Net Profit (Loss)	**3,750**	**7,380**	**10,550**	**21,680**
Net Margin	7.5%	11.4%	13.2%	11.1%

FINANCIALS CHECKLIST

Use the following checklist to determine which financial statements to include in the Financials section of your business plan:

Financials Checklist

- ☐ Three- or five-year projected income statement
- ☐ Current-period financial statement
- ☐ Three- or five-year historical income statement
- ☐ Current-period balance sheet
- ☐ Three- or five-year revenue projection (optional)
- ☐ Three- or five-year cash-flow projection (optional)
- ☐ Other: _____
- ☐ Other: _____
- ☐ Other: _____

HOMEWORK

In this hour, you learned how to create the Financials section of your business plan—and thus complete the main text of your business plan document. In Hour 19, "Appendixes and Attachments," you'll learn about other information you may want to include with your plan.

To prepare for the next hour, please do the following:

- Think about what other information, not currently in the plan document, you may want to present to potential investors.

- Assemble copies of your most recent or most important press releases.

- Assemble or arrange to print copies of any company profiles that have recently appeared in any newspapers or magazines.

- Assemble any key market data that was cut from the Opportunity section of the plan.

- Determine whether there are any analyst or research reports about your industry or your company that should be included with your plan.

- Consider whether product brochures, information sheets, or catalogs would be of value to potential investors.

- Read through the plan document as it currently exists and ask yourself whether it includes jargon, buzzwords, or acronyms that potential lenders or investors might not understand.

- Consider whether there is any value of including screenshots from your company's Web site in the plan.

PART IV
Plan the Package

Hour 19

Appendixes and Attachments

Chapter Summary

LESSON PLAN:

In this hour, you will learn about …

- Adding appendixes to your plan
- Supplying supplementary information
- Displaying less important information as an appendix

The best business plans are those that pack a powerful punch in a limited number of pages. When it comes to impact, shorter is always better.

In your quest to create a short and powerful document, however, you often have to excise all but the most essential information. There might be additional information that some lenders and investors might be interested in reading, even though it doesn't rightfully have a place in the main business plan document.

How can you keep your plan concise and effective yet still present interesting supplementary information? It's easy; all you have to do is add the extra information as an appendix or an attachment.

The difference between an appendix and an attachment is that an appendix is created as part of the document itself in your word processor, continues the numbering of your main document, and appears as part of your document's table of contents. An attachment is a separate document added to the end of your business plan document. Both are discussed in this hour.

How and When to Use Appendixes and Attachments

You use appendixes and attachments to include information that is important to your business strategy (and of interest to potential lenders and investors) but not integral to the presentation of your business plan. In other words, you put the less important information in the back of the plan, out of the way but still accessible.

Your appendixes should start after the last page of your main document's Financials section and should retain the numbering of the main part of the plan. Think of your appendixes as a new section, titled Appendixes, using the same level heading as the plan's other main sections.

Each individual appendix (and you can include as many as you want) should be assigned a distinct letter as its official head (Appendix A, Appendix B, and so on), should use the same level heading as other subheads in your document, and (this is probably different from other subheads) should each start on a new page.

When you view your appendixes in outline form, it should look something like this:

Appendixes

    A. Glossary

    B. Supplemental Market Data

    C. Company History

    D. Key Processes

        Product Development

        Shipping and Packing

    E. Web Pages

    F. Attachments

Note that this outline includes a separate subhead for Attachments. Since attachments are separate documents that are bound into the back of your plan document by your printer, they will not pick up the format or page numbering of the rest of your document. It's advisable, then, to make the last numbered page of your document lead into your (unnumbered) attachments. (Obviously, this Attachments page will be blank except for the header text itself.)

Adding appendixes to your document is easy; just keep typing in your word processor. Adding attachments, however, is slightly more complicated. You'll need to obtain the appropriate quantity of these supplemental documents to match the number of business plans you intend to print, and you should deliver the supplemental documents to your printer when you drop off your main document for printing. Your printer, then, will bind your attachments into the back of your document, immediately following the last printed page—this is why you want the last printed page to include your Attachments subhead.

JUST A MINUTE

If you don't have appropriate quantities of an attachment, you can ask your printer to make additional copies at the same time your plan document is being printed.

POTENTIAL SUPPLEMENTS TO YOUR BUSINESS PLAN

You could include any number of different items as appendixes or attachments to your business plan document. Essentially, any information that you think would be of value to potential lenders or investors (that does not fit well within the main narrative text) could be included as an appendix or attachment. The next few pages detail some of the more common items to consider.

ADDITIONAL MARKET DATA

It's sometimes easy to include too much market data in the Opportunity section of your business plan. Too much data results in overkill, however, and can often detract from the main points you're trying to make.

For that reason, supplementary market data is often presented in the form of an appendix. This may be data related but not directly relevant to the core data, or it may be detail several levels below the main data you presented earlier. In any case, if you think the data is important but you don't want to include it in the Opportunity section, throw it into an appendix labeled Supplementary Market Data.

Although you could include additional data as Web page printouts or copies of magazine articles, it would be much more professional to present supplemental market data as a full text-and-graphs appendix, in much the same style as your main Opportunity section.

ANALYST AND RESEARCH REPORTS

If your industry has been covered by financial analysts or market research firms, there may be information in those analyst or research reports that could prove interesting and useful to your potential lenders and investors. You may want to consider reproducing some or all of such a report and including it as an attachment to your plan.

Some research reports can be reproduced freely; some can't. Make sure you obtain any permissions necessary to reproduce a market report in your business plan. Reports that are sold for a high price might not be available to use in this manner—or may require you to pay a hefty fee to include them in your business plan.

If you choose to reproduce the entire report, consider asking the originating firm for official copies. If this is unfeasible for any reason, have your copy of the report professionally copied for your attachments; do *not* attempt to make copies on your own.

If you choose to reproduce only portions of the report, consider retyping the sections you want directly into your plan document (as an appendix) rather than photocopying only specific pages for inclusion. Some readers will see the "page 3" you included and wonder where pages 1, 2, and 4 are; if you retype specific sections (and format the contents similarly to the rest of your document), the information can be clearly positioned as an excerpt from the broader report.

NEWS STORIES

Along the same lines, if you or your company have been featured in a newspaper or magazine article, you may want to include a copy of that article as an attachment to your plan. (Do this only if it was a positive article, of course!)

The best way to include a newspaper or magazine article is to ask the originating publication for official copies and then have your printer bind those copies into the back of your business plan document as attachments. The copies you get from the original publication will be a lot cleaner and more professional looking than any photocopies you might make yourself.

If you can't get official reprints from the publication, let your neighborhood Kinko's-type printer make copies for you from the best available original article you can get your hands on. Your printer may be able to pull off some graphics magic to improve the printed quality of the article, making changes you wouldn't be able to achieve with a standard copier.

PRESS RELEASES

Another common attachment is the company press release—especially those announcing strategic initiatives, important additions to your management team, and major new products. Although you probably have the press release in an electronic format that could be poured into your business plan document template, it's better to leave the press releases in their native format so they stand out as separate documents from your main document.

Take care not to include too many press releases, however; some potential investors will view them as the company-produced propaganda they are and will automatically dismiss them. Along the same lines, you may want to consider adding any press releases as the last attachments to your plan, ensuring that the reader will get to the more important information first.

JUST A MINUTE

Recognizing the typically high fluff quotient of the average press release, you may want to rewrite any press release you include with your plan. Focus on the key information and feel free to delete the standard company blurb and press contact found at the end of most press releases.

PRODUCT INFORMATION

You should be able to spend a paragraph or two in the main narrative of your document talking about each of your most important products and services. If that isn't enough space, consider attaching one or more product information sheets to the back of your plan.

As with all attachments, any product information sheets you use should be bound into the back of the document when your document is printed. That means supplying your printer with the correct number of product sheets when you drop off your document for printing.

BROCHURES AND MARKETING MATERIALS

If product information sheets can be included with your plan, how about brochures, catalogs, and other marketing materials?

Most businesses choose *not* to include these types of blatant marketing materials with their plan documents, for one or more of the following reasons:

- Brochures push your products; your business plan pushes your business. Your marketing materials may not be relevant to an audience that is interested in your overall business, not your individual products.

- The style and image implied by your marketing materials may not be in synch with the image you choose to present in your business plan. (In other words, your product brochures may not present as professional an image as you're presenting in your plan document.)

- Brochures and catalogs most likely cannot be bound into the back of your business plan document. Any freestanding materials you provide to your readers increase the clutter factor and can possibly dilute the impact of your business plan.

- If your brochures and marketing materials are really great looking (good for you!), they may actually draw attention away from your main plan document.

On the other hand, brochures and other marketing materials do illustrate exactly what it is that your company is selling and help present your business's professional image. If you choose to include these types of items, make sure that they're of a sufficiently professional quality to advance your cause and that they reinforce the main points you stress in your business plan. Since you probably won't be able to bind these materials into your plan document, consider including them in a separate pocketed folder—which should bear your company's logo, of course.

HISTORY AND ACCOMPLISHMENTS

Whether your company has been in existence one month or one decade, it most likely has registered several important accomplishments. You may want to list those accomplishments in a Company History appendix in the back of your business plan. This type of appendix might also be called Accomplishments, Key Milestones, or Important Events.

When you list your company history or accomplishments, consider these points:

- Make sure the events you list are truly of strategic importance. Opening your first bank account might have been a moment of pride for you personally, but potential lenders and investors are likely to be less impressed.

- Don't list too many events; make sure you're picking only the relevant highlights.

- Consider grouping events by month or (for older businesses) by quarter or year.

- Present your highlights in a visual format that can be easily grazed. A table is always good (one column for date, another for event), as is the use of a graphic (see the following figure).

Q4 2000	Q1 2001	Q2 2001	Q3 2001	Q4 2001
Company founded	Senior management team hired	Software development launched	Prototype Web site launched	Software V1 released
Initial funding raised	Development team hired	Web site development initiated	Software enters beta testing	Web site goes live
	Company moves into current facilities	Sales and marketing staff hired	Initial teaser advertising	First sales recorded

Presenting your historical accomplishments via a graphical timeline.

WEB PAGES

You may have shown one or more pages from your Web site earlier in your plan document. If not—and if you have a Web site and it's of strategic importance—you should consider adding a page or two of Web site screenshots as a separate appendix.

What pages should you show? Your home page is always good, as are one or more representative product or service pages. If you have any unique features on your Web site, consider showing them as well. Don't overdo it, however, and remember to label each screenshot—and definitely include your site's URL so your readers can check it out themselves.

JUST A MINUTE

You can use any number of screen capture or graphics programs, such as FullShot or Paint Shop Pro, to take screenshots of your Web pages. Before you capture a screen, consider configuring your Web browser to full screen status, or at the very least remove any excess toolbars and menu bars. You want to show as much of your Web page as possible, with as little browser clutter as possible.

GLOSSARY

If you're in a particularly jargon-filled industry (and who isn't?), it's likely that some of your readers will be unfamiliar with the industry-speak you've undoubtedly peppered throughout your business plan. For the benefit of potential lenders and investors not fully familiar with your industry, consider including a short glossary of terms as an appendix to your plan document.

Any glossary you include should be short (a single page is good) and should include only those terms that you've actually used in your business plan. Each term should start on a new line; the term should be in bold, followed by a tab and then the term's definition (*not* in bold). Keep the definitions concise and remember to include definitions for any acronyms you've used in your plan.

The following figure shows what a typical glossary might look like.

ADDITIONAL FINANCIALS

If you chose to present a limited number of financial statements in your plan's Financials section, but you think that some potential lenders or investors might want more detailed financial information, consider including additional financial statements as appendixes to your plan. These supplemental financials might include revenue projections, asset inventories, and other similar schedules.

JUST A MINUTE

In reality, putting extra financial statements at the end of the Financials section has the same effect as creating a separate appendix for the additional financials. Alternately, you can prepare the additional financials but not include them in your plan document; instead, you can personally hand out copies of any requested documents direct to your audience.

B. Glossary

You can add a glossary to define terms with which readers might not be familiar.

2G	The second generation of cellular phones and networks; unlike the analog first generation, 2G phones and networks incorporate digital technology.
3G	The upcoming third generation of cellular phones and networks, designed for high-speed data transfer in addition to standard voice communication.
asymmetrical	A type of connection that operates at two different speeds upstream and downstream.
asynchronous	A type of connection that permits data to flow in only one direction at a time. Also known as *half-duplex*.
authentication	The process of verifying the identity of a device on the other end of a connection.
authorization	The process of granting a specific device access to a particular service.
bit	Describes a single binary digit, either a 1 or a 0. Eight bits equal one *byte*.
byte	Eight bits.
client	In a client/server relationship between two devices, the client is the device that pushes or pulls data from the other device *(server)*.
connect	The establishment of a temporary link between two devices.
device class	A particular type of device. For example, all Bluetooth-enabled mobile phones are in one device class, where all Bluetooth-enabled PDAs are in another device class.
device discovery	The process of identifying and paging another device.
discovery	The process wherein a remote device becomes aware of the network to which it is connected.
flow control	A procedure used to control the transfer of data between two devices.
frequency hopping	An RF technology that enables a single signal to jump from one frequency to another, in order to reduce interference and increase security.
full-duplex	See *synchronous*.
gateway	A device that connects one or more other devices to an external network.
half-duplex	See *asynchronous*.
handset	That part of a telephone that contains a microphone and an earphone speaker, and (in many instances) dialing and disconnect functions.
headset	A combination microphone and earpiece speaker used to facilitate telephone-based conversations.
hidden computing	The concept of accessing and controlling a computer from a remoter device.

IT Infrastructure

If you chose not to include a detailed list of your IT hardware and software in the plan's Organization and Operations section, you can use an appendix to present this information. Consider using a table or bulleted list and don't shy away from small type sizes to present fairly long lists.

SUPPLEMENTAL SCHEDULES

Along these same lines, there might be other schedules of interest to enough readers to include them as appendixes to your plan document. These schedules might include sales discount schedules, commission schedules, and other similar items.

DETAILED PROCESSES

There may be some processes that are key to your business that could stand to be illustrated—but not in the main narrative of your document. Consider presenting the appropriate graphics, flow charts, or tables for theses processes in one or more appendixes at the back of your plan.

INVESTOR LISTS

Potential investors may be interested in seeing how many previous investors have put money into your business. (In fact, some investors might demand to see this information.) Obviously, this is information that doesn't belong in the main part of your business plan, but it is ideally suited to presentation in an appendix.

As with any list, consider using a table or bulleted list to present the information. If you choose to include numerical data (shares owned, dollars invested, and so on) along with the basic list of names, definitely use a table to present the information.

JUST A MINUTE

If your investor list includes a lot of relatively small investors, you may want to list only large investors (above a certain amount) individually. Smaller investors can be grouped together into an "Other" category, enabling you to avoid publishing a potentially questionable long list of names.

MANAGEMENT BIOS

GO TO ▶
See Hour 16, "Management," to learn more about the management bios in your business plan.

If you didn't list management bios in a separate Management section, they should be included as an appendix. You may also want to use an appendix to list additional levels of your management team that would have been inappropriate to include as part of your main document.

OTHER DETAIL FROM YOUR MAIN NARRATIVE

Once you get the hang of using appendixes for supplementary information, you may want to revisit the main body of your plan document to look for any information that can be shifted from the front to the back of the document. Look for information—typically in the Opportunity and Organization and Operations sections—that doesn't absolutely positively support the main thrust of your business strategy. If the information is more interesting than essential, cut it out and put it in an appendix instead.

APPENDIXES AND ATTACHMENTS CHECKLIST

Use the following checklist to determine which supplementary information to include in your business plan:

Potential Appendixes and Attachments Checklist

- ☐ Additional market data
- ☐ Analyst and research reports
- ☐ News stories
- ☐ Press releases
- ☐ Product information
- ☐ Brochures and marketing information
- ☐ History and accomplishments
- ☐ Web pages
- ☐ Glossary
- ☐ Additional financials
- ☐ IT infrastructure
- ☐ Supplemental schedules
- ☐ Detailed processes
- ☐ Investor lists
- ☐ Management bios
- ☐ Other detail from your main narrative
- ☐ Other: _____
- ☐ Other: _____
- ☐ Other: _____

HOMEWORK

In this hour, you learned how to choose which information to include as appendixes and attachments to your main business plan. In Hour 20, "Table of Contents and Index," you'll learn how to improve the navigation of your plan document through the use of tables of contents, indexes, and other auxiliary elements.

To prepare for the next hour, please do the following:

- Acquaint yourself with the table of contents and indexing features of your word processing program.

- Examine your business plan document in outline view and evaluate your choice of headings and subheadings throughout.

- Read through your business plan and look for background information or references that don't need to be embedded in the narrative text— and that might be better presented as footnotes or endnotes.

Hour 20
Table of Contents and Index

Chapter Summary

LESSON PLAN:

In this hour, you will learn about ...

- Organizing your document
- Creating a table of contents
- Creating an index
- Incorporating footnotes and endnotes

At this point, we will assume you've written the first draft of your business plan document. We'll also assume you used some version of Microsoft Word to do the writing and that your business plan is contained in a Word document file. (Even if you used a different word processing program, such as WordPerfect, the navigational and formatting features should be similar.) Now it's time to start thinking about what the final form of your document will look like.

In the next hour (Hour 21, "Format and Print") you'll learn a variety of ways to format your business plan document. Before you begin your final formatting, however, this hour will show you how to add key elements that will help your readers navigate your plan document.

The concept of document navigation concerns the ability to find the things you want to find within a longer document. One reader might want to go directly to some key market information or jump directly to the financial statements; another might want to find information relating to a particular hot topic. The easier it is to find specific information, the more useful your business plan will be. It's definitely in your best interest to incorporate elements that improve the navigability of your document.

THE ELEMENTS OF NAVIGATION

If you have a very short document—a half-dozen pages or less—elements specific to navigation aren't really necessary; the document is short enough to thumb through and find anything you might be specifically looking for. With longer documents, however, it becomes increasingly more difficult to find information just by flipping through the pages.

In the case of your business plan, you have a document that is 20 or more pages in length—possibly much longer when you factor in appendixes. It would be expecting too much to ask your readers to reference specific information by scanning page after page after page; instead, you need to offer additional routes into your document to facilitate direct access to specific information.

The most basic navigational element is the page number. In fact, all other navigation elements depend on the presence of page numbers because they reference specific numbered pages. So if you do nothing else, make sure you number your pages!

When you're dealing with documents the size of your business plan, it's a good idea to organize the information into distinct sections, which you do by using varying levels of heads and subheads. This way, the information flows easily from top to bottom, and—when using Word's Outline view—you can visually see just how your document is organized.

If you've organized your document properly, you can create a kind of outline view for your readers by adding a table of contents (TOC) at the front of your document. The TOC lists the heads and specified subheads within your document, along with the page numbers of each section. A reader wanting to find a specific section of your document need only reference the TOC and then turn to the appropriate page.

Finally, some business plans will incorporate an index of important topics and terms. The index is located at the very end of the document and lists the key words and phrases used, along with the page numbers indicating where those words and phrases appear. A reader looking for a specific topic—market size, let's say—would look up that topic in the index and then turn to the page(s) where that topic appears.

You don't have to incorporate all (or any) of these navigation elements in your specific plan. Note, however, that the less navigation you accommodate, the more likely it is that your readers won't be able to reference key information—and we all know that dissatisfied readers diminish your plan's chances for success. Smart businesspeople embrace any opportunity to make their business plans more effective; adding navigational elements is a relatively easy task that can generate untold benefits.

ADDING PAGE NUMBERS

The easiest navigational element to add to your business plan document is numbered pages. Page numbers are typically incorporated in the *header* or *footer*, and can help readers find their place as they read through your document.

STRICTLY SPEAKING

The **header** is the thin strip across the top of a page, above the normal text. The **footer** is a similar strip along the bottom of a page, below the normal text. Headers and footers are typically used to present informational and navigational information such as page numbers, headings, titles, dates, and the like.

You can add page numbers to your document manually or automatically.

MANUAL PAGE NUMBERS

If your document includes subsidiary documents inserted within the normal page flow, you may need to manually number your pages. You can add manual page numbers in several different ways, including the following:

- Hand numbering—recommended only if you have very neat handwriting
- Stamps, using some sort of ink stamping device
- Press-on numbers
- Using a typewriter to type numbers at the bottom of each page

TIME SAVER

If you opt for manual page numbering, make sure you number the pages *before* the document is printed—otherwise, you'll have to manually number each individual copy of your plan!

AUTOMATIC PAGE NUMBERS

An easier and more versatile approach is to number the pages automatically within Microsoft Word. Not only can Word add page numbers (and update them interactively), the program can also use the page numbers to link to other navigational elements such as tables of contents and indexes. You will typically place page numbers in the header or footer of your document, by using Word's automatic page numbering feature.

WHERE TO START NUMBERING

If you add a basic automatic page number in Microsoft Word, every page of your document will be numbered—including the title page and the table of contents page. This isn't good form.

To make your business plan look as professional as possible, you want both your title page and your TOC to be unnumbered. In other words, you want the first page of your Executive Summary to be page 1 of your document.

ALTERNATIVE NUMBER FORMATS

In most cases, you want your pages to flow in the traditional 1, 2, 3 format. There are alternative number formats you can use, however, including the following:

- A, B, C
- a, b, c
- I, II, III
- i, ii, iii

You can even choose to number your document's "chapters" (first-level headings) and display page numbers in the format of "chapter-page," such as 1-2 or 2-A.

ASSIGNING HEADINGS

Back in Hour 7, "Create Your Outline," you learned how to create a basic outline for your business plan document. Key to that outline was assigning various levels of headings and subheadings to the different sections of your document.

You can create headings by formatting regular text to be larger and bolder, or you can use Microsoft Word's built-in *styles* to automatically format different levels of headings. The latter method is not only easier (once you get the hang of it) but also more versatile because it enables you to use the styles to automatically create a table of contents.

STRICTLY SPEAKING

Within Microsoft Word, a **style** is a set of preselected formatting options that can be applied to individual paragraphs within your document.

Word includes several built-in heading styles, labeled Heading 1, Heading 2, Heading 3, and Heading 4. These styles come preformatted, but you can change their individual formatting if you so desire. How these styles look is not important at this point; it's only important that you use these styles within your document.

GO TO ▶
See Hour 21, "Format and Print," to learn how to format Word's styles.

The best way to format your headings is to apply the Heading 1 style to the major headings within your document—Executive Summary, Vision, Mission, Opportunity, and so on. The next level of headings should be assigned to the Heading 2 style, and if you have a third level of headings, use the Heading 3 style.

PROCEED WITH CAUTION

You can create your own styles within Word to use with your headings, but you'll end up creating a lot more work for yourself when it comes to compiling your TOC. A better approach is to use the built-in Heading 1–type styles and then reformat those styles to match the overall design of your document.

BUILDING A TABLE OF CONTENTS

If you used Word's built-in heading styles for your document's major headings, you can easily create a table of contents (TOC) for your business plan. This TOC should be located just before the Executive Summary and ideally should occupy no more than one page.

As you can see in the following figure, a TOC is an essential overview of your entire document. You can choose various formats for your TOC, as well as select how many levels of headings to display. For example, you can choose to have your TOC display only your first-level headings (Opportunity,

Business Strategy, and so forth), or you can choose to also display second- and/or third-level headings. The most common approach is to include first- and second-level headings only; moving down to the third level complicates (and lengthens) the TOC unnecessarily.

Table of Contents

Microsoft Word has the capability to automatically generate TOCs, based on its default heading styles. This feature is found (in most versions of Word) by pulling down the Insert menu and selecting the Index and Tables command. (See the specific documentation for your version of Word for more detailed instructions.)

INCORPORATING AN INDEX

Although most business plans feature a table of contents, fewer incorporate an index. Indexes are definitely useful with very long documents (such as this book!) but have less value with shorter documents.

However, if you think your readers will want to look up specific topics that aren't easily referenced from the TOC, you should consider including an index such as the one shown in the following figure. Know, however, that creating an index is a much more complicated procedure than creating a TOC, and it will require quite a bit more time and effort on your part.

The reason indexing is so complicated is that your word processing program has no way to tell which words or phrases should be indexed. The program *could* index every word, but you don't want every word indexed; you only want to index the *important* words, and Word can't tell which words are important and which aren't.

Because of this, the only way to create an index in Microsoft Word is for you to manually select which words and phrases to include. As you might expect, this is very time consuming. (See the documentation for your specific version of Word for explicit instructions.) Once you've selected the word list, however, creating the index itself is a snap—as easy as creating a TOC.

USING FOOTNOTES AND ENDNOTES

Footnotes and endnotes are not navigational elements per se, but they do appear outside the normal text—even though they're connected to specific points in your text. Footnotes and endnotes are used to annotate your document, typically to reference data sources or add other information that doesn't need to appear within the narrative text itself. A common use of footnotes/endnotes is in the Opportunity section of your plan, to indicate the sources for the market data you quote.

An index enables readers to look up major topics that wouldn't normally appear in a TOC.

Index

As you can see in the following figure, a footnote appears at the bottom of your normal text, on the same page as the *reference mark*.

The **reference mark** is the number or other character that appears in the text and links to the information in the footnote or endnote.

Endnotes appear at the end of your document in a long list that includes all the endnotes inserted throughout your entire document. Whether you use footnotes or endnotes is a matter of choice—but you should use one or the other, never both. Footnotes are slightly more intrusive than endnotes; endnotes, however, require an added effort to reference.

You can use footnotes to include additional information about specific information in your text.

Factors contributing to this projected growth in U.S. wireless subscribers include:

- Declining airtime costs
- Simplified pricing plans and reduction (or elimination) of roaming and long distance fees
- Shift to digital service (PCS—a subset of the total digital market—currently represents 21% of all wireless subscribers, projected to increase to 40% by 2003[3]
- Improved wireless coverage
- Increasing availability of and demand for Internet-based wireless applications

---

[1] The Yankee Group National Tele-Trend Data

[2] Donaldson, Lufkin & Jenrette, *The Global Wireless Communications Industry* (Summer, 1999)

[3] Strategy Analytics

NAVIGATION ELEMENTS CHECKLIST

Use the following checklist to determine which navigation elements to include in your business plan:

Navigation Elements Checklist

- ☐ Page numbers in the header or footer
- ☐ Headings and subheadings
- ☐ Section headings in the header
- ☐ Table of contents
- ☐ Index
- ☐ Other: _____
- ☐ Other: _____
- ☐ Other: _____

HOMEWORK

In this hour, you learned how to incorporate navigational elements, such as tables of contents and indexes, into your document. In Hour 21, "Format and Print," you'll learn how to apply professional formatting to your document and how to shepherd the document through the printing process.

To prepare for the next hour, please do the following:

- Review other business plans in terms of their visual style and formatting.

- Refresh your Microsoft Word formatting skills—or find someone else who's a Word wizard.

- Create a preliminary list of people who should receive a copy of your business plan and use this list to estimate the total number of copies you need printed.

- Make some preliminary calls to Kinko's and other local printing firms to determine which ones offer the type of printing services you need.

HOUR 21
Format and Print

CHAPTER SUMMARY

LESSON PLAN:

In this hour, you will learn about …

- Choosing the right publishing program
- Formatting your business plan
- Arranging professional printing

Many businesspeople spend an inordinate amount of time and effort writing their business plans and still end up with a less-than-effective result. That's because they don't pay enough attention to the formatting, publishing, and printing of the document—and a poorly formatted or printed business plan can torpedo all your other work.

As much as some might hate to admit it, style is every bit as important as substance. You could have the most persuasive business strategy in the world, but if you present that strategy in a substandard and unprofessional manner, your readers will lose all confidence in your abilities. The way your business plan looks and feels is key to gaining acceptance for your strategy; just as a well-dressed candidate has an edge in a job interview situation, a "well-dressed" business plan document will give your business the edge when it comes to attracting financing.

This hour assumes you have a completed business plan to work with; it's relatively easy to format your document in the post-writing phase of the project. You can, however, apply the information and advice in this hour at any stage of the project, which will let you format "on the fly" as you pull together the individual sections and write your text.

DESIGN FOR SUCCESS

The actual formatting of your business plan should be in service to the document's overall design and should work toward attracting the reader's attention, improving the document's readability, and reinforcing the message of your business plan. Good design makes things easier to read and easier to find and helps direct the reader's journey through the business plan.

Good design does not draw attention to itself. It is most often clean and transparent and works to tie together all the different elements in your document. If a design works, you'll know it because the document itself works.

Bad design is easily noticeable. It is often cluttered and noisy, with different elements frequently competing with each other for the reader's attention. In a poorly designed document, the reader doesn't know which way to turn; there is no clear path from point A to point B, and it's difficult to tell which items are important and which aren't.

Bad design can also mean no design. If all you do is type text into your word processor's default template, with no regard for style or spacing or additional elements, you've just created a poorly designed document. You need to spend time deciding what size type to use, how you want your headings to appear, and what kind of graphic elements you want to incorporate. That means tweaking a fair number of program and document parameters, but the results will be worth it.

If you *don't* spend time on the design of your business plan document, you run the risk of losing your audience before it reads a single word. When an investor has dozens of similar business plans piled up on his or her desk, it's very easy to pass up the plain or ugly documents in favor of the attractive ones; when you have to perform triage, making the first cut on the basis of appearance is as viable as any other approach. The thinking, stated or unstated, is that a business that doesn't pay attention to the appearance of its own business plan probably won't pay attention to other important details of running the business.

In other words, pay attention to the details of how your business plan looks and feels—in contrast to the old axiom, investors *do* judge books by their covers and businesses by the appearance of their business plans.

FORMATTING YOUR DOCUMENT

The way your business plan looks is the result of the formatting you apply to the document itself. You can format every element of your document—the text, the headings, the headers, the footers, even the underlying page that holds all these different elements.

GO TO ▶
See Hour 20, "Table of Contents and Index," to learn more about headers and footers.

Most word processing and desktop publishing programs enable you to apply formatting through the use of document-wide styles. Each style contains a complete set of formatting parameters for typeface, type size, line spacing, justification, color, and the like; when you make a change to the underlying style, you automatically change the formatting of all the elements in your document that share that style.

Naturally, you can format individual elements without changing the underlying style. This is useful if you want to boldface a particular piece of text, force a page break, or tighten up the spacing of a bulleted list. Your final document will undoubtedly contain a mix of style-based formatting and spot formatting of individual elements.

CHOOSING A PROGRAM

When it comes to formatting your document, the first choice you have to make is which software program to use. In general, you have the choice of using your word processing program (such as Microsoft Word) or importing your base document into a professional desktop publishing program (such as Adobe PageMaker).

What type of program should you use? For most business plan documents, a word processing program works just fine. Today's state-of-the-art word processors (again, Word is the best example) incorporate a variety of formerly high-end desktop publishing features. While you might gain *some* formatting control in a dedicated desktop publishing program, it's unlikely you'll need to do anything to your document that you can't do from within Microsoft Word.

One major advantage of doing both your writing and your formatting in your word processor is that you don't have to separate the writing and formatting steps—you can format as you write. If you use a separate desktop publishing program, you have to finish your writing first and then import your document into the desktop publishing program. That's both time consuming and awkward, and it artificially splits your business plan process.

DOING THE WORK

Whichever type of program you choose, make sure you—or the person you've assigned to this task—know how to use all the ins and outs of the program. Formatting your business plan is too important a task to delegate to an overworked assistant who doesn't know how to use the features properly. You want someone who's a word processing or desktop publishing pro to put the finishing touches on your business plan; don't settle for less at this stage of the game.

If you're uncomfortable with this sophisticated level of program usage, hand off the formatting to someone who knows what he or she is doing. Within most larger companies, the marketing department is a good place to look for experts in this area. (If you have a design or publishing department, that's even better.) If no one in your company is up to the job, contact your local printer. Kinko's and other printing firms often offer desktop publishing services (for an additional fee); you give them your basic document (in Word format), provide some visual direction, and let them do the heavy lifting.

 To learn more about the powerful desktop publishing capabilities of Microsoft Word, read *Mastering Microsoft Word 2000, Premium Edition* (Sybex, 2000), also by the author of this book.

BLACK AND WHITE OR COLOR?

Another early design decision that needs to be made concerns color. Will your business plan be a black and white document, or will it incorporate color?

When making this decision, note the following advantages and disadvantages of each approach:

Comparing Black and White vs. Color Documents

	Black and White	*Color*
Visual impact	Weaker	Stronger
Versatility	Less	More

	Black and White	Color
Reproduction of graphics	Worse	Better
Cost	Lower	Higher
Printing schedule	Shorter	Longer

The bottom line is that color printing looks more professional, provides higher-quality reproduction of pictures and other graphics, and offers more versatility in terms of nontext elements. (For example, you can use color within the text to highlight headings or key phrases.) On the downside, color printing will cost you more per page (check with your printer to find out how much more) and adds a little bit of time to the printing cycle. (Color pages take longer to print than do black and white pages.)

Given that this business plan is key to the entire future of your business, a little time and money spent up front for color printing could be a very small expense to gain a very large impact.

PICKING A COLOR SCHEME

If you decide to go with a color document, what colors should you use?

The smart thing to do is pick a limited palette of colors that you then use for the key repeating elements in your business plan. For example, you might pick a medium blue for headers, footers, level-one headings, and chart and graphics backgrounds. You want to avoid using too many colors (except in pictures and complex graphics, of course); using too many colors is extremely visually confusing.

Whatever you do, if you pick a color for one element, use that same color for all related elements. For example, if you go with a blue header, *don't* change to a bright orange for your footer. Keep the same colors throughout to establish a visual consistency and theme.

JUST A MINUTE

Once you've chosen your colors, send a test document to the printer to see how the colors look on paper. Quite often, colors will appear different onscreen than they do in ink; go with what looks good when printed, even if it's slightly less appealing on your computer screen.

You should also carry your color scheme into any charts, graphs, and tables you incorporate in your plan. *Don't* expect that Word's default chart color scheme will suffice for your needs! For example, if you choose a medium blue as the primary color for your document, you might want to format all your charts so that the first element is light blue, the second is light green, the third is light yellow, the forth is dark green, and so on. You should then format every chart to follow this color scheme; this will give your plan a visual consistency that is extremely professional looking.

The colors you use are a matter of taste, of course—so make sure you use good taste. (If you don't have good taste—and you know if you don't!—employ someone else to make these color decisions for you.)

A good place to start is with your company's logo. If at all possible, pick up on the colors in your logo for the color scheme of your business plan. Likewise, if you use a particular color or set of colors in your marketing materials, your ads, or your trade show booth, you might want to incorporate those colors in your business plan. The key is to embrace *consistency* so that your business plan has a similar look and feel to everything else your company does.

PROCEED WITH CAUTION

If you find that all the different materials your company produces have different looks and feels, you have a potential company identity problem. Your company needs to present a consistent image to the public—think of the consistent red and white of Coca Cola or the corporate yellow of Hertz. If you don't currently have a strong corporate identity, take advantage of this opportunity and use your business plan document to establish a new and consistent identity for the rest of your business.

All that aside, it's better to use darker colors than lighter ones (they look more professional), although colors that are too dark might have trouble reproducing accurately. (As far as printing is concerned, lighter is better—so you'll have to make a compromise on this issue to some degree.) Going with overly bright or trendy colors might make your business plan—and thus your business—appear to be too lightweight. When all else fails, pick a deep blue, green, or maroon; they should reproduce well, and they lend an authoritative air to the look of your document.

FORMATTING THE PAGE

Most business plan documents are printed on U.S. standard 8.5-by-11-inch paper in regular portrait format.

So far, so good.

You'll want to include a margin around the edges of each page. While there is always the temptation to narrow the margins to squeeze more stuff on a page, you need to supply enough white space around the edges to give your document adequate "breathing room." Most documents incorporate one-inch margins all around—with one exception.

If your document will be bound—and it should be—you'll need to compensate for the space lost to the binding. To do this, change the left margin for your entire document to at least 1.5 inches. (Anything over 2 inches would be overkill.)

You also need to decide whether to print on one side or both sides of the page. Although two-sided printing is more efficient, it's also more difficult to organize and print. Plus, it's much less common than single-sided printing. Unless you have an extremely long document, it's best to go with single-sided printing.

JUST A MINUTE

If you choose double-sided printing, you'll need to adjust margins for both odd- and even-numbered pages so that the gutter (the inside edge) always has a 1.5-inch margin to compensate for the document's binding. You'll also want to use a relatively thick, relatively opaque paper, to minimize visual bleed-through from one side to the other.

FORMATTING HEADERS AND FOOTERS

The running information at the top of each page is called a header, and the similar space at the bottom of each page is called a footer. As described in Hour 20, "Table of Contents and Index," headers and footers can contain important navigational information such as page numbers, section titles, and the like. You can also use headers and footers to repeat your document's title, to show the date of the document, or to place the word "Confidential"—which needs to be *somewhere* on your document to protect its contents from prying eyes.

You probably want to set the type size for your header and footer at least 2 points smaller than the size of your document's body text (8 points is a good size). You should also consider using a sans serif font, such as Arial, for the header/footer text; sans serif is easier to read at smaller type sizes.

JUST A MINUTE

You can achieve a more sophisticated look by presenting your header/footer as a solid bar (in your main document color) with reverse (white) text. You can even play around with the color of the bar and incorporate various fade effects.

Formatting Headings

It's important for each major section of your plan to be easily distinguished. This is typically done by the formatting of the section headings.

Here are some items to consider when formatting your document's headings:

- When choosing a font for your headings, you should either use the same font as you use for your document's body text or choose a complimentary sans serif font such as Arial. You should use the same font for each heading level.

- Your level-one heading should probably be sized between 18 and 24 points; much larger looks cartoony, and much smaller doesn't have as great of an impact. You should make each descending heading level 2 to 4 points smaller than the one preceding it.

- Most designs utilize boldface for the first few levels of headings. For a slightly classier look, go with nonbold headings or use the narrow version of your chosen font.

- As you move to second- and third-level headings, the heading type size approaches the size of your document's body text. To differentiate a lower-level heading from the body text, italicize the heading.

- If you're printing in color, consider using color for at least your first few levels of headings.

- To better set off new sections, consider placing a line either above or below each first-level heading. Alternately, print the first-level heading in reverse against a colored bar.

- Consider starting each new first-level section on a new page. (This requires formatting the heading to always start with a page break before.)

- Make sure you put adequate space between the end of the preceding text and any second- and third-level headings. There should be more space before the heading than there is between the heading and the subsequent text.

- Consider using a hanging indent for at least the first level of headings. This pushes the heading out into the left margin and does an excellent job of breaking different sections in your text.

FORMATTING TEXT

Text formatting is vitally important but relatively easy. The main thing is to make the body text of your document as easy to read as possible—which means few, if any, fancy formatting effects.

Here are some formatting ideas to consider:

- Keep the type size between 10 and 12 points. Believe it or not, smaller text looks more professional and is actually a little easier for most people to read—especially in large blocks (recommended size: 10 points).

- Use a common and easily readable font. Most designers choose a serif font, such as Times New Roman, for readability. However, if your paragraphs are relatively short, you can risk a sans serif font, such as Arial or Helvetica, for a slightly more modern effect.

PROCEED WITH CAUTION

Never use the Courier family of fonts—they'll make your business plan look like it was typed on a typewriter!

- Format your body text style to put space both before and after each paragraph. You want a total of about 12 points between each paragraph, which you can get by leaving 6 points above and 6 points below.

- You can choose between left-aligned paragraphs and fully justified paragraphs. Full justification looks cleaner (straight lines down both sides of the page) but can leave ugly spaces in the middle of lines, especially if your text includes a lot of long words. Left alignment is a perfectly acceptable alternative.

PROCEED WITH CAUTION

Do *not* attempt to achieve paragraph spacing by adding an extra return after each paragraph—this can have unforeseen effects when you change the formatting of other elements in your document! Along the same lines, use only one space at the end of each sentence, not two. (These old conventions are carryovers from the days of typewriters; they're unnecessary today.)

- You may want to avoid breaking paragraphs at the end of a page; this will help you keep key information together. If you do this, however, be aware that you could end up with some awkward white spaces at the bottom of some pages.

FORMATTING LISTS

A list is a special case of text. Most of the lists in your business plan will be bulleted lists, and there are a few formatting issues you'll need to keep in mind:

- Choose a good-looking bullet. Most word processing programs let you change the default bullet style; you can use any number of "dingbats" or "wingdings" or symbols for your bullet characters. You can even use a separate graphic for your bullets, if so desired.
- List text can be either left aligned or fully justified. In most cases, left aligned is preferable because justifying bulleted text often leads to odd white spaces in the middle of lines.
- The standard spacing between bulleted items might be too large for your taste. Feel free to adjust the line spacing to tighten up the appearance of a list.

FORMATTING GRAPHICS

You probably have at least a half-dozen graphic elements in your business plan; these may be pictures, charts, flow charts, or something similar. When you add a graphic to your document, you have a handful of important decisions to make, including the following:

- **Size.** You want any text in your charts and graphics to be easily readable, but you don't want the graphic to overwhelm the rest of the page. In most cases, smaller will be better, at least to a point.

- **Position.** Where do you put the graphic on your page? Ideally, the graphic should be close to the text that references it. However, you don't want to just plop a picture in the middle of the page and let it be. You probably want to align each graphic to either the left or right margin—and position it in a way that helps add a little variety to the flow of the underlying page.

- **Text flow.** If your graphic does not extend the entire width of a page, you'll want to wrap the text around the graphic.

- **Borders.** Although a graphic can just sit on the underlying page, a more professional effect is to set off the graphic with some sort of border. You can choose from various border sizes and colors; something small and unobtrusive is always nice. Alternately, you can choose to add a drop shadow behind the graphic; this is a very professional-looking effect.

JUST A MINUTE

You should make sure you apply the same formatting to all the graphics in your document. For example, if you decide that a graphic should extend across the entire width of a page, then *all* the graphics in your document should have a similar width. If you decide to use a blue fade background behind one of your graphics, *all* your graphics should have a similar background. This similar treatment for all your graphic elements will lend a necessary visual consistency to your document, which increases its apparent professionalism.

FORMATTING THE TITLE PAGE

Finally, we come to the very first page in your document—the title page. This is the first thing your readers will see, even before they open your business plan.

Your title page should reflect the tone and style of your business but in a serious and professional manner. It should incorporate the design and color scheme of the rest of your document but in an understated manner. (No "in your face" blasts of color here.) It should also be designed in such a way that it won't look out of place among the dozens of similar business plans piled up on a potential investor's desk.

What elements need to be included on your title page? Here's a short list:

- Your company name or logo
- The words "Business Plan" (or something similar)

- The date of the plan (in month and year—day isn't necessary)
- The word "Confidential"

BEFORE YOU PRINT—PROOF

There's one more important thing you need to do before you take your plan to the printer. You—or someone you trust—have to go through the plan, page by page and word by word, and proofread it.

There's nothing more embarrassing than presenting a great-looking business plan and making your pitch for a large amount of money, only to notice that your name is misspelled throughout. Or maybe you find a partial sentence on page 3, an unmatched parenthesis in the first appendix, or a grammatically garbled passage in your first core competency. A few minor errors here and there probably won't derail your request for funding, but they definitely present your business in a less-than-favorable light.

The first proofing tool you should use is your word processor's spell checker. A built-in spell checker isn't perfect, however—it won't recognize some perfectly acceptable industry buzzwords, and it also won't distinguish between "there" and "they're" and "their" when only one of them is correct.

This means your document still needs a manual proofreading pass. Someone—hopefully someone who is very detail oriented and knows his or her way around a well-constructed sentence—has to read through the plan, carefully and front-to-back, to search for, identify, and correct any misspellings or grammatical problems.

Then—and only then—is your document ready to print.

PROCEED WITH CAUTION

You should avoid having the person who wrote the document do the proofreading. (You should also avoid doing the proofreading yourself.) This is because when you read something over and over and over, your mind starts to fill in any blanks and correct any mistakes. Your proofreader needs to bring a fresh set of eyes to the project to catch any mistakes you're now glossing over.

PRINTING YOUR BUSINESS PLAN

Once your business plan is completely done—all written and all formatted, from the title page to the last appendix or index page—it's time to turn it into a finished document. This calls for a trip to a printer.

Choosing a Printer

If your budget is tight, you're probably wondering why you can't use your office printer or copier to produce the printed copies of your business plan. The answer is that you can, but the results, in most cases, will disappoint.

You want the document that you hand to potential investors to represent the very best your company has to offer. If you have a high-quality, high-speed laser printer in your office, you can probably print your own copies of the business plan and approach the quality you'd get at Kinko's or another professional printer. Know, however, that if you want your document to be in color, you need to use a color printer—and a color *laser* printer, not an inkjet. If you're printing out a dozen or more copies of a 30-page document, *in color*, it's going to take a lot of time. If your laser printer isn't color, isn't fast, and isn't quite state-of-the-art, your results will be less than optimal—and slow.

The better approach is to let the pros do it. Check out your local printing houses (Kinko's is a good place to start but certainly is not the only option) and see what kinds of services they offer. Here's what you want:

- The ability to print direct from a computer file. Make sure they can accommodate the particular file format you used to prepare your document. (If you used Microsoft Word, you're probably okay with most printers; you should, however, confirm that they're using the same version of Word that you used.)

- Someone onsite with technical expertise to tweak or make changes to your file, if necessary.

- The ability to print the specific size document that you have and the quantity that you need.

- The ability to bind in additional material for attachments—even (and particularly) if you provide the material yourself.

- A willingness to show you a printed proof before they do the full print run.

- A variety of high-quality paper to select from.

- The ability to bind the document using your preferred binding method and a clear plastic cover (to show your title page).

- The ability—and a willingness—to meet your time schedule and on your budget.

If a printer meets all these criteria, you're probably in good shape. You should, however, ask for some samples of similar jobs performed. Ultimately, you'll have to be the final judge of quality and suitability.

FILE FORMATS

The first thing to worry about when it's time to print is the file format of your business plan document. Your printer's computer has to be able to read the file on your disk. If you used a program that the printer doesn't use, you're in trouble.

PROCEED WITH CAUTION

 For the best quality, you always want to initiate printing from the document file itself. You never want to make copies from a printed document—you're already a generation removed from the original, and you'll start to lose a lot of detail in your document's graphics and shaded areas.

Know, however, that most printers are capable of reading the most popular file formats for this type of project. Specifically, you'll find that most printers can work with Microsoft Word and Adobe PageMaker files; many can also work with QuarkXpress.

You'll need to find out whether your printer is an IBM-compatible or Macintosh shop. If you created your document on a Mac and your printer only has IBM-compatible computers, you may have a conversion problem.

Versions are also important. If you're using a newer version of a particular program and your printer only supports an older version, your file may not be compatible with the printer's system.

If worst comes to worst, ask about using Adobe Acrobat files. Acrobat is a file creation and printing program that enables precise printing of documents from almost any type of program. If you have Acrobat installed on your computer (and your printer may be able to loan you a copy), you simply "print" your document to an Acrobat .PDF file. Your printer then loads your .PDF file into its version of Acrobat and prints it out—exactly as it appeared on your computer.

FILE TRANSFER

No matter which file format you use, you also have the issue of delivering your file to your printing service. This isn't always easy because the files for some complex documents can be 10 megabytes (MB) or more in size—much larger than what will fit on a 1.4MB, 3.5-inch disk. When your file is this big, how do you get it from here to there?

There are actually several options available to you for transferring large files to your printer, including the following:

- **File compression.** If your file isn't *too* big, you can use a software utility, such as WinZip, to compress your file into a smaller .ZIP file. Depending on how many graphics are in your plan, you may be able to compress up to a 5MB file to fit on a 1.4MB disk.

- **ZIP disks.** If your file is so big that even in its compressed format it's too large to fit on a 1.4MB disk, consider using a larger storage medium. Particularly popular is Iomega's ZIP format; a standard ZIP disk will hold up to 100MB of data. Most printers have ZIP drives attached to their systems, and you may be able to borrow a portable ZIP drive to use on your end, if your PC isn't so equipped.

- **CD-RW.** Another option for storing large files is rewritable CD-ROMs. You can get up to 650MB of data on a CD-RW disk, which should be more than enough for your business plan document.

- **Removable hard drives.** Several other removable storage options are available to you, not the least of which are removable hard drives. If you use one of these, you can take your hard drive with you to your printer and connect it directly to your printer's PC.

- **E-mail.** Ask whether your printer accepts document files via e-mail. If this option is available, all you have to do is send your printer an e-mail message with your document file attached. When the printer receives your message, someone will save your file to the system and be ready to print, just like that.

- **Bring your laptop.** If worst comes to worst, just load your document file onto your portable PC and drag it to your printer. Hand your laptop to the people behind the counter and let *them* figure out how to get the file from your PC to theirs!

COLORS

If your document was formatted to be a color document, ask about the types of color printers to which your printing service has access. Different printers reproduce colors differently; output from a high-quality color laser printer will look a lot different than the output from a low-priced color inkjet. Ask to see full-color samples from the available color printers—and request the samples on a variety of different papers. (The paper quality can also affect color reproduction.) If you're still not sure, run a test of your document on the different printers and choose the one that looks best to you.

PROCEED WITH CAUTION

Once you see how your document prints on the selected color printer, you may need to go back and change some of the colors you originally used. It's not unusual, for example, to find dark blues printing closer to black on some printers; you may need to go through your document and universally choose lighter colors.

PAPER

Paper is paper, right? Wrong! There are hundreds and hundreds and *hundreds* of different types of paper you can choose from for your business plan document. Some papers are lighter and some are heavier; some are more opaque and some are more transparent; some are smoother and some are rougher; some are whiter and some are less white; some are more expensive and some are less expensive. And that's not even getting into colored, textured, or patterned papers!

You should choose the paper that looks and feels best to you (and that fits your budget), but here are some points to consider:

- A more opaque paper is less likely to show through the content of adjacent pages.
- A brighter white looks "cleaner" than an off-white paper. However …
- An off-white or lightly colored paper (light gray or beige) can lend a unique feel to your document—although the paper color might affect the reproduction of any colored graphics.

PROCEED WITH CAUTION

Never use a patterned paper for a business plan; not only does the cluttered background distract from the document's content, it simply doesn't look professional. (Patterned paper is for hobbies—or at least that's the perception!)

- Color typically looks better on glossy paper.
- Thicker paper—to a point—lends a more substantial feel to your document.

The thing to do is to ask your printer for recommendations and samples. If necessary, do some test printing of your document on different types of paper.

BINDING

Finally, you get to choose how you want your document bound. Depending on your printer, you'll have several choices, including the following:

- **Stapled.** A definite no-no—very unprofessional.
- **Three-ring bound.** Less than ideal, although for in-house use it does offer the flexibility of adding and removing pages at will over time.
- **Comb-bound.** Plastic comb binding is a good choice for most business plans. It's relatively low cost, has a professional look, and lays flat when spread open. You can also choose different colors for the plastic binding—although black is the most popular choice for the professional look.
- **Spiral- or wiro-bound.** This is similar to comb binding but uses a metal "coil" to bind the pages together. Wiro binding is also a good choice for business plans and is available in a variety of colors. Again, black is best.
- **Saddle-stitched or perfect-bound.** This is the type of binding used for books, and it will give a much different feel to your document. The problem with perfect binding is that it's difficult to lay a perfect-bound document flat on a desk—which a lot of people like to do with business plans. It also makes your business plan feel like something other than a business plan. For these reasons, perfect binding is seldom used for business plans and similar documents.

PROCEED WITH CAUTION

Never—*never!*—hand a potential investor a copy of your business plan that has been stapled or clipped together. This is *extremely* unprofessional and downright insulting. Always hand out complete, professionally bound versions of your plan—or risk immediate rejection from the very people you're trying to impress! (Even worse than a stapled or bound plan is a stapled or bound *photocopy* of your plan—a surefire way to guarantee rejection!)

When you talk about binding, you need to talk about any attachments you want bound into your document. You also need to talk about a clear plastic front cover (through which you can see the title page of the plan) and a dark back cover of a heavier material (to lend some rigidity to the document). In other words, think of how you want the complete *package* to look and feel. (Again, looking at samples of other business plans—or of similar documents that your printer has worked on—should give you some ideas.)

PRINTING AND PROOFING

Now it's time for the work to begin. If you have enough time in your schedule (and if you don't, make some!), ask to see a proof of the printed document before the final print run begins. Compare the printer's proof with your final copy of the plan (printed on your PC and printer, naturally), paying particular attention to page breaks, margins, headers, footers, placement of graphics, and color reproduction. If something doesn't look right, *fix it!* (Or, more precisely, ask your printer to fix it to make this version look more like your original copy.) You may even want to approve a bound version before okaying the full print run.

All of this printing and checking is time consuming—so make sure you've allocated enough of your time to make sure it goes quickly and smoothly. (This proofing process is also a good reason to use a printer close to home.)

PRINTING CHECKLIST

Use the following checklist to make sure you've included everything necessary to take to the printer:

Printing Checklist

- ☐ The formatted document in an acceptable file format (most printers can take Word-formatted documents)
- ☐ Any and all attachments that you want to bind into the back of the document; if you don't have enough copies, bring an original to your printer to copy
- ☐ A printed copy of the document (printed from your PC on your printer) to use for proofing
- ☐ The exact number of copies you need printed
- ☐ Other: _____
- ☐ Other: _____
- ☐ Other: _____

HOMEWORK

In this hour, you learned how to format and print your business plan document. In Hour 22, "Present the Plan," you'll learn how to present your business plan to potential lenders and investors.

To prepare for the next hour, please do the following:

- Memorize the key points of your business plan—including the key financial metrics.
- Brush up on your PowerPoint skills.
- Consider how to best translate your business plan document into a short PowerPoint presentation.

Part V
Plan for Success

HOUR 22

Present the Plan

CHAPTER SUMMARY

LESSON PLAN:

In this hour, you will learn about …

- Translating your plan into a presentation
- Developing a presentation strategy
- Fine-tuning your presentation

When it comes to obtaining funding for your business, the business plan itself is just one part of a complex process. This process typically starts with the identification of potential lenders or investors, then some preliminary discussions (the "getting to know each other" phase), then the delivery of the business plan—followed by a formal presentation of your business to one or more potential lenders or investors, a bunch of follow-up questions and requests for additional information that will have to be answered, and many, many further discussions and negotiations between them and you.

This book doesn't pretend to take you through the entire funding process for your business; the focus of this book is definitely on the business plan part of the process. This hour, however, picks up where the business plan document leaves off and teaches you how to use your business plan to accomplish your objectives.

YOU'VE PRINTED THE PLAN—WHAT COMES NEXT?

You've spent weeks—maybe months—putting together the perfect business plan. Now you're sitting in your office, surrounded by several boxes full of printed plans, hot off the presses. You've closed your office door, picked up your personal copy of the plan, rubbed your fingers across the pages, held it up and smelled that freshly printed smell, and smiled at how great it looks and feels (and smells). You've even read it once or twice or a dozen times and found a few mistakes you wish you would have caught but can probably live with. Now that you have all that out of the way, what comes next?

The very next item on your agenda is scheduling meetings with your largest potential lenders or investors. You can't just deliver a copy of your plan, ask your investors to read it, and then expect a funding check in the mail. The plan now becomes a tool that you use to kick off the funding process; it's used in conjunction with a formal presentation that you will make to all your potential investors.

The meeting you set up should be between you, your key management staff, and the key people at the lending or investing firm. The investor will probably call the shots, but you'll need at least an hour to present your business plan, possibly two. Unless you're having a one-on-one with your banker, you'll need a largish room with a conference table, an appropriate number of chairs, a computer projector, and a screen. In most cases, you'll be presenting at the investor's office; in rare cases, the investor will come to you.

JUST A MINUTE

If the investor wants to meet at your place and you don't really have a place (or at least you don't have a conference room suitable for the meeting), consider borrowing space from a neighboring business or leasing the conference room at a nearby Kinko's.

As you'll learn throughout the balance of this hour, you'll need to create a presentation around your business plan document. That means porting your document in some fashion to a PowerPoint presentation and then loading the presentation file onto a portable computer to take with you to your meeting. When you get to the meeting room, you'll plug your computer into the projector, fire it up, and start presenting—all the while being prepared for a barrage of questions from your audience.

It's helpful for your audience to have copies of your business plan before you begin your presentation. You can hand out copies while you're setting up the projector, but then you run the risk of your audience reading your plan while you're trying to present. A better course of action is to deliver copies of your plan the day before your presentation; this gives your audience members time to read and digest the important points of your plan, but not so much time that they start tearing it apart.

As redundant as it sounds, you should also create handouts of your Power-Point presentation so the audience can follow along as you present. Won't a handout just duplicate your business plan document, you ask? Yes and no. Yes, in that the main points will be the same. (They'd *better* be the same!) No, in that your presentation will have a slightly different flow to it and will lack a lot of the details of the printed plan. In any case, it's the right thing to do; audiences expect a hardcopy printout of any presentation they view.

PROCEED WITH CAUTION

Although you want to deliver the business plan itself a full day before your presentation, you do *not* want to deliver the presentation handouts at the same time—doing so would preclude the need for the presentation itself. Hand out the presentation materials at the beginning of your presentation, no earlier.

PORTING TO POWERPOINT

How do you turn your 20- to 30-page business plan document into a 20- to 30-slide PowerPoint presentation? It isn't that hard, as long as you know how to *condense* your plan into its core ideas and information.

You want your presentation to follow the same general outline as your business plan. This means you need a slide or two for each of the major and minor sections of your plan. For example, you'll have one slide for your Vision section and a separate slide for your Mission section. You'll have several slides for the Opportunity section, several more for the Market Strategy section, and so on.

Although there are other presentation programs available, this hour assumes you're using Microsoft PowerPoint to prepare your business plan presentation. To learn more about PowerPoint's powerful and versatile features, read *PowerPoint 2000! I Didn't Know You Could Do That* ... (Sybex, 2000), also by the author of this book.

Assuming you're following the basic outline discussed in this book, your plan should match up to your presentation as presented in the following table:

Converting Your Plan Outline to PowerPoint Slides

Business Plan Section	Number of Slides
Executive Overview	1
Vision	1
Mission	1
Opportunity	4 to 6
Market Strategy	4 to 6
Business Strategy	4 to 6
Organization and Operations	1
Management	1 to 2
Core Competencies and Challenges	2
Financials	1 to 2

In general, your slides should incorporate bullet points rather than complete sentences of text. You'll also need to condense the number of ideas you present in each section—you should present only the highlights and leave the detail for the printed plan.

You should also, whenever possible, represent ideas and information visually rather than through text; presentations need to be more visual than printed documents. This means you'll probably use all the charts you prepared for your document (you should be able to cut them from Word and paste them into the PowerPoint presentation), and you may want to create some new graphics to use in various places.

When timing your presentation, you should plan on spending two to three minutes on each slide—so a 20-slide presentation will run about an hour before any audience questions or interaction. Resist the temptation to include a large number of slides or to use very small type to put a large number of bullets on each slide. Also, don't assume you can get through more information by talking faster; you're really speeding if you click through more than one slide per minute, and your audience won't appreciate the rush.

Let's look at each of the sections of your plan and how they translate to PowerPoint slides.

JUST A MINUTE

To protect against any technology-related problems, you may want to create a separate copy of your presentation using slides or overhead transparencies; this way, you can switch from PowerPoint to the manual slides or transparencies if you run into problems with your computer or projector.

TITLE

Your presentation should start with a title slide, just as your document started with a title page. In fact, you should probably duplicate the graphics and text from your title page on your title slide; this lends an important consistency to your entire production.

You can reuse the title slide as the very last slide of your presentation. (*Never* end a presentation on a blank slide!) Just copy the first slide and paste the copy at the end of your presentation.

JUST A MINUTE

You should duplicate, as much as possible, the design of your business plan document in the design of your PowerPoint presentation. Use the same color scheme and graphic elements as well as the same fonts—as long as they work as well on slides as they do on paper.

EXECUTIVE OVERVIEW

This should be a single slide, with five to six bullet points detailing the key points of your presentation/plan. You should include bullets for the following:

- Opportunity
- Market Strategy
- Business Strategy
- Core Competencies (*not* challenges!)
- Financials (final-year revenue and profit)

GO TO ▶
See Hour 10, "Executive Summary," to learn more about writing the Executive Summary section of your business plan.

Vision

GO TO ►
See Hour 11, "Vision and Mission," to learn more about writing the Vision and Mission sections of your business plan.

The Vision slide is one of two exceptions to the bullet slide rule. (The other exception is the Mission slide, discussed next.) Assuming your vision has been stated in a single sentence—and assuming that sentence is relatively short—you should include the entire vision statement on this slide.

Mission

The Mission slide should resemble the Vision slide, with the mission statement included in its entirety.

Opportunity

The Opportunity section of your presentation, over the course of four to six slides, has to convince your audience of the viability and significance of the market opportunity you're choosing to pursue. A good way to do this is via a combination of bullet slides and charts.

JUST A MINUTE

When you get into the longer sections of your presentation, consider using title slides to separate each section—Opportunity, Market Strategy, and so on.

GO TO ►
See Hour 12, "Opportunity," to learn more about writing the Opportunity section of your business plan.

You may want to start, for example, with a bulleted list describing the market and the market opportunity. You could then follow this slide with two or three charts that illustrate the size of the market, the number of customers, or some other quantifiable data. A final slide in this section could summarize the key points in a bulleted list.

Market Strategy

This section of your presentation, like the similar section in your plan document, describes how you choose to pursue the identified market opportunity. You'll probably utilize a series of bullet slides, with a few possible exceptions:

- If you're describing a particular product, you can include a picture of that product on a separate slide.
- If your Web site is a key part of your market strategy, you can include a screenshot of your home page on a separate slide.

- If you already have an ad campaign planned, you may want to include a copy of a print advertisement (or a clip of a television or radio commercial) somewhere in this section.
- If there is a process component to your market strategy, you can show the process visually via the use of a flow chart.

BUSINESS STRATEGY

The Market Strategy section flows directly into the Business Strategy section. This section should contain a series of bullet slides, with a few possible exceptions:

- You can visually present your business's revenue streams via a chart (a pie chart is good) or some other type of graphic.
- You may want to illustrate your company's business model graphically, in a type of flow chart or organization chart.
- If there are any processes that are key to your business strategy, you can illustrate them with flow charts.

ORGANIZATION AND OPERATIONS

This section should be relatively short—in fact, a single org chart might suffice. The reason is simple; you need to keep your presentation high level and avoid the kind of detail that is representative of your plan's Operations section. The only exception to this is if there is a key operational component to your business strategy—and even if there is, you should present this operational component with a minimum amount of detail. (If the audience members want to know the detail, they can read about it in the plan document!)

MANAGEMENT

This is typically a one- or two-slide section, using bullets to present the names and titles of key members of your management team. If you feel that this is too self-serving—particularly if you have your management team with you in the meeting—you can delete this section.

GO TO ▶
See Hour 13, "Market Strategy," to learn more about writing the Market Strategy section of your business plan.

GO TO ▶
See Hour 14, "Business Strategy," to learn more about writing the Business Strategy section of your business plan.

GO TO ▶
See Hour 15, "Organization and Operations," to learn more about writing the Organization and Operations section of your business plan.

GO TO ▶
See Hour 16, "Management," to learn more about writing the Management section of your business plan.

Another valid approach is to use the org chart slide in the Organization section as a jumping-off point to discuss not only your key departments but also the management behind those departments.

CORE COMPETENCIES

GO TO ▶
See Hour 17, "Core Competencies and Challenges," to learn more about writing the Core Competencies and Challenges section of your business plan.

This will likely be your last text-based slide. It should contain four to six bullets that present your key competitive advantages and serve as a pre-financial summary for your entire business strategy.

There is seldom a reason to present your challenges/weaknesses in this sort of presentation—unless you feel you have some significant issues that are bound to be raised anyway.

FINANCIALS

You should end your presentation with a slide stating your key financial information. In most cases, this should consist of an abridged version of your projected income statement, showing the following information:

- Net revenues
- Cost of goods sold
- Gross profit
- Gross margin
- Operating expenses (combined)
- Net profit
- Net margin

GO TO ▶
See Hour 18, "Financials," to learn more about writing the Financials section of your business plan.

You should present this data in a table with a column for each of the projected years. You may also want to create a graph of the revenue and profit data to accompany this slide. If you use this type of chart, it should be placed before the detailed numbers.

PROCEED WITH CAUTION

No matter how loudly your accountant or CFO protests, do not under any circumstances include a complete income statement in your presentation. It is virtually impossible to present that level of detail in a readable fashion. To cram all those numbers onto a single slide, the type size will be much too small to read comfortably. If the audience members want to pore over the numbers (and some will), you can direct them to the full financials in your business plan document.

APPENDIXES

As a general rule, you shouldn't use any information from the appendixes in your presentation. If it's not important enough to be in your main document, it's not important enough to present.

JUST A MINUTE

Just as you pulled out all the stops to turn your business plan into a professional-looking document, you need to utilize all of PowerPoint's presentation features to create a sophisticated, professional-quality presentation. Work with PowerPoint's templates to create attractive backgrounds and slide designs and use the program's transition effects to animate the switch from slide to slide.

GO TO ▶
See Hour 19, "Appendixes and Attachments," to learn more about what items to include as appendixes or attachments to your plan document.

PRESENTING YOUR PLAN

The PowerPoint slides you prepare should represent a bare-bones version of your business plan—almost like an enhanced outline. You need to use these slides as the basis for a more complete verbal presentation so you can use your allotted time to paint a full and vivid picture of your business strategy.

TELL, DON'T READ

At this point, it's useful to return to the short story you told in Hour 7, "Create Your Outline." Essentially, that story should become the core part of your presentation. Your slides should follow along and reinforce that story—and, through the use of charts and graphics, elaborate on your basic points with key visual detail.

You see, the most common mistake businesspeople make in situations like this is to read their slides verbatim. This is a big no-no. After all, *anybody* can read what's on the slides—including everybody else in the room. If everything you need to say is on the slides, why give the presentation?

PROCEED WITH CAUTION

The tendency to read presentation slides verbatim sometimes leads to the creation of slides that contain way too much information. Avoid this problem by sticking to no more than six bullets per slide, with each bullet no longer than a single line.

Instead, you need to tell a story that goes well beyond what the audience can read off your slides. The key is to do more than just read the bullets; you need to use your slides as jumping-off points and then proceed to elaborate on each of the bulleted points. You add value by presenting the important detail that exists *between* the bullets, as only you can.

Prepare—And Practice

To talk between and around the bullets of your presentation, you have to have an in-depth knowledge of both your plan and your business. This means, for all practical purposes, that you have to have your business plan memorized. If someone asks you a question about the chart on page 7, you need to know the answer right then—without fumbling through the pages to look something up.

It's your plan, and you need to know it.

As to what you end up saying during the presentation, some businesspeople are comfortable "winging" it and some aren't. You may need only to jot down some brief notes about what to say for each slide, or you may need to write out a detailed script for the complete presentation. In any case, you have to be prepared; only then will you have the confidence you need to impress the potential investors in your audience.

One last thing: It helps to practice. Don't expect to deliver a perfect presentation without doing some dry runs first. Rehearse with the team that'll be with you in the real presentations and go after it like it's for real. Have some members of your staff pretend to be the audience and encourage them to ask tough questions and note any holes in your presentation. After a few "learning" sessions, you might even want to have a final dress rehearsal in which every word counts and you don't stop for anything.

The more you practice beforehand, the fewer surprises you'll encounter when you present for real.

It's important to practice under conditions that mirror as closely as possible conditions you'll face during the real presentation. Try to use the same equipment in practice that you'll have for real and use a similarly sized room. You don't want to be shaken by strange computer equipment or a room that feels way too big or too small. Make your practices as real as possible, and you'll feel like an old hand before you even start.

ADAPTING FOR DIFFERENT AUDIENCES

If you've ever given any speeches or presentations, you know that different audiences will react differently to what you're presenting. Some will sit back and listen quietly; others will raise their hands and jump up and down and ask question after question. Depending on your audience, you may be able to present your entire presentation from start to finish without interruption— or you may get thrown off-track from minute one.

THE PASSIVE AUDIENCE

In some ways, the easiest audience is the passive audience. This is a group of people that lets you do what you came prepared to do. They don't interrupt with questions, they don't roll their eyes and make little snorting sounds, and they don't get up and walk out of the room mid-presentation to "take an important call." They sit and watch and listen and absorb.

The problem with a passive audience is that it's hard to read. If the people are just sitting there, you don't know what they're thinking—are they buying what you're selling, or are they fantasizing about being somewhere else?

If you have passive audience members, you may want to make them a little more active by drawing them into the presentation. A good way to do this is with questions—*your* questions. When you get to a specific point in the presentation—toward the end of the Opportunity section, for example—you may want to stop and ask the lead person what he or she thinks of the market opportunity you've just presented. Or you may want to present a big chunk of your market strategy and then ask for feedback from the others in the room. These little tactics help keep your audience involved in what you're presenting, giving them a vested interest in your success. If they participate, then they're on your side.

JUST A MINUTE

When you're planning the flow of your presentation, you want to leave time for questions from the audience—and this is especially important if you have a quiet audience. Passive audiences are polite and won't interrupt your presentation with questions, so a formal Q&A session at the end of your presentation is a necessity. And don't just ask, "Are there any questions?" as you're packing up your laptop and running for the door. Put a full Q&A session on your meeting agenda and allocate at least a half-hour for it.

THE ACTIVE AUDIENCE

Active audiences are great for getting feedback, even if they're somewhat difficult to control. An active audience will interrupt you with question after question and will want to jump forward and back through your presentation like wayward time travelers. When you have this type of inquisitive audience, it's difficult to stick to your planned presentation; in fact, you may find yourself chucking the presentation completely to answer all the questions the audience poses.

The issue you have to face with an extremely active audience is, how much control do you retain? If you go completely with the direction of the audience, you won't get to tell your story; the meeting will likely get completely out of control, and you'll be perceived as reactive and directionless. On the other hand, if you disregard questions to stick to your prepared script, you'll be perceived as extremely rigid and unresponsive—also not good qualities for a successful businessperson.

The active audience is the most difficult situation for inexperienced presenters. That's because the proper response is a mixture of response and control, which is difficult to achieve. On the one hand, you want to answer any important questions that are raised; on the other hand, you want to stick to the general flow of your story and present your business on *your* terms.

How do you accomplish this delicate balancing act? Here are some tips:

- Some people will only be interested in specific topics—for example, the numbers guys will want to jump straight to the financial statements and ignore everything else. When you run into someone like this, you have to hold your ground, gently, by assuring the person that you've blocked off a full 10 minutes (or 20 minutes or a half-hour or *whatever*) just for that topic—*if* that person can be patient enough to wait for it.

- Some people want to question every little detail. Unfortunately, a one- or two-hour presentation is not the place to cover every little detail; if you let your presentation get dragged down to that level, you'll find that your audience has missed the forest for the trees. You have to maintain control in this situation by informing the questioner that the details are listed in the business plan document—or if they're not, that you'll be glad to supply more detail *after* the meeting.

- Some people will ask very legitimate questions. This is a good thing. You want to answer the good questions without hesitation. If at all possible, you also want to expand on those questions to make some larger points about your business or strategy. Embrace the good questions and use them to your benefit.

- Every now and then, someone will ask a question to which you don't know the answer. It happens. When it happens to you, don't get flustered, don't try to tap dance around the question, and above all, *don't lie*. If you don't know the answer, just say so and promise to get back to the group with an answer by the end of the day (or tomorrow, or whenever). Then comes the most important part—you have to do what you said. If you promised to get back to the group with the answer, *get back to them*. If you can't do it by when you said you would, get back to them and tell them you'll need a little more time. *Never* leave the audience hanging on an unanswered question—*always* provide an answer!

- When the questions start coming fast and furious, it's okay to hold up your hands, take a time out, and ask the crowd to hold their questions for a minute. Take a breather and get your presentation back on track; remind audience members that if they can hold their questions for a few more minutes, you have a full half-hour (or whatever) reserved for a complete question-and-answer session. After all, this is *your* presentation; although you want to satisfy the audience, you also want to get your point across and do as good a job as possible in selling your business. Learn how to go with the flow, but don't let the flow get away from you!

JUST A MINUTE

If you think an active audience will compromise the flow of your presentation, learn how to use PowerPoint's navigation controls to jump directly to specific slides. This way, you can jump to the slide that relates to a specific question and then jump back to the previous slide to resume the normal order of presentation.

After the Presentation

When your formal presentation is over, open the floor for questions. Make sure someone in your group is taking notes so you'll know which (if any) questions are left hanging. Also note any requests from the audience (most likely for more detail or for additional financials) that will need follow-up.

When all the questions have been asked, all the hands shaken, all the business cards exchanged, and all the equipment packed back up, head back to your own offices and debrief with your staff. Make sure someone is assigned to follow up on all hanging questions and requests and then get everyone's opinion of how things went.

PROCEED WITH CAUTION

If you're presenting somewhere other than your own office, make sure someone in your group is charged with collecting extra business plans and handouts when the meeting is over. You don't want to leave confidential strategic information sitting around in public where anyone—including your competitors—can read it.

If there were some rough spots or especially difficult questions in this presentation, you'll need to adjust your next presentation to compensate. You should get better with each presentation, and the only way to do so is to learn from what went right and what went wrong. Although no presentation will ever be completely perfect, it's not unreasonable to expect a certain level of performance from you and from your staff. When you reach this level—and you'll know when you do—success is bound to follow!

Presentation Checklist

Use the following checklist to make sure you're taking everything you need to your business plan presentation meeting:

Presentation Checklist

The day before the presentation:

☐ Send copies of your business plan document to all potential meeting attendees

The day of the presentation, bring the following items with you:

☐ A portable computer with both PowerPoint and the presentation file loaded

☐ A portable computer projector (if there won't be one in the conference room itself)

☐ A long extension cord and power strip (You don't want to run your PC on battery power—batteries can run out!)

☐ A spare copy of the presentation file on a disk or ZIP disk

☐ A backup copy of the presentation on slides or overhead transparencies

☐ A master copy of the presentation printout, marked up with your personal notes

☐ Copies of the presentation printout to hand out to all attendees

☐ Extra copies of your plan document (for any unexpected attendees)

☐ Copies of any detailed financials not included in the plan document (in case anyone asks for them)

☐ Notepads—and someone assigned to take notes throughout the entire presentation

☐ Business cards—and lots of them

☐ Other: _____

☐ Other: _____

☐ Other: _____

HOMEWORK

In this hour, you learned how to present your business plan to potential lenders and investors. In Hour 23, "Use the Plan," you'll learn how to put your business plan to work within your company.

To prepare for the next hour, please do the following:

- Think about which parts of the business plan are directly applicable to the day-to-day running of your business.

- Identify those parts of the printed business plan that might not be appropriate to present to all your employees.
- Consider how you might best present your business strategy to your staff—and ensure that they follow the strategies and tactics outlined in the plan.

HOUR 23

Use the Plan

LESSON PLAN:

In this hour, you will learn about ...

- Sharing the plan with your employees
- Encouraging buy-in throughout your company
- Using the plan to guide day-to-day decisions

The sad fact is that most business plans are used once (to obtain funding) and then filed away, never again to see the light of day. This is unfortunate, given the amount of time and effort that goes into producing a business plan and given how much real strategy resides in the average plan.

Wouldn't it be better if you could actually use your plan as a real plan to help guide and direct your business decisions over the next few years? Wouldn't it be great if all the employees in your organization read the plan and followed its instructions in their day-to-day labors? Wouldn't it be a good idea to check back with the plan every few months to see how you're progressing?

If you want to use your business plan to truly manage your business, you can. All it takes is a little effort—and a lot of will power.

WHY BUSINESS PLANS ARE OFTEN IGNORED

As you learned back in Hour 1, "Analyze Your Objectives," most business plans, after the funding process, end up sitting on shelves, collecting dust. Why is this?

There are several likely reasons why most businesses don't actually use their business plans to manage their business:

- **It's too much work.** It takes a lot of effort to present your long-term business strategy to all levels of your organization. It's not a simple matter of sticking copies of the business plan in everyone's mailboxes; you have to explain how the plan relates to each employee and provide direction on how to incorporate the plan into daily activities. That means one or more company meetings, maybe a few smaller group meetings, and even a number of one-on-one meetings with individual employees—and that's just at the beginning. To keep the plan alive, you'll have to monitor its implementation constantly. That's a lot of work—and it takes more effort than a lot of businesspeople are willing to put in.

- **Today's crises take precedence.** When long-term and short-term activities come into conflict, the short-term often wins. It's difficult to think about long-term strategy when today's fires are burning brightly out of control. Too many businesspeople manage like firefighters, going from one fire to another and never thinking about longer-term fire prevention. In this type of environment, the business plan is irrelevant—because there really isn't a plan.

- **The right people didn't see the plan.** You can't expect employees to embrace your business plan if they never see it. In the urge to maintain some degree of confidentiality, many businesspeople decide that they can't share information and strategy with the troops. In this situation, the employees really aren't part of the team—and the management toils on alone forever.

- **The plan doesn't really reflect the direction of the business.** This is the worst-case scenario—and it's not uncommon. When your plan is one thing and your actual business another, you're running a con game. It takes some skill to put together a business plan that wins the favor of investors, but if the plan doesn't reflect the true nature of your business, you've just sold your investors a total bill of goods. Lying to attract funding will eventually catch up to you, and you won't like what happens then.

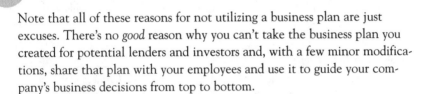

Although it's permissible—and advisable, in many instances—to put a particular spin on your business to gain the approval of investors, this does not extend to outright lying or pretending that your business is something it isn't. When push comes to shove, there is no substitute for telling the truth and no escaping from the reality of whatever situation you happen to be in.

Note that all of these reasons for not utilizing a business plan are just excuses. There's no *good* reason why you can't take the business plan you created for potential lenders and investors and, with a few minor modifications, share that plan with your employees and use it to guide your company's business decisions from top to bottom.

SHARING THE PLAN

The first step in using the plan in your day-to-day business is to share the plan with your employees. Before you call up the printer to order copies for everyone in your employ, you need to consider a few important points—who should see the plan, what should they see, and how should you present it to them?

WHO SHOULD SEE IT?

The answer to this question depends a lot on your management style. If you run a loose, family-oriented business, you'll probably want to share the plan with every employee, from the owner down to the guy on the loading dock. On the other hand, if you run a very tight ship in which all the decisions are made in the senior management boardroom, you may be less comfortable sharing company "secrets" with the rank and file.

As you can see, there's no one correct answer to this question—although there is much to be said about sharing information instead of withholding it. When you share your strategy with your employees—with *all* your employees—you ensure that they know where you want to take the business, and you start to steer them in the direction you want. While you might not convey every single financial detail to every employee (you don't have to distribute the entire plan verbatim), the fact that you share something important because the business plan itself will help to inspire employee loyalty.

On the other hand, there are times and places when you can truly have too much information. If you're managing a multinational conglomerate, the folks making widget parts in Iowa might not care about your grand plans for world domination. In addition, in situations in which there is vicious competition and low employee loyalty, you run the risk of having your key strategies leaked to competitors. In these types of situations, you may want to consider limited access to the business plan to select levels within your organization.

PROCEED WITH CAUTION

You should also be wary of distributing to employees a business plan that includes strategies that could be perceived as being anti-employee—such as instituting layoffs or moving operations to another location.

WHAT SHOULD THEY SEE?

In a perfect world, you could hand out the same business plan to your employees that you presented to potential investors. However, this may not be the way to proceed.

Remember that your business plan was custom-tailored for your audience of potential investors and lenders. It was not written with your employees in mind. Therefore, it is likely to contain some information of little interest to employees (but of great interest to investors), and it probably lacks a lot of detail that your employees might find useful (but that investors gloss over).

A better course of action is to rewrite the business plan, keeping in mind your new audience—employees. This doesn't have to be a major effort, but it will require some degree of reworking.

Let's look at each section of the plan and see what items you might need to change.

JUST A MINUTE

It's probably okay to retain the title of "Business Plan" for the employee version of your document. The cover should probably look similar to your original document, although you'll need to make some change so you can easily distinguish between the external and internal versions of the plan.

EXECUTIVE SUMMARY

The first thing you need to change is the title of this section. Most of your employees aren't executives, so they shouldn't be presented with an Executive Summary. Instead, they should see an overview of your plan. So change Executive Summary to Overview (or just plain Summary) and you're on your way.

The bulk of the existing Executive Summary should be fine as is, although you should check for any details (particularly financial details) that you plan to delete elsewhere in the plan. You should also run through the wording of the key points to excise any investor-focused phrasing.

VISION

Your Vision section should be exactly the same in the employee version of your business plan. In fact, both the Vision and Mission sections are potentially more important to your employees than to lenders and investors. Employees want to believe in the company, and your vision and mission statements give them something to believe in.

MISSION

Like the Vision section, the Mission section should be presented verbatim from the original plan.

OPPORTUNITY

There should be little in the Opportunity section that needs to be changed. Market data is market data; there shouldn't be any confidential information here that needs to be censored.

The only thing you might want to consider is how your competitors are presented. As long as the information is factual and nonbiased, you're probably okay as is. If, however, you put any spin on the competitor data in the original plan, you should examine what was written versus what your employees already know and make any changes as necessary.

MARKET STRATEGY

The Market Strategy section is the first section of your plan that may require major revision—or it may not. It all depends on the level of competitive

GO TO ▶
See Hour 10, "Executive Summary," to learn more about writing the Executive Summary section of your business plan.

GO TO ▶
See Hour 11, "Vision and Mission," to learn more about writing the Vision and Mission sections of your business plan.

GO TO ▶
See Hour 12, "Opportunity," to learn more about writing the Opportunity section of your business plan.

GO TO ▶
See Hour 13,
"Market Strategy,"
to learn more about
writing the Market
Strategy section of
your business plan.

strategy you revealed in the original plan. If you revealed a lot of detail, you may want to remove some of the detail for employee consumption—on the assumption that there will be some leakage of this version to competitors. In other words, don't include any details here that you wouldn't otherwise disclose publicly.

JUST A MINUTE

It may be more work than you want to undertake, but there might be value in editing the narrative text of your document to effect a less formal style. Changing "the company" and "management" into "we" or "I" will help to personalize the plan for employees—and will go a long way toward breaking down any barriers that exist between management and staff.

PROCEED WITH CAUTION

Below a certain level, your employees will be less concerned with confidentiality than you are. That means it's possible—and, in many cases, likely—that some employees will see nothing wrong with sharing your confidential business plan with other people. They may share it with their spouses, their relatives, or even friends who just happen to work for one of your competitors. If this really bothers you—*get over it*. It's just the way the world works, and you shouldn't be taken by surprise. *Expect* some leakage of the information you convey to your employees and compensate accordingly.

For example, it's probably okay to disclose some degree of product information—especially if the product is already out on the market. However, you might not want to disclose fine details about products that haven't yet hit the market—especially if competitors could use those details to mount a competitive threat. A good rule of thumb is that anything already public should stay public, and anything not yet public should only be talked about in general terms.

This does not mean, however, that you shouldn't share product strategy with your troops. If your strategy is to release new versions of a product every six months, you can't hide that; in fact, your employees need to know that information to do their jobs. Again, relate the strategy, even if you have to withhold a few key details.

BUSINESS STRATEGY

The Business Strategy of your plan describes how you intend to make money from your products and services. Some businesspeople might be uncomfortable sharing this information with their employees; these folks apparently don't want the troops to know that the company actually makes money or how much.

Know, however, that it's okay for your employees to know how you expect to make money—and it's even better if they know how the company making money matters to them personally. You'll probably need to add some text to this section to describe all the good things that happen when the company makes money—you can hire more employees, the employees can get paid more, the employees can get bonuses or profit sharing (if you offer either), the employees get to work in nice offices, the employees get nice perks, and so on. Personalize the company's revenues and profits, and you'll have more employees working harder to help you achieve your financial goals.

Along the same lines, it's also good to draw a strong connection between the work the individual employees do and the generation of revenues and profits. How does a salesperson doing his or her job affect the company's financials? How does a factory worker performing to normal levels affect the company? If you can directly relate what the employees do to the success of the company, you'll have a workforce that is more fully invested in how the company performs.

You should also examine the business model included in this section to ensure that it is presented in an employee-friendly manner. Make sure it doesn't include any proprietary information that shouldn't be shared publicly.

In addition to pure strategy and business models, this section might also include some high-level financial and market share projections. If you're comfortable sharing these numbers with employees, great. If not, you'll need to delete or revise this section.

GO TO ▶
See Hour 14, "Business Strategy," to learn more about writing the Business Strategy section of your business plan.

ORGANIZATION AND OPERATIONS

The Organization and Operations section of your plan is one that you might actually want to expand for employee consumption. The key is to avoid the appearance that you're playing favorites among departments or that any particular department is unimportant. This probably means beefing up some of the departmental sections or even adding sections for departments or groups that you didn't include in the original plan. And, of course, you should *always* include org charts for each department.

GO TO ▶
See Hour 15, "Organization and Operations," to learn more about writing the Organization and Operations section of your business plan.

You should also be very diligent when creating departmental org charts to make sure everyone in the department is included. Any people you leave off the chart are likely to feel slighted or "unimportant," so it's better to have too many names on the chart than not enough.

Another new consideration in this section is the accuracy of the information. While it might have been okay to generalize or condense information for potential lenders and investors, when you're describing to an employee what his or her department does, you better get your facts straight. Consider having someone from each department edit and comment on each department's section.

JUST A MINUTE

Another way to approach the Operations section is to ask each department to write its own description. See the "Expanding the Plan" section, later in this hour, to learn more about this approach.

MANAGEMENT

GO TO ▶
See Hour 16, "Management," to learn more about writing the Management section of your business plan.

As short as it is, the Management section might be the trickiest section to present. On one hand, you definitely want your employees to know who their managers are; on the other hand, you don't want them to know so much that they start to resent the upper levels.

The best way to approach this section is factually. Include the bare basics about each manager (schooling, prior job experience, current responsibilities) and avoid presenting any information related to salary or benefits. You should also edit the bios with a less formal style ("Bill" instead of "Mr. Williams") and consider including at least one more level of management than you did in the original plan. In this rare situation, more is better!

CORE COMPETENCIES AND CHALLENGES

GO TO ▶
See Hour 17, "Core Competencies and Challenges," to learn more about writing the Core Competencies and Challenges section of your business plan.

Laying out your company's strengths is a good thing—it inspires employee confidence and instills a sense of pride. Talking about your weaknesses, however, is more problematic. Although some employees will appreciate the candor, others will get nervous—and still others will find ways to use your weaknesses against you. If you feel you must present a Challenges section, be sure to include your responses to the challenges—and make sure the solutions are real and doable, not the kind of tap dancing you might have gotten away with in front of the investors.

FINANCIALS

Presenting financial information to employees is a hot issue. Some companies are open with all their information and readily share financials. (Public companies, of course, have to share the information—with everybody, including employees!) Other companies guard their numbers as they would their sister's honor and don't let anyone outside of a select few lay their eyes on them.

GO TO ▶
See Hour 18, "Financials," to learn more about writing the Financials section of your business plan.

Where you come down on this issue will determine how you approach the Financials section of the plan. At one extreme, you can simply excise the entire section. At the other extreme, you can leave it as is from the original plan.

A middle ground is to include the top-line numbers without the detail. The thinking here is that you want your employees to know that your goal is to become a $100 million company in three years, but they don't need to know the individual line items that get you there. If you take this approach, consider presenting the numbers as a graph rather than as pure numerics. You can even present the graph without presenting exact numbers (see the following figure), if you're really paranoid about that sort of thing.

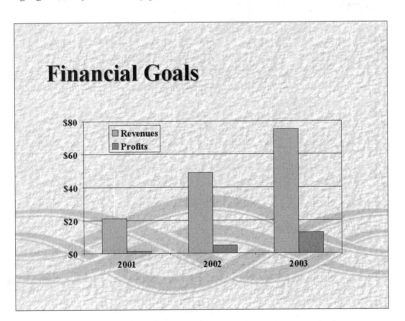

To share financial goals without all the detail, present your projections as a graph—without data labels.

Appendixes

GO TO ▶
See Hour 19, "Appendixes and Attachments," to learn more about writing the appendixes and attachments to your business plan document.

In general, you probably don't need to present the same appendixes to your employees as you did to potential investors. You're not "selling" your company as hard to your employees—and they probably already know most of this supplemental information anyway.

However, there may be different information that might be of value to your employees that is best presented in the form of an appendix. This supplemental information might include the following:

- A "who does what" chart, listing the individuals or departments responsible for common tasks
- A company phone list
- A list of important noncompany phone numbers and addresses—for the company health plan or retirement plan, for example
- A schedule of paid holidays for the coming year
- A list of current employee benefits, including number of vacation days, health and retirement benefits, and so on

JUST A MINUTE

If your original business plan document was in color, should the internal version of the plan also be in color? That's a tough choice because you could run up some hefty bills if you have a large employee base. While there no doubt is value in presenting the same level of professionalism to your employees that you presented to investors, it's better to give them a black and white document than to give them no document at all.

How to Present It?

Once you've created an employee-specific version of your business plan, it's time to present it to the troops.

PROCEED WITH CAUTION

Do *not* hand out the business plan to employees without any explanation. You need to explain to your staff members what the plan is, why you're distributing it, and how they should use it. A plan with no instructions is useless at best and potentially dangerous at worst.

The best way to present the plan is at a company meeting. This way, you'll be sure everyone in the company gets the same message, *from you*, unfiltered by the biases of any of your individual managers.

You can make this presentation a big production, or you can make it an afterthought. Given the significance of the plan, however, you probably want to present it with the same level of importance.

If it took you an hour to present the plan to potential lenders and investors, allocate at least an hour to present the plan at your company meeting. Use a similar PowerPoint presentation as you did before, edited (of course) to match the edits you made in the plan itself. This time, however, you don't have to present the entire plan yourself; you turn this into a real team project by letting other members of your senior management staff present particular parts of the plan.

For example, you might want to follow this approach:

- You (or the company's owner/president) should introduce the plan, explain its importance, and describe how the employees should approach and embrace the plan. Then you should tell what's coming up (the Executive Summary) and lead the company through your Vision and Mission. Take care to personalize these important sections —they're not only the company's vision and mission, they should be your personal vision and mission, too.

- The Opportunity section can be presented by your chief marketing executive—assuming that person is well-connected to the marketplace. If not, you might want to handle this section as well.

- The Market Strategy section can be presented by a team consisting of your chief marketing, sales, and product executives.

- The Business Strategy section can be presented by your chief financial officer—if that person is a personable presenter. If not, consider presenting this section yourself.

- The Organization and Operations section should be introduced by you but then turned over to the heads of each department to talk about their particular areas.

If you follow the recommendation for each department head to present his or her own individual departments, you'll probably need to allocate more than an hour for the total presentation. Even if you ask each manager to limit his or her presentation to five minutes (which probably won't actually happen), you could still end up spending an hour on this section of the plan alone.

- The Financials section—if you share financials—should be presented by *you*—not your chief financial officer. This is because the numbers need to be humanized and presented as business goals, not just abstract numbers. There should be no one better in the company at this than you.
- Finally, you should end with a formal Q&A period with your entire management team up front to answer questions. You probably want to discourage questions and comments during the presentation itself (the size of the group would make this virtually unworkable), but the audience *will* have questions, and you need to address them. As in the presentations you made to investors, make sure someone on your staff is assigned to take notes and follow up on unanswered questions.

You may find that one meeting like this isn't enough. You may want to follow up this meeting with a series of smaller, less-formal meetings for individual groups or departments. You may even, if you company is rather large, need to present the plan through a series of company meetings rather than a single meeting. In any case, listen to what your employees are saying and provide as much face time as necessary for them to fully grasp the plan and their relation to it.

One more thing … six months after your first presentation, hold another meeting. You don't have to re-present the plan, but you do want to follow up. Find out how the plan has been accepted and how employees are using the plan in their daily work. Reinforce the importance of the plan and introduce any changes or modifications that have arisen over time. Holding follow-up meetings like this—and you should probably schedule other meetings at six-month intervals—helps keep the plan alive and to emphasizes its importance to you, to your business, and to all the employees.

You should also hand a copy of the employee business plan to each new employee of your company on his or her first day on the job. Work with your HR department to make the business plan a part of the normal employee training and indoctrination process.

EXPANDING THE PLAN

Another way to encourage employees to embrace the business plan is to enlist them to write their own business plans. No, this doesn't mean you're abandoning your central business strategy; you want to use the employees' plans to *expand* the original plan down further into your organization.

In particular, what you want are separate business plans for each department in your company. You want your marketing department to create a marketing business plan, your sales department to create a sales business plan, and your product development department to create a product development business plan. You even want to get your support departments in on the act with their own human resources business plan and information technologies business plan. In short, you want each area of your business to have its own focused set of strategies that, when taken together, reinforce the larger company business plan.

JUST A MINUTE

Your expectations for these departmental business plans should be slightly different than for the full-company business plans. Ask for shorter documents (10 pages is probably an okay length) and revise or adapt the particular sections as appropriate. (For example, the Opportunity section for the human resources department won't be about the external marketplace; rather, it will describe the "market" for their services inside the company.)

Naturally, not all departments will be equally adept at putting strategy (and tactics) on paper. That's okay. You expect some variance. But you should offer your assistance if required, or the assistance of the people who helped you create the original business plan. If you have a business management or business strategy group, make sure it's tasked with helping the various departments prepare their individual business plans. Give your people the support they need to produce business plan documents that are just as important to their departments as the larger plan is to the company as a whole.

There are three chief benefits to creating individual department business plans:

- You end up with very specific strategies and instructions that each department can follow in the months and years to come.
- You get more individuals "owning" your company's strategy.

- Your company develops more strategies from the bottom up, fueled by those who are closest to the products and the customers.

If you plan things right, you can kick off the writing of the departmental business plans at your first company meeting and then make the presentation of the individual plans the focus of your first follow-up meeting. Then you should take the individual plans and adapt or edit your original plan to accommodate any new information or ideas raised. This, in turn, can feed the updating of the individual plans at a later date. The whole process, then, becomes ongoing—an essential and organic part of your business and a key driver and measurement of your overall strategy.

MANAGING BY THE PLAN

It's just not enough for everyone in your company to have a copy of the business plan; you need to somehow ensure that the company does what the plan said it would do from a strategic perspective. How do you incorporate your business plan into your day-to-day management?

Actually using your plan to make decisions and monitor progress requires discipline, but it can be done. Here are some useful ideas:

- Publicize (within the company) the financial and nonfinancial goals detailed in the plan. Draw up a large timeline chart, post it in the company break room or some other public place, and note the progress towards key milestones.

- At appropriate intervals, hold senior management meetings to evaluate progress toward the strategies and goals outlined in the plan.

- Whenever the company faces a key strategic decision (to buy a company, make an expansion, introduce a new product, or whatever), make sure you and your senior management team review the decision in relation to the strategies and goals outlined in the business plan.

JUST A MINUTE

It's not unusual for a company's goals and strategies to evolve over time. If you embrace strategic decisions that aren't quite in synch with what you originally put into your business plan, you need to adapt your business plan for these new strategic directions.

- As described previously, encourage each department to create its own department-specific business plan and use these plans to drive future changes in the main plan, as part of an ongoing planning-and-review process.

- Set a time schedule for a future review and revision of your business plan. It may be a good idea to update the business plan once a year; whatever your schedule, put the update on your calendar—and make sure it's a priority.

Probably the most important thing to do, however, is to *not* find a place for the plan on your bookshelf. Keep a well-used copy of the plan on your desk and on all your managers' desks. Reread the plan regularly and discuss it often. Keep the plan alive, and the plan will keep your business alive—just as you'd always planned.

IMPLEMENTATION CHECKLIST

Use the following checklist to help you implement your business plan across your entire company:

Implementation Checklist

☐ Create a version of the business plan with an employee focus.

☐ Distribute the new version of the business plan to all appropriate employees.

☐ Hold a company meeting to present the business plan.

☐ Ask each department to create its own department-specific business plan.

☐ Schedule periodic reviews of your company's strategic decisions and accomplishments as they relate to the goals and strategies presented in the business plan.

☐ Schedule regular updates to the main business plan document.

☐ Other: _____

☐ Other: _____

☐ Other: _____

HOMEWORK

In this hour, you learned how to apply your business plan in the day-to-day management of your business. In Hour 24, "Create a Private Placement Memorandum (PPM)," you'll learn how to use your business plan as the basis for a more formal PPM.

To prepare for the next hour, please do the following:

- Obtain copies of PPMs from other similar businesses.
- Contact your lawyers and let them know that you're getting ready to raise private capital and that you need to start work on a PPM.
- Make sure you have a copy of your business plan document file—and that you've marked up a hardcopy of your business plan with any comments or changes you want to make.

HOUR 24

Create a Private Placement Memorandum (PPM)

LESSON PLAN:

In this hour, you will learn about ...

- Understanding the differences between a business plan, a private placement memorandum (PPM), and an S-1 filing
- Creating a PPM
- Working toward a private stock placement

As you've learned throughout this book, a business plan is just a tool to help you obtain funding for your business. The business plan document doesn't obtain the funding —and legally can't be used (by itself) to ask for funding. When it comes time to actually sell shares in your company, you need a different document.

The type of document you use to solicit sales of your company's stock is dictated by the Federal government and hinges on just how you plan to offer the shares. If you're selling your stock privately—*not* on the public stock exchanges—you're making a private placement of your stock, and you need to provide potential investors with what is called a *private placement memorandum* (PPM). If you're selling your stock on a public stock exchange, you're making an *initial public offering* (IPO) of your stock, and you need to provide potential investors— and government regulators—with a document called a *prospectus* (which carries the official SEC designation of S-1). These documents are both similar to your business plan, but you must provide a good deal of additional information, in an accepted format, that further describes the details and the risks of your offering.

PPMs and S-1s are both highly legal documents and should only be created with the assistance of legal council. However, both of these documents can incorporate large chunks of what you created for your business plan— and must work hand-in-hand with your business plan to help you sell your stock to potential investors.

STRICTLY SPEAKING

A **private placement memorandum** (sometimes called an offering memorandum) is a legal document that presents the details of a pending offering of stock in a private company. An **initial public offering** is the offering of public stock in a company that was formerly private; this event is often referred to as "going public." A **prospectus** (also known as an S-1 document) is a document that is required to be filed with the U.S. Securities and Exchange Commission (SEC) and distributed to potential investors when a company is planning an IPO.

PRIVATE VS. PUBLIC OFFERINGS

There are two ways you can sell stock in your company—privately and publicly. Each is a valid way to raise capital, and each has advantages and disadvantages.

JUST A MINUTE

Private and public placements are not mutually exclusive through the course of a company's development. It's not uncommon for a growing company to raise several rounds of financing through private placements prior to pursuing an IPO.

PRIVATE PLACEMENTS

A private placement is a limited sale of securities (your company stock) that does not involve any public offering, advertising, or general solicitation. In other words, you offer shares in your company to selected individuals and institutions—privately.

To an investor, a private placement is more risky than buying shares in a public company. Since private companies are not regulated by the SEC—and are not required to publicly report financial and other important company information—there is a constant risk of not having enough (or good enough) information to make informed decisions. Further, there may never be a general market for privately placed securities—which means investors can't sell their private shares as quickly or as easily as they can shares in a public company.

These risks to investors translate into less work—and less stress—for the company itself. From the company's standpoint, there are several advantages to private placements (as compared to public offerings), including the following:

- You get to choose who will co-own your business with you; in a public company, anybody can buy a share and obtain an ownership role.
- Your company's stock price (and capitalization) is protected from the vagaries of the public stock market.
- You don't have to open your books for public inspection—and you won't be publicly pilloried when your company's performance doesn't meet expectations.
- You don't have to register a private placement with the SEC—and you aren't subject to the same level of initial and continuing government regulation.

This last point is the relevant one for this hour's lesson. A public placement, discussed next, has all sorts of SEC-mandated filings that have to be made—not just at the beginning of the process but every quarter until the end of time (or until your company ceases to exist, whichever comes first). A private placement, on the other hand, is subject to much less stringent overview.

Although Federal law restricts who may buy private placement shares and to whom and when they may be resold, there are few legal restraints concerning the offering of private stock and even fewer formal requirements for the documents that accompany the placement. In general, the offering company (you) is required to disclose—through a private placement document—certain information to potential investors; the format for that document is not rigidly dictated.

JUST A MINUTE

While Section 5 of the Securities Act of 1933 clearly states that "it is unlawful for any person, directly or indirectly, to sell a security unless a registration statement has been filed," Regulation D (effective April 15, 1982) provides a number of key exemptions that enable a small business to privately offer company stock without the onerous requirements of a full SEC registration.

Don't think, however, that you're completely free to write whatever you want in your offering document. Although there are no legal requirements, there are standards that should be adhered to if one wants to avoid litigation (from investors) at some future date. In other words, the format of the PPM is dictated by legal concerns, not by regulatory agencies.

The reality is that when you're ready to initiate a private placement of your stock, you'll need to give your lawyers a call. The legal beagles will work with you to write the PPM and will have very strong suggestions as far as what should and shouldn't be included. They can't order you to do one thing or another, but their advice should be strongly considered—they know what to do to avoid shareholder lawsuits in the future.

PUBLIC OFFERINGS

A public placement is a sale of securities (your company stock) to anyone who wants to buy. By law, a public offering is truly *public*—you can't limit sales to a select group. Your stock is sold on the public stock exchanges and is publicly available to any investor.

While any company can go public, few should. In reality, the IPO market is limited to larger firms with high growth potential; unless your company has annual sales in excess of $10 million, projected growth rates in excess of 30 percent, and a post-IPO capitalization of at least $60 million, you're probably not a candidate for a public equity event.

If your company is a viable IPO candidate, however, there are some real benefits to going public:

- Lots of money—which you'll need to fund aggressive expansion plans
- Liquidity for your original shareholders
- The ability to entice current and future employees with stock options and employee stock purchase plans
- The ability to fund future acquisitions with company stock
- Some degree of marketing awareness generated by the IPO process

Of course, there are also disadvantages to being a public company:

- Quarterly reporting requirements—which not only are time consuming to prepare, but also result in everything you do becoming immediately visible to your competitors.
- Loss of management control and flexibility.

- Sometimes-intrusive performance pressures.
- Investor relations are time consuming.
- The IPO process itself is complicated and expensive—costing up to 10 percent of the initial capital generated.

Regarding this last point, filing for an IPO requires adhering to a bewildering number of SEC regulations. You'll have to hire a team of lawyers and auditors and consultants to create your S-1 filing, and you'll have to partner with one or more underwriters for your offering. (Unlike Regulation D offerings, full public offerings can only be sold by accredited underwriters—typically investment banks.) It's also less likely that you can use your business plan as the core of the S-1 document; there are so many Federal regulations inherent in the process that you're probably better off starting from scratch.

THE PRIVATE PLACEMENT PROCESS

Since this book is targeted more at private companies than public ones, the balance of this hour will focus on the private placement process and the creation of a PPM.

In general, there are four phases of the private placement process:

1. **Prepare.** This phase is when you get your act together. If you haven't completed your business plan, you'll need to finish it off before you go much further. You'll need to consult with your financial advisors to determine how many shares to offer and how to price them. You'll also need to consult with your legal staff to create the PPM and to prepare for the solicitation process.

2. **Solicit.** This phase begins with the identification of potential investors. Once you have a list of prospects, you start making phone calls to judge their interest. Those responding favorably to your overtures then sign nondisclosure agreements and receive numbered copies of your PPM. This is followed by a formal presentation of the offering, either individually or in groups.

3. **Negotiate.** If you're presenting to smaller "friends and family" investors, there isn't much negotiation involved; you've stated the terms of the placement, and they decide whether they want to play or not. If you're presenting to larger investors or venture capital firms, it's likely

that they'll propose to you how they want to do the deal. They'll send you a letter of intent, and you'll start negotiating.

4. **Close.** After you come to terms with all your investors, it's time to close the deal. The lawyers get involved again to make sure all the i's are dotted and t's crossed, and then you're ready to deposit the checks.

JUST A MINUTE

It's not uncommon for the entire private placement process to take six to nine months. Your costs will consist primarily of ongoing legal fees and any necessary fees for consultants and financial advisors. (Expect fees to range between one and five percent of the total capital raised.)

WHY YOU NEED A PPM

Whenever you offer securities (such as your company stock) for sale, in either a public or private fashion, the SEC requires you to provide to potential investors a disclosure document of some sort. This document is used to inform potential investors of the details of your offering, certain risks inherent in the investment, and other obvious and not-so-obvious information.

In the case of a private offering, the document you need to create is called a private placement memorandum (PPM).

INVESTORS EXPECT IT

A PPM serves as a sales document for your company (or, to be more specific, for your company's stock), as a reference and instruction manual to your private placement, and as a warning of the potential risks in investing in your company. Any firm or individual interested in investing in your company will want to see the information you put into your PPM; by using the PPM to distribute the information, you've supplied this necessary information in a format familiar to frequent investors.

The PPM differs from your business plan in that it must contain specific information about your private placement, about potential risks to the business, and about specific types of business dealings. A good PPM will also contain much of the same information as in your business plan, which means you can use your business plan as a cornerstone when building the official PPM.

LAWYERS DEMAND IT

When you prepared your business plan, you didn't need to get a lot of outside input. When you prepare your PPM, however, it will most likely be driven by outsiders—in particular, your lawyers. They will pour over the document word by word and demand all sorts of twiddly changes that seem insignificant to you but will cause apoplexy among the legal beagles if you don't comply.

The reason for this is that an additional audience for your PPM—in addition to potential investors—is potential plaintiffs. What this means is that anything you do wrong in a PPM can come back to haunt you in the form of lawsuits. (That's right, there are lawyers out there just waiting to sue over any inaccuracy that creeps into your PPM. Really!)

Let's take an extreme example. If you do not disclose a particular business dealing in your PPM, and for whatever reason, the investment in your company does not pay out, then every single investor may have a legal right to recover his or her investment from the company—and also from the company's officers and investors. (The basis of the lawsuits? Nondisclosure of essential information.) The company and its officers and directors (which includes you, of course) may also risk severe civil and criminal penalties for violating various aspects of the securities laws.

A well-prepared PPM does not guarantee immunity from, but rather acts as insurance against, such risks. If you're completely open and honest about your business and its accompanying risks, you'll be less liable to potential lawsuits from investors claiming that they were misled. Of course, if you disclose all the information that the SEC says you should disclose, you'll also be in compliance with the securities regulations, which is another good thing.

CREATING A PPM

Whereas your business plan presents your business in the way you want to present it, a PPM presents your business in the way that investors (and lawyers) want to see it. To meet the investors' needs, a PPM should lay out what capital is needed, what risks are likely to be incurred, what state and Federal regulations apply, for what types of investors this investment is suitable, and so on—in addition to the basic information about your business that appears in your business plan.

For the nonPPM-specific items in the PPM, you should be able to reuse elements from your business plan. Whether you cut and paste whole sections or individual paragraphs, there is no need to reinvent the wheel with this new document. Of course, your lawyers might suggest some rewording here and there, but at least you won't be starting from scratch.

JUST A MINUTE

Your lawyers will probably advise that your PPM be devoid of all flash and splash, insist that all charts and graphics be deleted, and roll their eyes at the thought of fancy headers and footers and the use of color. In this instance, you should listen to their advice but follow your own best judgment. There is no law or regulation that says PPMs have to be boring; in fact, some of the most effective PPMs utilize the same style and formatting options found in the best business plans!

Although there are no formal requirements as to the precise structure and contents of a PPM, there are certain Regulation D disclosure requirements that must be met. To fulfill these SEC requirements, a PPM should include (in no set order) the following elements:

- Suitability standards for investors
- Description and price of the securities offered
- Amount of the offering (minimum and maximum amounts)
- Plan for distribution of the securities
- How you plan to use the proceeds from the securities offering
- Description of prior offering, stock plans, and stock options
- Risk factors (should include the Challenges identified in your business plan plus additional issues)
- Identification of the officers and directors of the company
- List of principal shareholders
- Disclosure of "certain transactions" (described later in this chapter)
- Description of the restrictions on the resale of the company's securities, along with a statement that no market currently exists or may ever exist for them
- A statement detailing that neither the SEC nor any state securities commission has approved or disapproved this securities offering, nor commented on the adequacy or accuracy of any disclosures in the PPM

- Description of your company's business (from your business plan)
- Discussion of the market for your company's products and services (from your business plan)
- Key financial statements, including a current income statement, balance sheet, and cash flow statement (from your business plan)
- Projected income statement (from your business plan)
- Current capitalization of the company
- Calculation of dilution of shares

In addition, your lawyers want you to elaborate on selected information that you reuse from your original business plan. For example, you may be advised to include management salaries in the Management section or to provide more detailed (or different) financial statements. You will definitely be advised to provide detailed information about your data sources and financial assumptions; everything you say in the plan will have to be confirmed and backed up; otherwise, you'll be asked to delete it.

Although the creation of a PPM could fill up another separate book, we will discuss some of the key elements of a PPM in the following sections.

COVER PAGE

The cover page of your PPM will contain much of the legalese either required by the SEC or suggested by your lawyers. In fact, the cover page of a PPM closely resembles the cover page of a public prospectus, including some or all of the following:

- The date (including month, day, and year) that the PPM was created
- A blank for numbering (Each individual PPM must be *hand-numbered* when it is handed out to a potential investor—you can then track each copy by following the assigned number.)
- The word "Confidential" or a statement that the document is not to be reproduced
- A line indicating that this is an offering of a specific type of stock
- A paragraph summarizing the offering (purchase price and size)
- A termination date for the offering
- A sentence stating that "the securities offered are speculative and involve a high degree of risk"—followed by a reference to the Risk Factors section of the document

- A statement that no person is authorized to give out any information other than that contained in this document

- A legal-type paragraph stating that the securities being offered have not been approved or registered by the SEC, for example:

"The securities being offered have not been approved or disapproved by the Securities and Exchange Commission or any state securities commission nor has the Securities and Exchange Commission or any state securities commission passed upon the accuracy, completeness, or adequacy of this Memorandum. Any representation to the contrary is a criminal offense. The securities being offered have not been registered under the Securities Act of 1933, as amended (the "Act"), in reliance upon an exemption from registration afforded by Section 4(2) of the Act and Regulation D."

JUST A MINUTE

Although your lawyers will most likely protest to the contrary, the official PPM cover page doesn't have to be the first page of your PPM document. You can, if you want, insert a title page similar to your business plan title page *before* the text-dense PPM cover—as long as this first page is dated, numbered, and marked confidential.

DESCRIPTION OF THE OFFERING

The next few pages of the PPM describe the offering in mind-numbing detail.

JUST A MINUTE

It is common to find, between the cover page and the description of the offering, one or more pages of additional disclaimers, along the lines that the PPM contains forward-looking statements, that the company's actual performance may differ materially from these statements, and that the offering is subject to withdrawal without notice. If you're not sure what to include here, just listen to your lawyers; they'll know.

The description is likely to include the following:

- The purchase price per share
- The number of shares offered or aggregate offering price (number of shares times price per share)

- Whether any commissions are being paid on the sale of shares (probably not)
- The fact that the transferability of the shares is restricted by Federal and state securities laws
- The fact that no market for the shares or the underlying stock exists and that none may develop in the future
- Information regarding the conversion of the shares (especially in regards to the automatic conversion upon the consummation of an IPO)
- Any antidilution provisions
- Information about any potential dividends
- Information about redemption of the stock
- Information about what happens to the stock if the company is sold, dissolved, or liquidated
- Shareholders' voting rights

Depending on the specifics of a given placement, this section might also include information about registration rights, the right of first purchase of new securities, protective provisions, and other such items.

RISK FACTORS

The Risk Factors section of a PPM is the favorite section for lawyers everywhere. According to the legal beagles, any conceivable risk that could be faced by investors—up to and possibly including the coming of Armageddon—must be here. As a result of this extreme full-disclosure approach, the Risk Factors section is typically the longest section of the PPM. This section goes well beyond the one-page Challenges section of your business plan; literally anything that can go wrong is fair game for inclusion.

Your lawyers will undoubtedly do a good job imagining every possible doom-and-gloom scenario that could face your business, you can start writing the Risk Factors section with this relatively short list of possible risks:

- The company has no operating history.
- The company has had no profits from operations.
- The company has an uncertain financial position.

- The company will probably need more than one round of financing to survive.

- The company might not survive, anyway—it may, in fact, become insolvent or go bankrupt.

- The company is highly dependent on a few key individuals (including you!), none of whom have run a company of any size before.

- The company is highly dependent on just a handful of major customers.

- The company's products, services, and underlying technologies are unproven.

- The company's products and services are subject to substantial pricing pressures.

- The company's products could face technological obsolescence.

- The company may not be able to obtain government approval for various things it wants to do.

- The company faces intense and established competition.

- The company's core technology or content is not wholly protected by patents or copyrights.

- The company may come under government scrutiny at some time in the future.

- The company's securities aren't liquid.

- The securities are likely to be substantially diluted.

- The investor might lose his or her entire investment in this company.

This list can go on and on, but you get the point. Unfortunately, all this caution is necessary, because several Federal statutes have virtually immunized companies from lawsuits if their "forward-looking statements" are accompanied by "meaningful cautions." This section is a downer (and is typically placed right up front, before you get into opportunities and strategies), but it's important.

CERTAIN TRANSACTIONS

Another section unique to the PPM is the Certain Transactions section. This is simply the revealing of any dealings that may impact the valuation of the pending investment. These typically include grants of shares to management or other large stock-based transactions. An example would be the exchange of stock for services or assets rendered by a third-party firm. The point is to reveal any transaction that diminishes or dilutes the apparent value of the available stock; although there are no legal guidelines as to what to or not to reveal, you're better off legally if you don't hold anything back. Any transaction you conceal can potentially come back and bite you.

EVERYTHING ELSE

From here on out, the PPM will contain information that was presented (at least in part) in your original business plan. These sections should include the following:

- Opportunity (with all data fully referenced)
- Market Strategy
- Business Strategy
- Organization and Operations
- Management (with all references fully checked out and the probable inclusion of management salaries)
- Financials (with all assumptions clearly stated)

Lawyers will frown on the inclusion of a Core Competencies section (you can't promise investors that these things will actually happen!), and given the huge Risk Factors section at the beginning of the PPM, you don't need to list competitive Challenges.

JUST A MINUTE

Your lawyers will probably argue against the need for the Vision and Mission sections; there's no legal reason not to include them, so it should be your call. Note, however, that after a dozen or so pages of risks and disclaimers, a high-minded vision statement might seem quite out of place.

PPM CHECKLIST

Use the following checklist to gather the information necessary for a comprehensive private placement memorandum:

PPM Checklist

- ☐ Number of shares to be offered and at what price
- ☐ Complete details of the stock placement
- ☐ Lawyer-approved list of disclaimers
- ☐ Comprehensive list of risk factors
- ☐ Disclosure of any large stock transactions that might dilute the value of the shares offered
- ☐ Verification of any data or information reused from the business plan
- ☐ Your lawyer's approval of the final document
- ☐ Other: _____
- ☐ Other: _____
- ☐ Other: _____

HOMEWORK

In this hour, you learned how to turn your business plan into a private placement memorandum. This completes your 24 one-hour lessons—you're now ready to create a business plan for your own company!

APPENDIX A
20-Minute Recap

HOUR 1: ANALYZE YOUR OBJECTIVES

This hour explains what a business plan is, why you need one, and what kind of results to expect when you present your plan to potential lenders and investors. If you know nothing at all about business plans, this hour is a must-read.

HOUR 2: ANALYZE YOUR AUDIENCE

In Hour 2, you learn about three potential audiences for your business plan, and then you focus on the most important audience, potential lenders and investors. More important, you find out why it's necessary to tailor your business plan to a particular audience and how to give them what they expect while still presenting your business in the best possible light.

HOUR 3: ANALYZE YOUR MARKET

The next few hours focus on some of the most important business fundamentals for any business—startup or established. This hour is all about market analysis, and you learn how to define your market (in terms of products, customers, and competitors), how to quantify market size, how to estimate market growth, and how to determine competitor market share. In addition, you learn how to conduct important market research and analysis, which you can then feed into the Opportunity section of your business plan.

HOUR 4: ANALYZE YOUR STRENGTHS

Hour 4 continues to focus on business fundamentals, in particular the ability to evaluate your company's strengths and weaknesses. You learn how to identify unique competitive advantages as well as competitive and marketplace challenges. You also find out how to respond to these challenges and the best way to present weaknesses and challenges in your business plan.

HOUR 5: ANALYZE YOUR STRATEGY

The cornerstone of your business plan is your long-term business strategy, or how you intend to get from point A to point B. This hour discusses the differences between vision, mission, goals, strategy, and tactics and presents the basics of creating a winning strategy.

HOUR 6: ANALYZE YOUR OPTIONS

A business plan is a key tool for obtaining financing for your business, and this hour examines the various types of funding available to you. You learn how to determine the best source of money to fund your business, as you evaluate the pros and cons of bank loans, so-called "friends and family" funding, strategic investors, and venture capital money. Equally important, you find out how to tailor your business plan for each different type of lender or investor.

HOUR 7: CREATE YOUR OUTLINE

With the fundamentals out of the way, you now turn your attention to the business plan itself. This hour focuses on the contents of the plan and what components you need to include. By the end of Hour 7, you'll have constructed the basic outline for your business plan, and you'll be ready to start preparing for the major project ahead of you.

HOUR 8: MARSHAL YOUR RESOURCES

Putting together a business plan is a lot of work, and you need to assemble the troops to get it all done on time. This hour is all about the management of the project; it discusses the type of work that needs to be done and the type of people best suited to do it. You learn how much time you'll need to reserve for the entire project, as well as what outside resources you may need to enlist.

Hour 9: Build Your Numbers

You measure the performance of your business by the numbers, and your business plan will include a *lot* of different financial metrics. To prepare you for the numerical parts of your business plan, this hour presents the how and the why behind a variety of financial statements, from income statements to balance sheets to cash flow projections. If you're an account (or otherwise well-versed in the numbers), you can probably skip this hour; if you're a little shaky numerically, then this hour is a great refresher course for financial basics.

Hour 10: Executive Summary

This hour begins the actual writing of your business plan—which continues through Hour 18. Starting at the front of the plan, Hour 10 discusses the Executive Overview section—why it's important, what it should contain, and how long it should be.

Hour 11: Vision and Mission

Every business is driven by a vision and a mission, and this hour discusses the Vision and Mission sections of your plan. You learn how to create powerful yet concise vision and mission statements and how to present them in the context of your business plan.

Hour 12: Opportunity

The Opportunity section of your business plan describes the market you've chosen to pursue and quantifies the magnitude of the market opportunity. In this hour, you learn how much and what kind of data to include in the Opportunity section, how to present that data (in text, lists, tables, and charts), and how to address other key market factors.

HOUR 13: MARKET STRATEGY

Once you've identified the market opportunity, you now describe your strategy for exploiting that opportunity. As discussed in this hour, this is done in the Market Strategy section of your business plan. This is a key part of the plan, and you learn how to present your products and services, marketing activities, sales strategies, and distribution plans. You also find out how to present your competitors and how to address their strengths and weaknesses.

HOUR 14: BUSINESS STRATEGY

The next section in the business plan is the Business Strategy section. As you learn in this hour, this section is where you present the details of your business, including (and especially) your business model. This hour also shows you how to describe the business you're in and how you'll make money in that business.

HOUR 15: ORGANIZATION AND OPERATIONS

This hour focuses on the Organization and Operations section of your business plan. This is where you present your company's structure (through the use of an org chart) and discuss the operations of all the key departments in your organization—in a fair amount of detail.

HOUR 16: MANAGEMENT

The Management section of your business plan includes short bios of your company's senior management team. This hour shows you how to prepare those bios—what to include and what to leave out—as well as other bios you may want to include in the plan (additional managers, the board of directors, and key advisors to your company).

HOUR 17: CORE COMPETENCIES AND CHALLENGES

The text part of your business plan concludes with a short Core Competencies and Challenges section. This hour provides advice on how to choose which items to present, as well as how to present them in a way that puts your company in the best possible light.

HOUR 18: FINANCIALS

Your business plan concludes with the Financials section. This hour tells you which financial statements you definitely need to include and which are optional. You'll also learn *how* to present the numbers in terms of detail and formatting.

HOUR 19: APPENDIXES AND ATTACHMENTS

If you have additional information that didn't fit in the main body of your business plan, you can include that information as an appendix or attachment. This hour discusses different items you can include at the back of your business plan, including glossaries, press releases, screenshots of Web pages, and product information.

HOUR 20: TABLE OF CONTENTS AND INDEX

It's important that the readers of your business plan be able to navigate their way through the plan to find the specific information they need. This hour presents several different navigational elements, including page numbers, section heads, tables of contents, and indexes. (You'll also learn how to incorporate footnotes and endnotes in your text.)

HOUR 21: FORMAT AND PRINT

When your business plan is completely written, it's time to format the document and get it printed. This hour shows you various formatting options that can provide a highly professional look and feel to your plan, and it teaches you everything you need to know about getting your plan professionally printed and bound.

HOUR 22: PRESENT THE PLAN

Preparing the business plan is just one part of the funding process; presenting the plan to potential lenders and investors is equally important. In this hour, you'll learn how to convert your printed plan into a PowerPoint presentation and the best ways to give that presentation to various types of audiences.

Hour 23: Use the Plan

The business plan isn't only for potential lenders and investors. Since your plan details your core business strategy, you should be able to use the plan to guide short-term and long-term decisions that your company needs to make to be successful. To help you fully utilize your business plan throughout your entire organization, this hour discusses various ways to share the business plan with your employees and how to integrate the plan into the day-to-day management of your business.

Hour 24: Create a Private Placement Memorandum (PPM)

As useful as the business plan is, it is not the document you use to actually ask for funding. When you're talking about private investment, you need to create a private placement memorandum (PPM), which describes your stock offering, details the risks of the investments, and fulfills various Federal regulatory requirements. This final hour shows how to use the information in your business plan as the cornerstone for your PPM and what kind of additional information is needed to create the required document.

APPENDIX B
Glossary

10-K   The official report of a company's yearly performance, filed annually with the *Securities and Exchange Commission*. Not to be confused with the company's *annual report*, which is distributed separately to the company's *shareholders*.

10-Q   The official report of a company's three-month performance, filed quarterly with the *Securities and Exchange Commission*.

annual report   A company-prepared report, targeted at current and potential *shareholders*, that presents the previous year's financials and other important information. Unlike the more formal *10-K* statements required by the SEC, annual reports are often glossy, four-color pieces with an equal mix of marketing and informative value.

asset   An item, physical or otherwise, that you or your business owns.

balance sheet   A financial statement that describes what a company owns (*assets*) and what it owes (*liabilities*).

breakeven point   That point in time when expenses and gross profits become equal.

budget   A plan for how much money your business will spend during a specific timeframe.

budgeting   The process of creating a month-by-month (or, in some cases, week-by-week) expense *budget*.

business plan   A formal presentation of a company's vision, goals, opportunities, strategies, and financial goals, typically used as a tool to obtain funding.

CAGR   See *compound annual growth rate*.

capital   Money invested in a business.

capital asset   An item that you expect to own for an extended period of time—at least several years.

cash flow   The available cash for a given period, calculated by adding depreciation and any other noncash charges to a company's after-tax profits.

cash flow projection   A projection of *cash flow* over a specified future period.

cash on hand   The amount of cash you have available at the start of a given measurement period.

cash paid out   The amount of cash spent over the course of a given measurement period.

cash position   The amount of cash projected to be on hand at the end of a given measurement period.

cash receipts   The cash generated over the course of a given measurement period.

CEO   Chief Executive Officer.

CFO   Chief Financial Officer.

CIO   Chief Information Officer.

CMO   Chief Marketing Officer.

COGS   See *cost of goods sold*.

compound annual growth rate   The year-over-year rate of growth for a specified period of years.

COO   Chief Operating Officer.

cost of goods sold   Costs directly associated with the manufacture or purchase of the goods that contribute to your revenues. Also called *product costs*.

costs   See *expenses*.

current assets   Items that a company owns (*assets*) that can be converted into cash within the next 12 months.

current liabilities   Debts or monetary obligations (*liabilities*) payable within the next 12 months.

dividend   A payment made by a company to each of its stockholders, typically based on some percentage of the profits generated during a specific time period.

earnings   See *profit*.

EBITDA   Stands for earnings before interest, taxes, depreciation, and amortization. On an *income statement*, the net profit a firm generates during a specific period, after all actual costs have been accounted for but before the company pays taxes and the interest on its loans and before it amortizes or depreciates any capital assets.

EBITDA margin   Describes *EBITDA* as a percentage of *net revenues*.

equity   The part of the business that is owned by its owners and investors, typically in the form of stock, as calculated by subtracting total liabilities from total assets.

exit strategy   How one intends to liquidate a specific investment or business.

expenses   The money you have to pay for various goods and services. (Also called *costs*.)

fixed assets   *Assets* that are not easily converted into cash. (Also called *long-term assets*.)

goal   An end or objective, specific to your mission, that your business strives to attain.

gross margin   Describes *gross profit* as a percentage of *net revenues*. (Also called *gross profit margin*.)

gross profit   The direct profit a company makes from sales during a specific period, calculated by subtracting the *cost of goods sold* from *net revenues*. Also reflects the difference between an individual product's revenues and its cost of manufacturing.

gross profit margin   See *gross margin*.

gross revenues   Total dollar sales for a specific period, not counting any damaged or returned goods.

HR   Human resources.

income   See *profit*.

income statement   A financial statement that reflects the revenue your company generates, the expenses you pay, and the profit (or loss) that filters down. Also called a *profit and loss statement* or *P/L*.

initial public offering   The first offering of securities (such as company stock) to the general public via the public stock exchanges; sometimes referred to as "going public."

IPO   See *initial public offering*.

IS   Information systems.

IT   Information technology.

liability   An item that someone else owns and for which you owe.

liquidity   A reflection of how quickly *assets* can be converted to cash.

long-term assets   See *fixed assets*.

long-term liabilities   Debts and obligations (*liabilities*) that are due to be paid over a period exceeding 12 months.

market share   The percentage share of industry revenues generated by a specific company, calculated as total industry revenues divided by individual company revenues.

MIS   Management information systems.

mission   The overall purpose of your business; more specific than your vision but not directly quantifiable.

net earnings   See *net profits*.

net income   See *net profits*.

net margin   Describes *net profit* as a percentage of *net revenues*.

net profits   Reflects the reported *profit* or loss after interest expenses, taxes, depreciation, and amortization (*EBITDA*) costs have been factored out. (Also called *net earnings* or *net income*.)

net revenues   On an *income statement*, the result of *gross revenues* minute *returns*. (Also called *net sales*.)

net sales   See *net revenues*.

net worth   See *equity*.

offering memorandum   See *private placement memorandum*.

operating expenses   All the indirect costs of the ongoing, day-to-day operation of a business—rent, payroll, utilities, advertising, and the like. Operating expenses do *not* include costs related to the manufacturing of a product.

P/L   Profit and loss statement; see *income statement*.

penetration   A measurement of the percentage of potential customers currently using a specific type of product or service, as calculated by dividing the number of current customers by the number of potential customers.

PPM   See *private placement memorandum*.

private placement   A limited sale of securities (such as company stock) that does not involve any public offering, advertising, or general solicitation.

private placement memorandum   A legal document that presents the details of a pending offering of stock in a private company. (Also called an *offering memorandum*.)

pro forma   A forecast or "what if" analysis.

product costs   See *cost of goods sold*.

product mix   The complete range of products that your company offers.

profit   How much money you have left after subtracting expenses from revenues. (Also called *income* or *earnings*.)

profit and loss statement   See *income statement*.

prospectus   See *S-1*.

return on investment   The payback on a specific dollar investment for a specific time period. (Also called *ROI*.)

returns   On an *income statement*, the cost of any returned or damaged merchandise as well as any allowances and markdowns.

revenues   The dollars you generate by selling your products and services. (Also called *sales*.)

ROI See *return on investment*.

S-1 A document that is required to be filed with the *Securities and Exchange Commission* and distributed to potential investors when a company is planning an *IPO*. (Also called a *prospectus*.)

sales See *revenues*.

SEC See *Securities and Exchange Commission*.

Securities and Exchange Commission The Federal agency, created in 1934, charged with regulating the sales of securities to public and private markets.

share A specified ownership piece of a company.

shareholder A person or entity that owns shares in a company.

stock Ownership of a company in the form of *shares*, which represent a piece of the company's *assets* and *profits*.

stockholder See *shareholder*.

strategic investor A large investor, typically another company, that sees some synergies between what it does and what your company does.

strategy A plan of action designed to achieve your business goals.

tactic A method used to implement a specific strategy.

tangible net worth Equity in a company less the book value of intangible assets, such as goodwill.

TOC Table of contents.

total cash available The amount of cash, in total, that you have available to pay out over the course of a given measurement period, as calculated by adding *cash receipts* to initial *cash on hand*.

VC See *venture capital*.

venture capital A type of private investment in a company by an investment fund willing to take a higher level of risk predicated on a company's prospects for above-average growth.

vision The reason you're in business; it's what drives your company and everything your company does.

APPENDIX C
Outline

SAMPLE BUSINESS PLAN OUTLINE

The following generic business plan outline is meant to be adapted to the specific needs of individual businesses.

Title Page

Table of Contents

Executive Summary

Vision

Mission

Opportunity

    Market Size and Growth

    Customer Dynamics

    Market Trends

    Competitive Dynamics

Market Strategy

    Product

        Positioning

        Pricing

        Packaging

    Sales and Distribution

        Targeted Channels

        Sales Strategy

Marketing

    Advertising and Promotion

    Public Relations and Trade Shows

Competitive Comparison

Business Strategy

    Business Model

        Revenue Streams

        Profit Margins

        Market Share

        Growth

    Strategic Initiatives

        Acquisitions

        Expansion

    Timeline

Organization and Operations

    Organization Structure

    Key Operations

        Product Development

        Manufacturing

        Warehousing and Distribution

        Sales

        Marketing

        Information Technology

        Finance and Accounting

Human Resources

Facilities

Copyrights and Patents

Management

Senior Management Team

Board of Directors

Key Advisors

Strategic Investors

Core Competencies and Challenges

Core Competencies

Competitive Challenges

Financials

Revenue Projection

Income Statement (Projection)

Income Statement (Current)

Income Statement (Historical)

Balance Sheet

Cash Flow Projection

Appendixes (Optional)

Glossary

History and Accomplishments

Web Pages

IT Infrastructure

Supplemental Schedules

Detailed Processes

Additional Market Data

Additional Financials

List of Major Investors

Index (Optional)

Attachments (Optional)

Analyst and Research Reports

Featured News Stories

Press Releases

Product Information

Brochures and Marketing Information

APPENDIX D
Financial Formulas

ASSETS

ASSETS = LIABILITIES + EQUITY

CASH POSITION

CASH POSITION = CASH ON HAND + CASH RECEIPTS − CASH PAID OUT

COMPOUND ANNUAL GROWTH RATE (CAGR)

CAGR = ((YEAR LAST ÷ YEAR FIRST) raised to the (1 ÷ YEARS TOTAL) power) − 1

CURRENT RATIO

CURRENT RATIO = CURRENT ASSETS ÷ CURRENT LIABILITIES

DEBT-TO-EQUITY RATIO

DEBT TO EQUITY RATIO = LIABILITIES ÷ TANGIBLE NET WORTH

EARNINGS BEFORE INTEREST, TAXES, DEPRECIATION, AND AMORTIZATION (EBITDA)

NET PROFIT = GROSS PROFIT − (OPERATING EXPENSES − INTEREST − TAXES − DEPRECIATION − AMORTIZATION)

EBITDA MARGIN

EBITDA MARGIN = EBITDA ÷ NET REVENUES

EQUITY

EQUITY = ASSETS – LIABILITIES

GROSS MARGIN

GROSS MARGIN = GROSS PROFIT ÷ NET REVENUE

GROSS PROFIT

GROSS PROFIT = NET REVENUE – COST OF GOODS SOLD

NET MARGIN

NET MARGIN = NET PROFIT ÷ NET REVENUE

NET PROFIT

NET PROFIT = GROSS PROFIT – OPERATING EXPENSES

JUST A MINUTE

The term "net profit" can be used interchangeably with the terms "net income" and "net earnings."

NET REVENUE

NET REVENUE = GROSS REVENUE – RETURNS – DISCOUNTS - MARKDOWNS

PROFIT (GENERAL)

PROFITS = REVENUES – EXPENSES

QUICK ASSETS RATIO

QUICK ASSETS RATIO = (CURRENT ASSETS – INVENTORY) ÷ CURRENT LIABILITIES

RETURN ON INVESTMENT (ROI) I

ROI = NET PROFIT ÷ TANGIBLE NET WORTH

RETURN ON INVESTMENT (ROI) II

ROI = EXIT VALUE ÷ INITIAL INVESTMENT

Index